STREET FIGHT

STREET FIGHT

The Chicago Taxi Wars of the 1920s

ANNE MORRISSY

Essex, Connecticut

An imprint of Globe Pequot, the trade division of
The Rowman & Littlefield Publishing Group, Inc.
4501 Forbes Blvd., Ste. 200
Lanham, MD 20706
www.rowman.com

Distributed by NATIONAL BOOK NETWORK

British Library Cataloguing in Publication Information available

Library of Congress Cataloging-in-Publication Data available

ISBN 978-1-4930-6867-8 (cloth: alk. paper)
ISBN 978-1-4930-6868-5 (ebook)

∞™ The paper used in this publication meets the minimum requirements of American National
Standard for Information Sciences—Permanence of Paper for Printed Library Materials, ANSI/
NISO Z39.48-1992.

Contents

CONTENTS

Introduction

As far as the record is concerned, John D. Hertz and Morris Markin never once stood in the same room. Hertz—tall, bespectacled, and affable—would go on to become a household name for an almost incidental transportation innovation he pioneered: the rental car. Markin—heavy-browed, balding, and enigmatic—preferred to keep a lower profile. In the 1920s, both men stood at the dawn of an industry that still plays an important role in modern city life to this day: taxis. Each man ran a successful business in the taxi industry, businesses which, for much of the 1920s, happened to be in direct competition with each other. In those days, like today, there was a lot of money to be made by besting the competition. These business rivals would leave a deep and lasting impression on the taxi industry for decades to come, not just in Chicago, but throughout the United States.

Yet as far as we know today, Hertz and Markin never shared a podium at a business conference. They never sat together for an interview with an assistant state's attorney in preparation for a grand jury hearing. And even when the companies they founded decided to sue one another, they preferred to send their attorneys to do their negotiating for them. When Hertz suspected Markin of attempting to tank the stock value of Hertz's company on the New York Stock Exchange, he does not appear to have demanded an audience with his rival. When cabs were destroyed, and drivers murdered, and taxi garages bombed, and even when some of the top leaders of the taxi industry ended up dead in a series of events that ranged from unusual accidents to outright murder, neither man appears to have sought an appointment with the other in an attempt to get to the bottom of the violence.

Despite this practiced distance, Markin and Hertz remained the leaders of two of the biggest and most influential companies in the Chicago taxi industry during the Roaring Twenties, that era of bootleg bathtub gin and scantily clad flappers, of jazz cabarets and audacious political corruption, of well-dressed gangsters with their Tommy guns, of a building boom that sent architecture soaring to scrape the sky. Chicago in the 1920s had it all, or was in the process of building it. And whenever possible, the city wanted to hold world records: By the end of the 1920s, Chicago boasted the largest fountain (Buckingham Fountain, constructed in 1927), the world's largest hotel (the Stevens Hotel, also completed in 1927), and was in the process of building the world's largest single building (Merchandise Mart, opened in 1930). Chicago did nothing by degrees; like a racehorse, it ran full out in every aspect of urban living. As the "hog butcher for the world," its stockyards drew as many as five hundred thousand visitors every year. Its politicians were known around the country for their big personalities and their brazen corruption. Even its murderers and organized criminals became international celebrities. Chicago in the 1920s "stood at the peak of its economic power and influence," according to one modern historian. A New York critic, writing of Chicago in 1930, described it as the "extrovert of cities" and marveled at its confidence: "never embarrassed, never apologizes, never blushes."

There was so much to see and do, and suddenly there was a new way to get there. Around the country, but especially in Chicago during this time, taxis were an exciting new phenomenon, and a taxi ride around the city was suddenly an everyday luxury available to the average person. People took taxis to work, to the theater and to dinner, to go dancing in ballrooms, to brave the thrill rides at amusement parks, to visit friends, to meet trains, to go shopping, to watch ballgames, to check out library books, to visit museums, to listen to jazz music . . . or sometimes just to see the sparkling city from the window of a moving automobile. Gone were the days of the staid and slow horse-drawn hansom cabs: Automobiles were thrilling and modern, and although the average person couldn't quite afford to buy a car, the taxi industry allowed everyone in the city to experience a taste of the good life. All they had to do was throw out their hand at a street corner, or telephone a request to the main garage, and they could have their own, personal, on-demand automobile at any time.

Hertz, the cofounder and president of Chicago's Yellow Cab Company, and Markin, the founder and president of the Checker Cab Mfg. Co., had an outsized influence on this taxi landscape in Chicago. They were visionaries in a burgeoning industry. They were business rivals in an era of nearly unlimited growth and unprecedented wealth. They were extremely ambitious men. They had other things in common too. They were both Jewish immigrants to America, born thirteen years apart— Markin in Russia and Hertz in a village in Slovakia, then part of the Austro-Hungarian Empire. They both started on unrelated career paths before falling into the automobile industry, almost by accident. They both went on to enormous success. And through their respective companies, they both provided unparalleled employment opportunities for Jews, Black people, women, and other marginalized groups thanks to their progressive ideas about employment, and their egalitarian views about who had the right to pursue the "American dream."

But at the same time that these two men held the majority of the Chicago taxi industry in their palms, there was a dark side to the business as well. As taxis became more and more popular beginning in the late 1910s, taxi drivers started skirmishing over things like union membership, cab fares, and turf protocols. By the dawn of Prohibition in 1920, these smaller battles had erupted into organized acts of business-related terrorism and deadly violence that often took place in full view of the public, and killed innocent bystanders on more than one occasion. The vast amounts of money being made by the cab companies in the 1920s attracted gangsters who sensed an opportunity to line their pockets through graft, embezzlement, and extortion. And so, these gangsters muscled their way into the industry as well. The many incidents that erupted along the way became known in the newspapers as the "Taxi Wars," and they spanned a period of more than a decade, from 1916 to around 1929.

All told, the Taxi Wars involved everything from sophomoric pranks to cold-blooded murder, from domestic terrorism and mass shootings to extortion, voter intimidation, bribery, jury tampering, and securities fraud. The body count was truly stunning. And yet even at the time, the story was eclipsed by other crime happening in the city during the Prohibition era. Over the years, the Taxi Wars were nearly forgotten, so that when the industry began to shift again in the early twenty-first century with the introduction of ride-hailing companies, no one even remembered how some of the longstanding taxi regulations had come to exist in the first place.

At its core, the story of the Taxi Wars is a story of two men—Hertz and Markin—and the companies they founded, vying for dominance in the market. At Yellow Cab, Hertz adopted a public-facing approach, often communicating directly with the taxi-hailing masses. At Checker, the always-secretive Markin preferred to operate through trusted proxies and associates, and rarely made public statements. But his influence was always there—steering the actions, steering the response. These two rivals knew that only one of them could win the ultimate Taxi War—the battle for corporate dominance in this lucrative new industry. By the early 1930s, one of these men would obtain control of more than 85 percent of the taxis on the streets of Chicago and be well on his way to dominance in New York, Cleveland, Minneapolis, and Pittsburgh as well. The other would be out of the business entirely. This is their story.

It is also the story of the thousands of drivers, mechanics, factory employees, washers, instructors, agents, supervisors, starters, dispatchers, operators, inspectors, stenographers, and bookkeepers, all of whom gave untold hours of tireless work to expand the cab industry in Chicago in these early days. Some of them were forced to give their lives as well. But before that, in the beginning, there was just a foggy day in downtown Chicago, and a few dozen yellow cars emerging from the mist, ready to pick up their very first fares.

Part I

Get Your Motor Runnin', 1908–1920

CHAPTER 1

Whistle for a Ride

From Luxury Auto Livery to Taxis for Everyone (1908–1915)

JUST BEFORE 5:00 P.M. ON MONDAY, AUGUST 2, 1915, NINETEEN-YEAR-old aviatrix sensation Katherine Stinson climbed alone into her signature Stinson-Partridge tractor airplane in Chicago's Grant Park. At a petite 5'2" and about one hundred pounds, Stinson defied the public's stereotype of a pilot. Aviation was such a new phenomenon that she was only the fourth woman in the United States to receive a pilot's license. (Amelia Earhart would be the sixteenth American woman to earn her license, in 1921.) Bucking traditional gender expectations, instead of a skirt, Stinson wore a sealskin suit with bloomers, as well as knee-high leather boots and a round hat suggestive of what later became known as an aviator's cap. Starting her engine, Stinson bounced along the ground until she lifted the plane into the air, "defying gusts of wind and low-hanging clouds and banks of fog," according to the *Chicago Tribune.* The previous month, Stinson had perfected a loop-de-loop at Chicago's Cicero Flying Field, the first woman to do so. Although the weather on Monday did not permit her to attempt the trick, she promised to return to Grant Park later in the week to try again.

In the park below, thousands of people watched her twelve-minute flight through the air from their decidedly pedestrian vantage points. It was the first day of Market Week, a convention for retail shop owners and buyers around the Midwest, sponsored by the Chicago Association of Commerce. Market Week provided an opportunity for store buyers to see the latest offerings from Chicago's retailers, wholesalers, and manufacturers, and to decide what they might want to stock in their stores in the coming year. Already hundreds of visitors had arrived in town—many buyers brought their wives and families for a trip to the city. Market Week planners expected almost one hundred thousand attendees before the end of the week.

The city was still recovering from tragedy. Just nine days earlier, a passenger steamship called the *Eastland* had capsized at its mooring in the Chicago River, trapping many of the passengers underwater and throwing many more into the busy, filthy waterway. In total, 844 people were killed in the disaster, the deadliest maritime incident in American history. As the crowds watched Stinson take to the air, crews were still working to recover bodies from the wrecked steamer. Just the day before, three new victims—two eighteen-year-old women and a twenty-two-year-old man—had been hauled out of the river. Every day, the newspapers carried information about the latest *Eastland* victims to be identified and the various relief funds established to help support the grieving families.

The Market Week attendees in Chicago that Monday may not have realized it, but they were also present for another historic moment in Chicago. At 5:00 p.m., just as Stinson was taking to the air over Grant Park, the first forty-five Yellow Cabs appeared for business on the streets of the Loop. Marked by their distinctive yellow paint and the new Yellow Cab logo on the door, these identical vehicles boasted an enclosed cab that could seat four passengers, two facing forward and two facing backward, while accommodating packages or hand luggage in the open area beside the driver. The cars were designed to be both tough and lightweight, to improve fuel efficiency and reduce operating costs, and their debut represented a new approach to taxi operation in the city of Chicago. As Yellow Cab boasted in its ads, the company would operate on a "European system": "The Yellow Cab will be picked up on the street and by telephone. There will be no charge accounts associated with them," the ad explained.

The new service was the brainchild of two men, partners in an already successful automobile livery business: Walden W. Shaw and John D. Hertz. They were the president and vice president, respectively, of Walden W. Shaw Livery, which they had formed in 1908, in the first decade of the automobile transportation revolution. Walden Willard Shaw had been just thirteen years old when inventor William Morrison of Des Moines, Iowa, had brought his newest invention to the city to demonstrate it to a prospective manufacturer, the very first "horseless carriage" in Chicago. It was an electric model. Seeing the potential in the new vehicle, John B. McDonald, head of the American Storage Battery Company, bought it from Morrison. He became the first person to commute by automobile in Chicago when he began driving to work downtown, and within a decade, more and more automobiles appeared on the city's streets.

It is hard to overstate the benefits a horseless carriage offered over other forms of road transportation at the time. It is also difficult today to imagine the level of pollution, chaos, and crowding on many of Chicago's streets in the 1880s and 1890s. The city was messy and difficult to travel around. The streets themselves were generally no more than dirt roads (occasionally covered with wooden boards) and turned into mud whenever it rained or when the frost slowly melted throughout the spring. In 1895, a book called *The History of Chicago* declared that for much of the city's history to that point, Chicago's streets "were in a condition which rendered travel vexatious and perilous to both man and beast."

The "beasts" were particularly problematic. When the first automobiles appeared in Chicago, the vast majority of vehicles on the street were pulled by livestock: jitneys, hacks, wagons, omnibuses, broughams, buggies. In the 1880s, an estimated seven thousand horses pulled public transit vehicles alone, and many times more pulled personal and commercial transportation. The amount of animal waste on the city's streets in 1880 is unimaginable today: "millions of pounds of manure and tens of thousands of gallons of urine" per year, according to historian Greg Borzo. In addition to being unpleasant and noxious, the vast amounts of animal waste presented significant sanitation and public health problems. (The tetanus virus, for example, is carried in horse manure.) An 1897 *Chicago Tribune* survey of Chicago civic planners asked them to envision what the city might look like in 1990, and one respondent hoped that by that time, "such a vulgar thing as a horse will never be seen upon the downtown streets of the city."

Adding to this mix was an ever-increasing density of pedestrians. The city was suffering growing pains, brought on by the period of enormous growth that began shortly after the Great Chicago Fire in 1871. Industrious Chicagoans rebuilt the central business district, "The Loop," with startling speed after that catastrophe. It must have seemed to the Chicagoans of the era that every day the city got bigger, the buildings got taller, and the streets got more crowded with people, vehicles, and animals.

By the late 1880s, Chicago was eager to prove its place as a world-class city. As a prelude to the ambitious World's Fair they would host in 1893, the city leaders began expanding the boundaries of Chicago. In just five short years, they annexed over 120 square miles of adjacent land into the city grid. Areas that had previously existed as outlying villages or suburbs suddenly boasted city status. As a result, Chicago's population more than doubled between 1880 and 1890. By 1910, more than 2.1 million people would live in Chicago, and nearly half of those within four miles of the Loop.

Given all of these factors, it is no surprise that forward-thinking Chicagoans like John B. McDonald had high hopes for the new "horseless carriage" as a way to move people throughout the city. On Thanksgiving Day, 1895, the *Chicago Times-Herald* sponsored America's first automobile race, from Chicago to Evanston and back. A $5,000 reward would go to the inventor who could design a "practicable, self-propelling road carriage" that achieved the fastest speed on the course. Although eleven motorists registered for the contest, cold temperatures and high snow drifts up to two feet deep meant that only six automobiles started the race. Of these, only two managed to finish. Seven hours and fifty-three minutes after starting from the Museum of Science and Industry, J. Frank Duryea crossed the finish line first in his "wagon," a vehicle based on a model invented by Carl Friedrich Benz, which had already found some commercial success in Europe. Duryea had averaged around 7 mph for the duration of the trip, and used a total of 3.5 gallons of gasoline.

This demonstration, though painfully slow-going by modern standards, proved that the horseless carriage could travel long distances over preexisting roads in Chicago's inclement winter weather. Race promoter H. H. Kohlsaat declared at the finish line that, "a better test of the utility of road machines could not have been made, and I feel assured that the beginning has been made in a new method of transportation." He was correct. By 1899, several wealthy Chicagoans had acquired early automobile models. There were soon enough automobiles on the streets to spur the Chicago City Council to pass some of the first laws in the United States regulating them. These laws established a speed limit of 8 mph and required that anyone who wanted to drive one must appear before the newly formed Board of Examiners of Operators of Automobiles, a committee of three officials, which constituted the earliest predecessor to the modern-day Department of Motor Vehicles. In 1902, just ten years after John B. McDonald started commuting in the first known horseless carriage in Chicago, the Board of Examiners had granted driving privileges to eight hundred city residents.

Walden Willard Shaw had a front-row seat to this technological revolution. Born in 1879 to William W. Shaw and Sarah Bogardus Shaw, he and his brothers, Robert and E. B., were the heirs to a large fortune their father had made when he took control of the Dake Bakery, a Chicago wholesale bakery, and then sold it for a huge sum to the American Biscuit Company. (The American Biscuit Company was later acquired by the National Biscuit Company, which is still operating today as Nabisco.)

As a boy, Shaw was fair and lithe, as he would remain all his life. He was raised in an atmosphere of Gilded Age bonhomie, in a home on Ashland Avenue in what was then an aristocratic part of the city's West Side. He attended Chicago's Marquette School, then Princeton-Yale Preparatory School and Phillips Academy in Andover, Massachusetts. When Shaw's father sold the Dake Bakery in 1897, he told his sons "not to worry about money and to just go off and enjoy life for a while," according to Shaw's granddaughter, who said that Shaw followed that advice well. In 1900, he married Bessie Kennedy and they settled into a home in Chicago's Hyde Park neighborhood. They went on to have two daughters together, Margaret Elizabeth and Bessie K. Shaw.

Both Shaw and his brother Robert became true automobile enthusiasts. In 1901, Walden Shaw bought his first automobile, a Hanriod, and in November that year, the two brothers and their wives left for Europe to take a nearly six-month-long, ten-thousand-mile tour of the continent by automobile. They started in Paris, the epicenter of automobile technology at the time, and made plans to visit Germany, Austria, Italy, Spain, Egypt, and North Africa. The trip appears to have been a success. In late 1904, following his father's death and the brothers' inheritance of the estate, Shaw returned to Europe with his wife for a second automobile tour, this time visiting France, Italy, Spain, and England in a large open-air car called a Panhard. Shaw preferred to drive the vehicle himself, rather than hire a chauffeur, "on the theory that if there are going to be any road mishaps, he prefers to have control of the car himself."

It was during one of these two trips to Europe that Shaw first drove a French make of automobile called a Berliet. He immediately fell in love with its design, which included a twin-cylinder engine. Shaw loved the Berliet model so much that he purchased one on his trip and shipped it back to America. It inspired great envy among his Chicago friends, who started placing orders for their own Berliets through Shaw. He suddenly found himself the de facto Berliet dealer for Chicago, corresponding with the factory in Lyon, France, and placing orders on behalf of his friends and acquaintances.

In 1906, Shaw formalized that role when he incorporated the Walden W. Shaw Company as an auto dealership on the city's growing Motor Row, which stretched along Michigan Avenue from 12th Street (modern-day Roosevelt Road) to 26th Street. Chicago's Motor Row was impressive and internationally famous at a time when automaking was a new and decentralized industry. The area got its name beginning around 1903, when the early automakers from around the world began to locate luxurious showrooms there, attracted by the abundance of flat roads for test drives and the number of potential customers who passed through the city each year. An article in the *Chicago Tribune* on February 10, 1906, claimed that, "Chicago has the most imposing automobile row of any city in the country, and claim for a world's record might well be made without much chance of there being any dispute." Eventually, the area boasted more than one hundred automakers showcasing their latest models, including Winton, Ford, Studebaker, Pierce-Arrow, and Packard.

By November of that year, the Shaw Company was the sole Chicago distributor of Berliets, as well as automobiles manufactured by the Wayne Automobile Company of Detroit. Unfortunately for Shaw, demand for the Berliet cooled significantly after that initial burst of interest. These were unquestionably luxury items, and, even in Gilded Age Chicago, very few people could afford to spend $4,500 (more than $125,000 in today's money) on such an extravagance. By late 1907, the Walden W. Shaw Company had incurred around $45,000 in debts. With interest in the Berliets petering out, Shaw recognized that he needed fresh ideas to jump-start his business plan.

Luckily for Shaw, automobiles continued to capture the consumer imagination. More and more dealerships were springing up along Motor Row, and one car salesman would emerge as an important player both in the future of the Shaw Company, as well as in the automobile landscape of the city itself. As it turned out, the solution to Shaw's business problems would require ingenuity, creativity, and above all, hard work. John D. Hertz had all of these skills, and an unparalleled business instinct that would serve him extremely well in the decades to come.

JOHN D. HERTZ: A PARTNERSHIP BEGINS

The Chicago Athletic Association building towers an imposing eleven stories over South Michigan Avenue, its red brick, Venetian Gothic façade hinting at the luxury still contained within. The building, designed by club member and revered Chicago architect Henry Ives Cobb, was completed in 1893 on land leased from another founding member, Marshall Field. The private club was intended as a meeting place and sporting venue for the city's business and cultural elites, "to encourage all sports, to promote physical culture, and to cultivate social intercourse and friendly relations among the members."

The large building contained tennis and racquet courts, billiards and game rooms, a boxing ring, an indoor pool, a bowling alley, a basketball court, an indoor track, and space for a bicycle club, in addition to sixty-one hotel rooms, a library, and multiple lounges and dining rooms. In the words of architectural historian Edward W. Wolner, it was a "single, highly urbanized venue for exercising, competing, socializing, dining and sleeping—the unique convenience of all the satisfactions of sporting life within walking distance of work." From the start, the club attracted some of the city's wealthiest men—First National Bank president Samuel Nickerson, inventor Cyrus Hall McCormick, and president of the Art Institute of Chicago Charles Hutchinson among them. One contemporary author has described the Chicago Athletic Association of the turn of the twentieth century as a "unique mix of sports and clout." It was likely inside this rarefied club that Walden W. Shaw first encountered a tall, dark-haired man nearly always seen wearing round spectacles and an amiable expression: the entrepreneurial car salesman, John D. Hertz.

John Daniel Hertz was no stranger to hard work. He was born Sandor Herz in 1879 in the small village of Ruttka in what was then Hungary (now called Vrútky and part of modern-day Slovakia). When Hertz was just five years old, his family—father Jacob, mother Katie, and four, soon-to-be five siblings—immigrated to America, settling in Chicago. "My first sight of America," he remembered later, was "from the window of an immigrant train . . . from Newark to Chicago, a red ticket in my hat-band, and my nose pressed against the glass, a very small boy looking out at a strange, bewildering country."

The family was Jewish and working-class, and they chose to settle on West Taylor Street, in Chicago's Little Italy neighborhood. Although there was a sizable enclave of Italian immigrants living in the area, the neighborhood was settled by working-class immigrants from throughout Europe and had a large Jewish population. Newspaperman George Ade would later describe Hertz in his early life as "so poor, and the soles of his shoes were so thin, that he could stand on a dime and tell the difference between heads and tails . . . except that he didn't have a dime to stand on."

Growing up, Hertz had a difficult relationship with his father, a hardware and crockery merchant and a strict man. At age eleven, after receiving a particularly severe beating from his father ("doubtless richly deserved," Hertz later demurred), he dropped out of school and ran away from home. "My problem was that I had to eat, and I had to sleep, and it was a day-to-day struggle to see whether or not I could stay independent of a home that had become distasteful to me," he remembered later in life.

He started out as a newsboy, one of the hundreds of young boys who "stood in a long line to pick up the bundles at the old *Daily News* office" before heading to the streets to hawk the days' headlines to passersby. The work was dangerous and physical, demanding that the boys lug heavy newspapers through the city streets in all weather conditions, shouting to be heard above the street noise, constantly hustling to sell their day's allotment. Typical pay for this job was around 50 cents per one hundred newspapers sold. During this time, Hertz lived in the Newsboys' Home, a "waif's home" for these working children, which provided shelter and "good, plain food to eat," as well as Sunday church service and a Monday evening cultural concert. Fending for himself at such a young age, Hertz frequently ended up in situations where he had to defend himself with his fists on the streets. "I was as wild and untamed as the grass on the prairie," he later remembered.

Even at that young age, Hertz was clever and resourceful, and it wasn't long before he landed a position at the *Chicago Record*, working the night shift as an office boy, physically running the copy between various editors' offices on tight deadline. While the job was a big step up from being a newsboy, the hard lifestyle was already taking a toll on his health. "Working nights, picking up a meal here and there and with being a growing, gangling child, I was pretty frail, pinched in the chest," he remembered. Recognizing this, Hertz's boss sent him to his own personal doctor, who determined that an immediate lifestyle change was necessary to improve the boy's health. "The doctor warned me I would have to quit working nights," Hertz remembered, "that I should be outdoors in the fresh air, and that I must join a gym and develop my body." Hearing the doctor's recommendations, Hertz's boss fired him, saying it was for his own good, though Hertz admitted that it "hardly seemed like a favor at the time."

Let go from the newspaper office, Hertz found an "outside job" as a freight wagon driver, driving a team of horses and a delivery wagon ten to eighteen hours a day at a rate of six dollars a week. He also started training as a boxer at Gilmore's Academy of Boxing, and to further supplement his income, Hertz began a modestly successful boxing career under the pseudonym "Dan Donnelly." However, he never lost his instincts for the news business, and he kept in touch with Ed Sheridan, the sports editor at the *Chicago Record*, supplying boxing tips and gossip for which Sheridan paid him on space by the inch, depending on which tips made it to print. Despite Hertz's lack of formal education, Sheridan recognized a spark of potential in his young source. He began to mentor Hertz, coaxing the insecure boy to take over writing the stories himself. "I wouldn't have dared to write anything on my own initiative," Hertz recalled. "Sheridan had to push, persuade and bully me into doing it, convince me there was nothing to be afraid of." More than any other experience in his youth, Hertz said it was that moment of first becoming a writer that he "always considered the real turning point of my whole life." By the age of twenty-one, thanks to Sheridan's support, Hertz was a regular sports reporter for the *Chicago Record*.

However, the turn of the twentieth century was a particularly volatile time to be working in the Chicago newspaper industry. The city boasted ten rival daily newspapers, all competing for the same readers—bankruptcies and buyouts were a common job hazard for those working in Chicago journalism at the time. Around 1901, when the *Chicago Record* merged with the *Chicago Herald*, Hertz lost his job. Instead of looking for another newspaper job, he decided to pursue a career as a boxing manager, taking on professional featherweight boxer (and former newspaper colleague) Benny Yanger, "The Tipton Slasher," as his client, while also freelancing occasional sports stories to the *Chicago Tribune*.

Yanger proved to be a lucrative client, bringing in nearly $10,000 in prize money in 1902 alone. However, on July 15, 1903, Hertz's life took a turn that would lead him away from the professional boxing world: He married Frances "Fannie" Kesner. Kesner was born in Chicago to wealthy Dutch parents, and she was four years younger than Hertz. The elder Kesners did not approve of professional boxing as a suitable profession for their daughter's husband-to-be. As Hertz later recounted, "I was making fairly good money [as a boxing manager] and getting lots of experience, but my girl vowed that she would not marry me until I gave up this kind of life." Hertz was smitten with Fannie, and so he did. "As I simply could not think of living long without her, I began looking around for other work," he explained. His desire to prove his worth to Fannie's parents became an animating force in his life. "I was determined that my wife's folks should not be in a position to point their finger at us," he later remembered. "This fired me with ambition." The couple went on to have three children together—Leona, born in 1905, John D. Jr., born in 1908, and Helen, born in 1910.

Around the same time their first child was born, Hertz entered a new career field: automobiles. "It was by chance, rather than by any design or prophetic sense on my part, that I was first drawn into this young industry," he later said. He took a job as a "demonstrator" for the Columbia automobile agency. His first full year in the business—1905— Hertz did not exactly prove himself a wildly successful salesman, making only around $800 in commissions. The following year, he applied for a $50-per-week managerial role at a rival dealership, and found his stride, earning more than $12,000 once commission was factored in, or more than $350,000 in today's money. "The main reason I succeeded was because I sold, not automobiles, but service," he remembered.

> When I sold a man a car, I was his servant from then on. If one of my customers had a breakdown at 2 o'clock in the morning, he knew that I would be on my way to help him out—cars broke down rather often in those days. I bought supplies for them at cost and did everything I could for them. The result was that my customers sold most of my cars for me.

This focus on customer service made him one of the most successful salesmen on Motor Row. But more importantly, the lessons he learned about the importance of providing unparalleled customer service would go on to play a significant role in Hertz's future endeavors.

In 1907, both Shaw and Hertz were working in the fledgling auto-mobile industry in Chicago, Hertz as a very successful salesman, and Shaw as the owner of a struggling dealership. Sensing an opportunity, Shaw offered Hertz a one-third share in the Walden W. Shaw Company if Hertz would invest $2,000 and come to work for him for an initial salary of $65 per week. A partnership was born.

Hertz and Shaw's success together was almost immediate. By the end of their first year as partners, the Shaw Company's debt was eliminated, and the books showed a profit of $15,000 (more than $450,000 today). Hertz was now the vice president and general manager of the Shaw Company. One of his methods for stimulating sales included an offer to buy back a customer's earlier model automobile—one of the earliest "trade-in" deals. Because of this, a majority of the profits Shaw and Hertz saw in that first year were represented by this fleet of used vehicles for which there was not yet any consumer demand. "As my customers weren't buyers of second-hand cars, I had to put on my thinking cap to find some way of disposing of them or making them earn their keep," Hertz explained. From this dilemma emerged a brilliant business idea. "Having driven a delivery wagon, I figured that there should be money in the passenger delivery business," Hertz continued. "Joy-riding was beginning to become popular. Families were taking to hiring a car for outings, especially on Sundays. And a few taxis were beginning to make their appearance."

Shaw was initially skeptical of the idea, but Hertz convinced him to use a few of the secondhand cars from their trade-in fleet as an automobile livery service. Hiring a handful of chauffeurs at 20 percent commission, Shaw and Hertz started the service by raising $50,000 in capital from investors. They assembled a fleet of ten vehicles—both used trade-ins and new models—and bid on the exclusive livery contract at the Chicago Athletic Association. This initial fleet consisted of Thomas Flyer "touring cars," large-bodied, open-air cars (some with a retractable cloth top) that could seat four to five people. Shaw and Hertz succeeded in winning the contract, which meant that any Chicago Athletic Association member could arrange a Shaw car through the club. No money exchanged hands between the passenger and driver—the fee was attached to the member's bill.

Within two months, the livery service proved so popular that Shaw and Hertz expanded the fleet to forty Thomas Flyers. Shaw Livery contracts followed at other private clubs, hotels, theaters, and restaurants, with the Walden W. Shaw Company stationing uniformed attendants at such venerable locations as the Blackstone Hotel, Marshall Field &

Co., the South Shore Country Club, and the Green Mill Gardens. At these locations, members and patrons found that the in-house car service was a convenient way of arranging and paying for a car, and this drove additional business to Walden W. Shaw Livery. Individual passengers could open their own accounts with the company by completing and returning an account request card, upon receipt of which they were issued a small silver-and-enamel key with their account number printed on it. (For discretion, the women in the household could be issued a separate identifying token.) Account holders arranged a ride by calling the garage at Wabash 5100.

By September 30, 1908, the livery business had grown so rapidly that Shaw and Hertz incorporated the Walden W. Shaw Livery Company to separate the auto dealership and auto livery businesses. At that time, the Shaw Livery fleet of vehicles included touring cars that could be hired by the hour, and two new metered cabs, the taximeter being an emerging technology the company was piloting. In the spring of 1909, the fleet expanded again, and included more than thirty Keeton metered cabs and a fleet of seven-passenger, limousine-style touring cars. Shaw and Hertz had succeeded in securing so many contracts with private businesses that an article in a trade publication in 1909 called Walden W. Shaw Livery the "'Contract Company,' the reason being that they have contracts with the majority of the hotels and clubs to furnish the cabs."

Just two years earlier, Shaw had been a struggling auto dealer. After partnering with Hertz, he was now the owner and president of an extremely successful automobile taxi company. In the fall of 1909, the two men closed the auto dealership to focus entirely on the livery side of the business. And there was still room for considerable growth in the industry—in Chicago in 1909, horse-drawn cabs and hacks still outnumbered metered automobile taxis by a rate of three to one. But that would soon change.

CREATING A BETTER CAB COMPANY

Six years later, on March 31, 1915, Chicagoans opened their *Chicago Tribune* newspapers to page three and learned of "Shaw's New Plan": a new "European-style" and "cut rate" taxi service. "Company Will Operate

'Yellow Cab' Service as Result of Council Action," the subhead read. The news item announcing the Yellow Cab venture in Chicago detailed the many differences between the new service and the previous Shaw Livery experience, chief among them lower prices and the general method by which passengers would hail a cab and pay for the ride:

> The Yellow Cabs will be placed at the public cab stations, of which there are twenty-six in the Loop district, and you will be obliged to go into the street or telephone the main garage to summon them and pay the driver cash, according to the meter, at the end of your ride.

Shaw and Hertz envisioned Yellow Cabs parked at cab stands throughout the city, ready to be hailed by passersby or quickly deployed to the nearest request.

Why did Shaw and Hertz choose the color yellow to brand their new cab venture? The answer to that question remains somewhat elusive. It's possible that Hertz first saw a taxi painted yellow on a trip through New York City in 1914, while he and Fannie were on their way to Paris upon a doctor's recommendation. In Paris, he certainly would have experienced "European-style" taxi service, including the lower rates and the method of hailing a cab directly from the street, all of which would go on to inform his launch of Yellow Cab in Chicago. And undoubtedly Hertz realized that if passengers would be hailing the cabs directly from the street, then visibility was key. Writing several years later about the decision to paint the new cabs yellow, the company's general manager wrote, "When the Yellow Cab Company began operations . . . we purposely selected a conspicuous color, one which every cab user would recognize not only when it was close to him, but when it was a block away."

Addressing the question of the color yellow, a biography of Hertz published in 1926 claimed that Hertz "commissioned a local university to ascertain scientifically which color would stand out strongest at a distance. Tests then conducted gave birth to the bright yellow color." However, a Yellow Taxicab Co. existed in New York City at least as early as 1912, when the New York State Supreme Court determined that the company could not claim an "exclusive right to paint its taxicabs yellow."

Although the article announcing Shaw and Hertz's new Yellow Cab venture referenced "council action" as the inspiration for the new service, in reality, the two men had been working on plans for the new company for over a year. They had seen the need for a new kind of service by March of 1914, when smaller cab companies and independent operators took direct aim at Walden W. Shaw Livery. That month, around two hundred independent cab operators sent a letter of complaint regarding the high, city-regulated taxi rates and a lack of fair competition to the City Council.

Seven months later, on October 5, 1914, the Department of Public Service's Bureau of Valuation Statistics of the City of Chicago had released a report on taxicab rates and vehicle traffic. The report's authors had spent the previous months conducting extensive research on the streets of the Loop in downtown Chicago, investigating vehicle usage and counting the number of taxis, delivery trucks, and other vehicles standing at the curb at any given time. With an eye toward reducing the amount of traffic, they interviewed the professional drivers of these vehicles for their suggestions on how to fix the city's traffic congestion problems, and then conducted a comprehensive review of the methods implemented by other cities around the world to manage congestion.

One of the report's key recommendations was to encourage greater taxi use in Chicago, with the hope of reducing the number of privately owned cars driven and parked in the Loop. "In London and in Paris, a large proportion of the people of ordinary incomes are habituated to the use of taxicabs," wrote the authors. "London has 10,486 motor cabs; Paris 10,088; while Chicago has but 915 . . . advantage will be gained by increasing the number of authorized cab stands."

According to the report, one of the biggest problems in Chicago was that cab rides remained a luxury that only the wealthy could afford. For context, a taxi ride for four people from the Hotel Sherman to the La Salle Street train station, a distance of about eight blocks, cost $1.10, or nearly $28 in today's money. The prices were steep, but the ride was luxurious compared to taxis in many other cities at the time. An editorial in the *New York Tribune* on August 4, 1915, described the author's experience in a Walden W. Shaw taxi-limousine on a recent trip to Chicago: "A

Chicago taxi doesn't look like one. It looks like—it is, in fact—a seven-passenger limousine with the front side-curtains knocked out. It has electric lights and a self-starter. It is upholstered in Spanish leather. It is lighted on the inside. It is clean, inside and out." Chicago's taxi service was tailored specifically to the wealthy, and this was reflected in the price.

The report's authors took direct aim at these practices. Under subheadings like "Present Rates Too High," "Present Service Too Restricted," and "Popularized Service Needed," the report criticized the cab companies' arrangement of exclusive contracts with the clubs, hotels, and restaurants, as well as the city's regulations that set high rates as standard.

> The taxicab companies in this city have apparently found it more profitable to . . . assure to themselves the patronage of those stopping at the first-class hotels by a working agreement with the managements. . . . These hotels give space in their lobbies for a taxicab office, assume the accounts of their guests and receive therefore a commission which is believed to be 10 percent or more in some cases.

The cab companies benefited immensely from these relationships, which ensured a steady pipeline of wealthy clientele. But they were not the only beneficiaries. The system benefited the hotels and clubs as well, as the cab companies often extended reduced rates to an organization's passengers, while the establishments themselves collected increasingly significant commissions and fees from the cab companies as part of their contracts. One Chicago hotel of the era reputedly reaped $20,000 in commissions from a cab company contract in a single year, or more than $500,000 in today's money. These private arrangements were a recipe for tension between the drivers for the big cab companies and the smaller, independent operators. Their animosity toward each other sometimes spilled into the streets.

The same month that the report was released, a handful of diners were enjoying a late supper at the College Inn, the popular restaurant inside the Hotel Sherman at the northwest corner of Clark and Randolph Streets, when a taxi drivers' feud suddenly interrupted their meal. Today, a visit to the former site of the Hotel Sherman reveals nothing of the history of the block. Instead, a building that looks like a bloated spaceship wedges itself into the middle of the Loop—the architecturally daring James R. Thompson Center, all glass and rounded walls, built in a spurt of public building in the 1970s. However, in 1914, the Hotel Sherman rose authoritatively over the busy intersection, rebuilt just three years earlier in the grand Beaux-Arts style and designed by the venerated Chicago architects Holabird & Roche. The 757-room hotel was one of the most well-regarded hotels in Chicago at the time, and its basement level contained the popular College Inn, which drew locals as well as out-of-town visitors looking for a trendy restaurant experience. Walden W. Shaw Livery had secured the taxi contract for the Hotel Sherman and the College Inn restaurant, which billed itself as the "World's Most Famous Restaurant."

At 9:00 p.m. on October 19, 1914, the elegant lobby of the Hotel Sherman began to fill with a noxious scent. The smell intensified, quickly creeping into the basement-level College Inn, where diners feasted on meals of whole squab chicken, roast prime rib, or broiled, fresh-caught lake trout. Guests in the restaurant and on the main floor of the hotel abruptly fled the scene to avoid the terrible smell, which was so potent it could be detected as high as the eleventh floor. The driver of a Walden W. Shaw taxi posted outside the Hotel Sherman later alleged that a rival cab driver threw a stinkbomb toward him, which landed inside the Clark Street entrance of the posh hotel instead.

A newspaper item about the incident the following day declared, "Stink Bomb Hurled in Taxi War Hits Hotel," marking the first time the words "Taxi War" appeared in print in Chicago. It would not be the last. Though it was a relatively small gesture of protest against the exclusivity of the relationship between Walden W. Shaw Livery and the Hotel Sherman, the stinkbomb evoked a strong response from those who were present that night. The public was fed up.

Following the release of the city's report, and the incident at the Hotel Sherman, public sentiment began to turn against the clubby luxury of the current taxi landscape. Shaw and Hertz must have sensed this shift, intuiting that the regulations, which were currently so favorable to their company, could not survive long given the public feeling. In January of

1915, they had quietly incorporated a new cab entity under their names, filing the articles of incorporation in Maine, where tax laws were particularly favorable at the time. They called the new company Yellow Cab.

A few months later, when the City Council passed a compromise version of the rate reductions requested by the independent cab operators, Shaw and Hertz had this ace up their sleeve. If they were prohibited from making the kind of profits they were accustomed to with a luxury taxi, they would just have to create a new kind of cab service, one that would reduce overhead and hopefully attract a wider demographic to the convenience of taxi rides. They were ready to roll out their new business.

THE DAWN OF MODERN TAXIS

When they announced this new venture, Shaw and Hertz made it clear that the new Yellow Cab Company rates not only adhered to the recently passed city rules, but in fact they were 25 percent lower. Shaw and Hertz felt it was important to assure riders that the price reduction did not mean the service was similarly cut-rate, so they made sure that the first Yellow Cab ads emphasized that the cars would be "clean as a whistle, sanitary to a [high] degree, subjected to careful daily inspection and have all the devices that contribute to absolute safety." For riders who may have expressed skepticism about the quality of the drivers themselves, Yellow Cab's ads boasted that every cab would be driven by a married man who was fully insured. As general manager, Hertz required that all Yellow Cab drivers be clean-shaven and well-presented. This included a strict uniform: well-shined shoes, a hat, a white collar, a coat, and puttees (leather wraps that covered the driver's calves and protected his pants from dirt and mud). Hertz also required his drivers to carry whisk brooms to sweep the cabs after every load, and wool lap blankets for passengers to use in the unheated automobiles during the winter months, which drivers were required to carefully refold in the backseat after each use. To ensure full adherence with these policies, he required drivers to present themselves to the main dispatcher for inspection at the start of every shift.

To further assure riders of the quality of the drivers, early Yellow Cab ads explained the company's intention to give the drivers "every inducement to become courteous and accommodating business men" by initiating an employee profit-sharing plan whereby drivers would split 20 percent of the total profits of the company among them. Before the employees could share in the profits of Yellow Cab, however, the company had to be operating in the black. The startup costs of a new taxi service were significant: It took a large outlay of funds to manufacture the first fifty cars in the fleet. Early Yellow Cab ads minced no words about the financial risk Shaw and Hertz undertook in forming this new kind of taxi service. "The burden of expense that is necessary to operate the present Shaw [Livery] Service is too great to be borne by a company that charges as low rates as the Yellow Cab Company," the ads announced flatly. Shaw Livery operated what amounted to luxury cars, and the cost to ride in one reflected the high-end experience. Yellow Cab would lower its rates by streamlining and modernizing its operations, but the experience to the average rider would change slightly, Shaw and Hertz wanted the city to understand. Despite this, the ads promised potential riders that Yellow Cab would "afford every convenience that is possible at the low rates to be charged."

Shaw and Hertz called it the "European model" to impart a certain air of sophistication on the endeavor, and also because this type of affordable taxi already existed elsewhere in the world—Paris, London, and even New York City—but it had yet to be tried in Chicago. "So we are making this experiment," Hertz explained to a *Chicago Tribune* reporter. "In a word, we will compete with ourselves, for the Yellow Cab Company will be a separate concern [from Shaw Livery]. . . . Such conveniences as calling a cab at a hotel, café, or club and simply signing a ticket are not possible at the rate we propose to charge. The experiment will be surrounded by the fairest possible conditions and the public will have to be the referee. Personally, I believe that mighty few people who use taxicabs steadily will sacrifice convenience and luxury to save a few cents a mile. But we shall see." In the first ads for Yellow Cab, Shaw and Hertz continued this tone of skeptical acquiescence. "The whole thing is an experiment and we are going to give Chicago the chance to choose between the Yellow Cabs and the luxurious limousines operated by the Walden W. Shaw Company," the ad copy read. "It's up to the public whether or not the experiment succeeds. If it does succeed, we will flood Chicago with Yellow Cabs. We will put them everywhere."

"Your move, Chicago," the ads seemed to be saying. Show us how much you want an affordable taxi service. Open your wallets and prove it to us.

CHAPTER 2

License to Drive

Yellow Cab's Rapid Rise Inspires Bad Blood (1916)

IN FACT, CHICAGO DID OPEN ITS WALLETS. BY JANUARY 1916, JUST FIVE months after Katherine Stinson took to the air over Grant Park and the first Yellow Cabs appeared on the streets, the Yellow Cab Company was thriving and outgrowing its space in the shared Shaw Livery garage. To gain the space necessary for the expansion they already envisioned for Yellow Cab, Shaw and Hertz worked out an agreement with a local contractor to build a new garage for the company. It would be located on 21st Street between Michigan and Wabash, just off the city's famed Motor Row.

The new Yellow Cab garage would reportedly be one of the largest in the country, measuring one hundred feet by two hundred feet and four stories high. It would be made of concrete, a new and revolutionary building material. In addition to housing the company's fleet of vehicles, the new garage would provide space for Yellow Cab's mechanics and car wash staff. While other taxi companies expected drivers to perform all of the cleaning and maintenance of their vehicles, Shaw and Hertz preferred to hire dedicated staff for each task, with the intention of prolonging the lives of the vehicles by ensuring expert care. Another notable feature of the new garage space was the dispatch center, where a team of telephone operators served as the nucleus of the operation, receiving taxi requests from customers and passing those requests along to the starter at the nearest cab stand. The top floors of the garage contained office space for a team of bookkeepers and in-house lawyers and, eventually, even a company tailor, dentist, doctor, and nurse.

CHARLES W. "CHARLIE" GRAY

The move into the new garage was overseen in part by Yellow Cab garage superintendent Charles Wellington "Charlie" Gray, already a fixture in the young company and destined to play an even more important role in Yellow Cab's future. Gray was born in Saint Louis in 1874 and moved to Chicago with his family at the age of eight. Very soon after that, Gray started working as a newspaper boy to help supplement the family income. He eventually made enough money selling papers to attend one year of college at the University of Illinois at Champaign. Returning to Chicago, he took a job as an office boy at a Chicago newspaper called the *Inter Ocean*, rapidly working his way up to treasurer and business manager.

Gray grew into a very tall and athletically built young man (described by his colleagues as a "tower among men"), with a genial smile, dark hair, and brown eyes set beneath thick eyebrows. He was naturally friendly and outgoing, well liked by almost everyone who met him. In 1894, at the age of nineteen, Gray had married Mae Fitzpatrick, and the two had quickly gone on to have three children together. Unfortunately for the young family, by the turn of the twentieth century, the *Inter Ocean* was struggling to stay afloat financially. Around the age of thirty, Gray suddenly found himself unemployed from his salaried newspaper job. "I didn't have a dime, and I had debts," he told a friend in the newspaper business many years later. "I could have borrowed from friends of more prosperous days, but I didn't want to do it. I had determined to come back, and I wanted to do it alone." Luckily, Gray had one passionate hobby that would prove to be fortuitous: Like Shaw and Hertz, he was mad for automobiles.

Gray was what Chicagoans at the time called "an avid automobilist." In 1903, when his finances were still strong, he bought a new make of automobile called a Peerless (one of fewer than five hundred in existence at the time). He served as the president of the Chicago Automobile Club (CAC), then in its infancy and soon to merge with several other automobile clubs around the country to form the American Auto Association (AAA). As president of the CAC, Gray spent his free time driving from Chicago to points around the country, on dirt and gravel roads, attempting to break time records set by other automobilists. Through his connections at the CAC, Gray may have met Walden W. Shaw.

Crucially to his future, Gray was also close friends with John D. Hertz. Gray was just five years older than Hertz, and the two men grew up not far from each other on the city's working-class West Side. Both Gray and Hertz started out as newspaper boys, and went on to work in the industry: Hertz at the Chicago *Morning Herald*, Gray at the *Inter Ocean*. Hertz and Gray were lifelong friends.

Gray initially sought out a job as a driver for one of the city's first automobile cab companies by single-handedly reassembling a broken-down car left abandoned in the company's garage. The manager was so impressed with Gray's mechanical abilities that he offered him a job on the spot. Gray went on to become a hugely successful taxi driver, one of the highest earners in the Loop in the earliest days of the industry. Though it was a step down in status from his previous newspaper position, the job of driver was a good fit for him. Gray's natural affability meant he was popular with his colleagues as well as his passengers, and, as a chauffeur, he spent his days doing the thing that he seemed to love best: driving around the city in an automobile. However, by the time Gray began his new career in the cab industry, the reversal of fortune had taken a toll on his personal life. In 1904, he and wife, Mae, had divorced, and she moved to the city's North Side with their three children. What Mae could not have known was that Charlie Gray's fortune was about to turn around, in a big way.

As soon as Shaw and Hertz formed Shaw Livery in 1908, John Hertz offered his old friend Gray a management position in the operations department, but Gray initially turned it down. "I cannot afford it," he said, calculating that he could make more money as a driver than he would be paid as a manager. Gray continued as a driver until he had repaid all of his debts and built up a comfortable savings once again. Then, in October of 1909, Gray joined Shaw Livery as a "road man," inspecting Shaw cars on the street for $20 per week. He was eventually promoted to garage superintendent of Shaw Livery (and eventually of Yellow Cab when it was formed in 1915). By that time, Gray's personal life was looking up as well. On September 17, 1914, the thirty-nine-year-old Charlie Gray married his second wife, twenty-six-year-old Johanna Margaret Berg, a Chicago native born to Scandinavian immigrants. Family lore indicates that the two met when Berg, a stenographer, had been hired to work as Gray's secretary at Shaw Livery, retiring from this position when she married Gray. Between 1915 and 1922, Charlie and Margaret Gray would go on to have six children together: five girls and a boy they named after Gray's boss and lifelong friend—John Hertz Gray.

CABS FOR EVERY CHICAGOAN

It didn't take long after its debut for Yellow Cab's new European-style cab service to become a fixture of daily life in Chicago—and an exciting form of transportation for the many visitors who arrived in the city every day. In fact, it is not an overstatement to say that Yellow Cab's appearance on the streets of Chicago revolutionized the city's nascent taxi industry. For the first time, the practice of standing on the street and whistling for a taxi became a reality for a majority of city-dwellers. Cabs were no longer the exclusive domain of the wealthy, who could call them from their expensive clubs and hotels. Due to the more egalitarian cab-hailing methods and the more affordable rates, taxis became a part of modern, daily life for Chicago's average citizen. As a result, business was booming. On New Year's Eve, 1915, Hertz estimated that there were three times as many cab requests as on an ordinary night (a cold rain that year helped boost the numbers). "It was by far the biggest taxi business the city ever experienced" to that point, he said. Between Yellow Cab and Shaw Livery, Shaw and Hertz estimated that they collected around nineteen thousand fares in that single night. By contrast, Atlas Cab Company claimed the next-highest number of fares at 4,352.

Without question, the European-style taxi service was proving to be extremely lucrative for Shaw and Hertz. However, it had one significant drawback over the earlier Shaw Livery model: In the absence of charge accounts, drivers were now required to carry cash, leaving them vulnerable to robbery. In the first year of Yellow Cab's operation, several drivers reported being robbed. In one newsworthy incident in January 1916, a Yellow Cab driver was shot in the hand and robbed at gunpoint by three assailants, two men and a woman. They were eventually caught after Hertz offered a $1,000 reward for information, but the arrest did little to stop the problem: Robberies continued to plague the company.

Early Strikes: A History of Tension Between Labor and Management

Another point of contention for Yellow Cab involved ongoing tension between the drivers affiliated with the union, and nonunion drivers. Bad blood between labor and management in the taxi industry dated back more than six years. It first arose in 1909, when nine hundred taxi drivers, all members of the International Brotherhood of Teamsters, Chauffeurs, Stablemen and Helpers, had voted to strike for reduced hours. Standard driver pay rates at the time stood at $12 per week, with drivers expected to work a grueling schedule of seven days a week at twelve hours per day. The striking drivers had demanded a reduction of that standard schedule to a six-day, seventy-two-hour work week, for the same wages. To counter the union's demands, a coalition of the owners of nine of the city's livery companies—Shaw Livery among them—had formed the Automobile Transportation Association of Chicago, and together they refused to compromise with the drivers. The striking drivers had ultimately been forced to give up their protest and returned to work at their original hours and wages. Stung by their failure and still angry at their working conditions, the drivers had returned with a bitter resentment that only grew stronger.

Their dissatisfaction had come to a boiling point a year later, on the evening of April 4, 1910. That night, Chicago's wealthiest citizens had stood in their well-stocked dressing rooms, donning their finest dresses, silks, suits, hats, and jewels as they eagerly anticipated the opening of the "grand opera season," which was about to open in a typically glittering triumph. On the program was the Metropolitan Opera Company of New York performing *La Gioconda*, led by the world-famous Italian conductor Arturo Toscanini. One of the soloists listed for the performance that evening was the world-renowned lyric tenor Enrico Caruso. It would be one of the great social events of the season.

Dressed in the latest Edwardian fashions, many of the opera-goers had headed out first for an early dinner at the finest restaurants in the city, or made their way to their luxuriously appointed private clubs to enjoy an aperitif and a little gossip before curtain time. Many of them had then arranged to take auto taxis to 50 E. Congress Avenue, where the regal stone façade of the Auditorium Theater rose above them, imposing and impressive. As the opera-goers arrived and stepped out of their taxis, they could not have guessed that none of those taxis—not a single one— would return to take them home that night.

The time had come for the union drivers to renegotiate their contracts, and they were demanding their standard salary of $12 per week plus 20 percent of any cab fare in excess of $60 that they earned in a week. They also demanded that they be required to work no more than fifteen hours out of each twenty-four-hour day. But the cab company owners refused to even respond to these demands. So while the city's elite had been dropped off at the Auditorium Theater that evening, off-duty drivers from six of the main cab companies gathered in a meeting room above a restaurant just two blocks away. After three hours of deliberation, the union drivers decided to order a general strike—about an hour before the final curtain call at the opera. As scouts spread the news among idling taxis on the streets, the drivers, "no matter where they were or what the conditions, immediately put on full speed for the garages," knowing that this would leave the opera-goers scrambling to find a ride home.

As Chicago's wealthiest had emerged from the Auditorium Theater after the performance, they found only horse-drawn cabs waiting for them, many of which had been quickly harnessed to their carriages and hastily deployed from their stables as news of the auto taxi drivers' strike spread. When all of the horse-drawn cabs were claimed, some of the city's elite trudged up the steps to the L or crowded into horsecars, resigned to taking common public transportation while dressed in their finest clothes.

Despite the strike, no resolution to the auto taxi drivers' demands was forthcoming. By early May, the strike had already dragged on for almost a month when the cab companies had sued the striking drivers for breach of contract, and warned them that the taxis would be returned to the streets with "scab" replacement drivers. On May 9, 1910, a picket line of union drivers had gathered at the Owen H. Fay garage as that cab company for the first time loaded six taxis with scabs as drivers and placed a sheriff's deputy in each car for protection. The taxis had pulled out of the garage, tailed aggressively by union leaders in a large touring car. As the procession had passed under the railroad viaduct on Motor Row, another group of union taxi drivers standing on the railroad tracks threw bricks at the passing cabs, smashing car windows and injuring at least one of the scabs.

Particularly galling to the striking drivers had been the cab companies' use of the sheriff's deputies and other armed police for the protection of the scabs. By June, the Chicago Federation of Labor, backing the union taxi drivers, had publicly questioned the "right of the city to pay for police protection for the taxicab companies" and went on to "pledge its moral and financial support to the fullest extent of its ability to the striking chauffeurs." The mayor replied that he had ordered the police protection at the request of the cab company owners because he agreed that "their property was in danger of destruction."

The strikers had continued to disrupt the work of the scabs by a variety of methods. A favorite means of labor resistance involved throwing stinkbombs into the lobbies of the upscale hotels that held cab contracts. This tactic so enraged Walden Shaw that he had directed his legal team to file an injunction against the strikers, after it was reported that the Hotel La Salle had considered dropping its Shaw Livery contract due to the incidents.

A circuit court judge granted Shaw the sweeping injunction—"prohibiting the strikers, officers of the chauffeurs' union and their 'associates, allies and confederates' from picketing or in any manner assaulting, intimidating or persuading employees of the company and interfering with its business and the operation of taxicabs." But shortly afterward, the strikers were at it again. They had placed sharp tacks on Diversey Boulevard, along a route they knew many of the scab-driven Shaw taxis would be navigating on their way to transport passengers from a downtown conference to a private event at Riverview Park, Chicago's answer to Coney Island. Upon arrival, about a dozen of the cars reported punctured tires.

By the end of July 1910, with the strike about to enter its fourth month, the skirmishes continued when two men had been arrested for physically assaulting the business agent for the union. When questioned by police, one of the assailants, Henry Hunt, claimed he had been offered $7 a day by the cab companies for the work of assaulting striking taxi drivers and labor leaders, at a guaranteed contract rate of at least one beating per day.

Not long after this conspiracy was made public in the newspapers, the strikers had retaliated with several attacks of their own. On August 11, a man and a woman in town for the Knights Templar convention were riding in a scab-driven taxi when strikers threw a bottle containing a concoction of benzine and phosphorus through the open passenger window. It broke on impact, burning the hands of the two tourists and destroying the woman's clothing. A few days later, another scab driver for Shaw Livery had been hit in the head by a brick thrown by a striker, necessitating treatment at St. Luke's Hospital.

By September of that year, the strike had taken a significant toll on the cab companies. Of the initial seven companies involved in the labor dispute, two of them went bankrupt, and one—the City Motor Cab Co.—had faced such steep financial losses that the owners agreed to merge with Shaw Livery. Facing similar fates, the owners of two of the remaining major cab companies had agreed to settle with the International Brotherhood of Teamsters. On September 2, 1910, at 6:00 p.m., twenty-five of the striking drivers had returned to work at a rate of $18 per week for a seventy-hour work week, or no more than ten hours a day, seven days a week. The remaining cab companies had settled within a few days, ending the five-month-long strike. The first cab company to settle the dispute cited "a dearth of nonunion drivers" for their decision to compromise, suggesting that the intimidation tactics employed by the union drivers against the scabs had proved extremely effective. For better or worse, it was a lesson that the cab drivers would remember in future battles.

Early Skirmishes Across the Union Divide

Since founding Yellow Cab in 1915, Shaw and Hertz had not changed their attitude toward organized labor, and so they still did not recognize or allow unionization at their company: Like Shaw Livery, Yellow Cab was a staunchly nonunion shop. As a result, in the earliest days of the company, Yellow Cab drivers often fell afoul of unionized labor. In January, 1916, the *Chicago Day Book*, a union-friendly daily newspaper catering to the working classes, publicly lambasted Shaw Livery and Yellow Cab for their refusal to recognize unions. The *Day Book* later alleged that a Yellow Cab driver had been fired for "being disloyal to the company and his fellow workers by negotiating with the union and promising to join." The unionized taxi drivers continued to deem Yellow Cab a "scab concern," and conflicts on the street reminiscent of the 1910 clashes continued intermittently. On January 22, 1916, eight union teamsters beat a Yellow Cab driver into unconsciousness on Division Street after they all found themselves drinking together at a nearby bar. Four months later, two more Yellow Cab drivers were robbed by striking union drivers. Tensions between the union drivers and Yellow Cab drivers only seemed to escalate with Yellow Cab's increasing success.

By May 1916, that success was undeniable. A little more than a year had passed since Hertz made his dramatic prediction that the City Council's new rate regulations would force him to "withdraw the finest taxicab service of any city." In fact, it was just the opposite. It had forced Shaw and Hertz to invent the most popular taxicab service in the city. The Yellow Cab Company could barely keep up with rider demand. Shaw and Hertz had already reduced the rates once in the beginning of 1916, but by June, business was so profitable that they decided to reduce their rates by an additional 30 percent, a move that only served to further increase ridership. (Drivers' salaries were unaffected by the rate change.) After starting their fleet with forty-five cabs just ten months earlier, Shaw and Hertz were on track to have three hundred Yellow Cabs on the street by the end of the year.

EXPLOSIVE ESCALATION

Just before 9:00 p.m. on July 28, 1916, Shaw Livery driver James V. Anderson sat parked in front of the Hotel La Salle, hoping to pick up a fare among the several hundred people inside who were dining and drinking on a typically busy night. The city was in the middle of a deadly heat wave, with seventy-nine Chicagoans dying as a direct result of the heat that day alone. As Anderson sat sweltering in his car that evening, two pedestrians ambled down the sidewalk past him. A streetcar headed south down the block.

Anderson didn't know it, but in the shadows of a nearby alley, a man, about twenty-five years old, five-foot-six-inches tall and "wearing a cap," according to witness reports, lit a match and put fire to a homemade bomb of paper, rags, and black powder. He threw it toward Anderson's cab and ran, fleeing eastward. The bomb exploded with a loud bang, stopping conversations in the hotel and knocking the tobacco pipe out of one nearby pedestrian's hand. Despite its loud noise, the bomb did no lasting damage to the cab. Upon investigation, the police attributed the incident to the bad blood between the union cab drivers and the nonunion Shaw employees. "Bomb Exploded in Loop Near Hotel; Taxi War Blamed," read a headline in the *Chicago Examiner* the following day.

Just ten days later, on August 7, a Shaw Livery garage was again targeted by bomb-throwers. That garage contained an automobile elevator, and the bomb exploded when it hit the steel elevator gate. The sound of the explosion woke people in the nearby Blackstone and Congress Hotels and caused minor damage to the structure, but no one was hurt. By this time, Hertz was angry. In the *Chicago Tribune* the following day, he announced that the Shaw company was offering a $5,000 reward to anyone who could provide information leading to the arrest and conviction of the person responsible. "We have evidence that the attack on our garage was inspired by a one-man organization that has been trying to blackmail us and our employees for six years," he added, referencing the 1910 union skirmishes.

The offer of a reward did not stop the attacks, however. The following week, on August 13, three men in a black touring car threw a bomb at a Yellow Cab that was parked at a busy intersection northwest of the

Loop—the driver had just stepped out of the cab and into a nearby shop. The touring car quickly drove away, but the bomb failed to detonate. A pedestrian who witnessed the bomb attempt retrieved the failed explosive and turned it over to the police. They noted that the bomb was made of iron pipe filled with powder and nails, nested into a pasteboard candy box and wrapped in paper. Two months later, on October 19, the bomb-throwers hit their target when a bomb on a timer exploded at the Yellow Cab manufacturing plant on the West Side, injuring one employee and blowing a hole in the roof.

Hertz's assertion that the perpetrator was a one-man operation may have been designed to ignore or intentionally misdirect attention away from the escalation of the labor tensions surrounding the taxi companies in 1916. By that time, the union had gained enough strength to establish a standard pay rate of $18 per week plus 35 cents per hour overtime. The union also demanded that taxi drivers be allowed to take at least one day off every two weeks. The nonunion Shaw and Yellow Cabs defied these requirements, and the relationships between union drivers and Shaw and Yellow Cab drivers frequently escalated to violence. The tensions were not limited to these companies. In fact, the Atlas Company had similar problems: Some of its drivers joined the union, while others did not, occasionally leading to open hostility that endangered passengers, as when a union driver threw a brick through the window of a cab driven by a nonunion driver, hitting a woman riding in the backseat. She was more stunned than hurt, but the incident demonstrated that, for the average bystander, the combative exchanges between cab drivers could leave the taxi-riding public caught in the middle.

The Formation of the Walden W. Shaw Manufacturing Company

Although these labor battles created a charged environment on the streets of the city, Shaw and Hertz continued expanding their fleet of cabs. The biggest challenge to this expansion involved the auto manufacturing itself. Shaw and Hertz had initially designed the Yellow Cab themselves, customizing the car specifically for taxi use to meet the demands of their new business venture. To ensure that Yellow Cab would have enough automobiles in their fleet to meet the escalating demand, they had been manufacturing the cabs as quickly as they could, using an initial $50,000 capital investment. At their downtown manufacturing location, eighty employees turned out about one cab per day. The company had recently expanded to a similar operation on the West Side. So in September 1916, Shaw and Hertz incorporated the manufacturing arm of the business as the Walden W. Shaw Manufacturing Company.

By manufacturing the taxis in-house, Shaw and Hertz were able to control production quality and quantity to guarantee an adequate supply of new cars to keep up with demand. They were also free to experiment with innovations that would make Yellow Cab drivers' lives easier, and make passengers' rides more enjoyable, including the invention of the "first automatic windshield wipers" and early adoption of the first balloon tires. It turned out to be a very successful endeavor. Soon, Walden W. Shaw Manufacturing was selling exclusive car parts direct to automobile owners, as well as manufacturing cabs for taxi affiliates in other states. By the end of 1916, the Yellow Cab Company boasted 270 cabs on the street, with thirty more already in progress or scheduled for production. Having nearly achieved the promised three hundred Yellow Cabs on the city's streets, the company aimed even higher. In an announcement that would have sounded preposterous just twelve months earlier, Hertz promised a huge expansion plan. "As rapidly as possible," Hertz promised in the *Chicago Tribune* in December 1916, "700 new Yellow taxicabs will be constructed and put into service, bringing the total to an even 1,000."

Less than two months after forming Walden W. Shaw Manufacturing, Shaw and Hertz incorporated the Shaw Corporation, a parent holding company to oversee the rapidly growing Shaw empire. To guide the parent company, they attracted several powerful names to serve as directors, including F. B. Hitchcock, an insurance broker whose father was the vice president of the First National Bank of Chicago, and M. S. Rosenwald, brother of Sears, Roebuck and Co. president Julius Rosenwald.

Shaw Corporation stocks went public on October 27, 1916, with $900,000 in preferred stock and forty thousand shares of common stock. Less than a month later, on November 22, Shaw and Hertz made good on their promise to make the employees part-owners of the company: The

Shaw Company purchased $100,000 of the preferred stock and resold it to the company's four hundred drivers, mechanics, office workers, and other Shaw employees. Through an agreement with the common stock holders, any employee who purchased two shares of the Shaw Company stock received a third share as a gift. The demand from employees was so great that Shaw and Hertz were forced to devise a system based on seniority to dole out the stock options. "Our men are salesmen of taxicab service," Hertz explained to a reporter. "Our great success is due to our profit sharing with employees."

With this development, the vast majority of Yellow Cab drivers were now employee-owners, thereby cementing their nonunion status. While they may have celebrated their new status and enjoyed the promise of increasing financial success, the profit-sharing plan also laid the groundwork for ongoing and escalating tensions between the International Brotherhood of Teamsters and the Shaw Livery and Yellow Cab employees. Everyone involved would soon find themselves on the front lines of a street battle that grew more heated by the day.

The Hotel La Salle Taxi Fleet
The report arrived on the desk of Ernest J. Stevens, vice president and manager of the Hotel La Salle, on November 29, 1916. It was marked "strictly confidential." On three carefully typewritten, mimeographed pages, the anonymous author laid out in minute detail every financial aspect of the newly formed Walden W. Shaw Corporation, down to even the family history and personal financial stability of the principal shareholders and decision-makers. (Secretary-Treasurer John Borden, an adventurer who was one of four heirs to a lead mining fortune, was described as "prompt pay and absolutely responsible for any obligation he incurs.") This marked the first time that Stevens had hired a private investigator to conduct significant opposition research on his rival, Yellow Cab.

Stevens was no pushover. He was a respected hotelier and a shrewd businessman, and he was well connected among Chicago's social and business elites. He was born in 1884 in the small farming town of Colchester, Illinois, one of two sons born to Jessie and James W. Stevens, the latter of whom would go on to found the Illinois Life Insurance Company before entering the hotel business. The family moved to Chicago when Stevens, "Ernie" to his family, was just five years old, and his brother Ray was seven. They rented a house in a then-fashionable part of the South Side. In Chicago, Ernie's father sought out new business opportunities, and, in the 1890s, he did not have to look far to find them. Around the same time he was starting what would become the Illinois Life Insurance Company, James Stevens also bought two adjacent, empty lots in the Oakland neighborhood and funded the construction of an extravagant house with seven marble bathrooms.

Although he had hoped to flip the house for a profit, the home sat empty, its price tag of $40,000 (more than $1.1 million today) too high to attract buyers. Instead, his wife secretly arranged to have all of the family's furniture transferred from their rental into the spec home, surprising her husband with the move. So Ernie and Ray grew up in this grandiose home, built "in the florid style of the nineties," as a reporter described it many decades later. While the Stevenses may have presented the image of a happy family to the outside world, the marriage of James and Jessie Stevens was in fact severely strained. Finally, in 1903, when Ernie was a student at the University of Chicago, his parents divorced. James and Jessie Stevens never saw or spoke to each other again. At the time of the divorce, James moved out of the grand Oakland house, but Ernie continued to live there with his mother until he finished school. Despite his parents' estrangement, he remained close to his father, and they grew to develop similar business interests. After college, Ernie continued on to Northwestern University Law School. In 1907, he married Elizabeth Street and they moved together to Hyde Park.

By this time, James W. Stevens had expanded his reach beyond insurance to real estate and dry goods, and he also had his eye on an ambitious new endeavor: hotels. In the first decades of the twentieth century, Chicago hotels were internationally famous for their opulence and enormous size. The world-famous Palmer House Hotel at that time boasted a twenty-five-foot-high rotunda, an Egyptian parlor, furniture imported from Europe, and a grand dining room with Corinthian columns, marble floors, and Italian frescoes. The Auditorium Hotel featured four hundred luxuriously appointed rooms, a theater that could seat forty-two hundred people, and a tower rising 238 feet in the air from which guests could enjoy a panoramic view of the Loop below. The twenty-three story Blackstone Hotel, built in 1910, laid claim to being the site of the largest pane of glass in America (a window in its main dining room), and featured private elevators for its wealthiest guests.

Seeking to join the rarefied world of Chicago hoteliers, in 1908, James Stevens and a group of investors began construction of the Hotel La Salle on the northwest corner of La Salle and Madison Streets in the heart of the Loop. Ernie joined the family business as the hotel's vice president and manager. As partners, Ernie and his father proved to be smart and ambitious. When the Hotel La Salle opened the following year, the Stevenses demonstrated that they knew exactly what wealthy guests wanted in a luxury hotel. The building stood twenty-two stories tall and contained more than a thousand guest rooms. Designed by Holabird & Roche, the Hotel La Salle was one of the most stylish hotels in the city in the 1910s. Visitors entering through its doors would find themselves passing through an ornate, Circassian walnut-paneled lobby decorated in a lavish Louis XIV style, perhaps heading for the lush palm room or one of the elegant dining spaces, each full of fine furniture, marble, brass, and crystal. The hotel's Blue Fountain Room became a popular post-theater dining spot for the city's patrons of the arts. Famous Chicago journalist-turned-screenwriter Ben Hecht once described the Blue Fountain Room as a place where "a single meal meant bankruptcy." During a brief trip to Chicago to participate in the city's annual St. Patrick's Day Parade in 1910, President William Howard Taft even occupied the Hotel La Salle's second-floor Presidential Suite.

To travel around the city, guests of the Hotel La Salle were able to walk or take advantage of the city's patchwork of public transportation, including trains, streetcars, and horse-drawn omnibuses. But for most of the wealthy hotel guests, they preferred to ride in a private automobile. When the Hotel La Salle was first built, prior to the City Council's taxi rate reduction ordinance of March 1915, taxi rides were still mostly reserved for the upper classes. The wealthy and fashionable guests of the Hotel La Salle liked to travel in style and comfort, and they represented exactly the clientele whose attention a taxi company of the time hoped to attract. Shaw and Hertz knew that, to have a successful cab business in the early 1910s, they needed access to exactly the kind of people who stayed at the Hotel La Salle.

So, in keeping with the predominant practice in the city at the time, they had worked out an arrangement with hotel manager Ernest J. Stevens, who agreed to lease his posh establishment's cab privileges to them—for a price. During the Hotel La Salle's first full year of operation in 1910, Walden W. Shaw Livery took over the hotel's cab stand. It was a lucrative arrangement for Stevens. Each year, he raised the price that he demanded of Shaw and Hertz to hold on to that cab stand privilege. By 1916, Yellow Cab was paying $1,000 per month (more than $23,500 per month in today's money) for the right to operate an exclusive taxi stand in front of the Hotel La Salle, and gain more or less unchallenged access to the taxi business of the hotel's wealthy guests.

But with the introduction of Yellow Cab and the "European" system of taxi hailing in 1915, the exclusivity contract with the Hotel La Salle must have seemed less and less necessary to Shaw and Hertz. If guests of the hotel could simply walk outside and whistle for a Yellow Cab, the large sums of money Shaw and Hertz paid to the Hotel La Salle suddenly seemed unnecessary. The old system no longer benefited them in the same way it once had, and the two men were ready to end their contract payments to the hotel.

THE BEGINNING OF A WAR

The streets around the Hotel La Salle were filled with record-breaking crowds of holiday shoppers when James W. Stevens discovered among his mail one morning an envelope from the Walden W. Shaw Corporation. In it, he found a standard, corporate holiday card—creamy white stationery with the word *Shaw* inscribed inside a respectable green wreath—the printed text below it reading, "We count among our assets the good will you have shown during the past year and it prompts us to wish a happy new year to you." Tucked in with the bland holiday greeting was a typewritten letter from John Hertz.

"Dear sir," it read. "Effective January 1st, 1917, the station heretofore maintained at the Hotel La Salle will be discontinued. Our contract terminates on that date. THERE WAS NO QUESTION OF SERVICE INVOLVED." The letter went on to describe a new arrangement between Yellow Cab and the hotel. "A new station has been located directly across the street from the Hotel La Salle at 17 N. La Salle Street."

The news that Yellow Cab was discontinuing its arrangement with the Hotel La Salle probably did not come as a surprise to James Stevens that day. In fact, the looming deadline for the agreement's renewal appears to be the event which prompted Ernest J. Stevens to hire a private investigator and order that first report on Yellow Cab in November. All the parties involved knew that the contract was due to renew on January 1, 1917. Stevens later claimed that during contract renewal negotiations, Hertz had refused to accept his proposed rate for the exclusive rights to a cab stand, rejecting the current rate of $12,000 per year and offering instead only $8,500 per year. Stevens rejected the counteroffer, and as the end of the year drew closer, he began quietly assembling the necessary components for the Hotel La Salle to begin operating its own in-house fleet of cabs, amassing a handful of Willys-Knight touring cars. This was no small investment. Records from the Hotel La Salle taxicab department indicate that Stevens spent nearly $80,000 on taxis and taxi equipment in 1917 to get the service up and running.

By establishing an in-house fleet of cabs at the Hotel La Salle, both James and Ernie Stevens knew they were entering into direct competition with Yellow Cab and its new cab stand directly across the street. What the Stevens father and son could not have realized at the time were the repercussions that would reverberate through the city, costing lives and endangering the welfare of an untold numbers of drivers, riders, and innocent bystanders. Years later, when a grand jury was tasked with investigating the Taxi Wars, all of the involved parties agreed that there, in that slim holiday greeting, was the opening salvo of what would eventually become an all-out war.

CHAPTER 3

The Rubber Meets the Road

The Earliest Battles of the Taxi Wars (1917–1918)

THE FIRST WEEK OF 1917 BROUGHT WINDY AND RELATIVELY WARM weather to downtown Chicago, with the temperature reaching an unseasonably balmy high of 44 degrees, though the wind howled and raged and rattled the windows, making it feel much colder to the pedestrians who hurried in the streets clutching their coat collars closed. Like the rest of the country, Chicago's mood was anxious, as local newspapers kept one eye turned toward the war in Europe, still hoping the United States might be able to avoid involvement, while increasingly warning that American entry to the war seemed likely. As a distraction from the darkness of a Chicago winter, local movie theaters carried a wide selection of silent films with titles like *The Girl Who Did Not Care*, *The Honor of Mary Blake*, *An Enemy to the King*, and *Nanette of the Wilds*.

Visitors staying at the Hotel La Salle that week may have considered themselves lucky to have avoided the worst bitterly cold temperatures that a Chicago winter can produce. They also had the distinction of being the first guests of the hotel to experience the La Salle's new in-house fleet of taxis, advertised as the first hotel-owned fleet of cabs in the world. Following the discontinuation of its contract with Yellow Cab, the Hotel La Salle taxi fleet went into service just after the first of the year.

The hotel's new taxi department consisted of a fleet of touring cars painted a shade of hazel brown, verging on burgundy, that earned them the nickname the "Purple Cabs." The Hotel La Salle taxis advertised rates of 25 cents for the first half-mile, in accordance with the city regulations. Like the Shaw Livery cabs, the passenger interiors featured thick upholstery with Spanish leather backs and trim. As with Yellow Cabs, the space beside the driver was reserved for hand luggage. In their brochures, the Hotel La Salle boasted "comfortable, easy-riding, luxuriously appointed taxicabs" that were "attractive in appearance and manned by carefully selected, well trained, cautious chauffeurs." With this marketing language, the Hotel La Salle taxi department took direct aim at Yellow Cab's business. Because of this, the presence of the Hotel La Salle cabs created tensions on the streets almost immediately, tensions which would eventually escalate to violence between the cab drivers.

On the evening of Monday, January 8, 1917, several Yellow Cab drivers began an overt harassment of the La Salle taxis, crowding the streets around the entrance to the hotel. "A stranger would have imagined that a Yellow Cab convention was being held," the *Chicago Tribune* declared under the headline "Yellow Cabs and Purple Stage a War." Several Yellow Cabs parked along both sides of the street outside the hotel. When a La Salle taxi would move toward the hotel entrance to pick up a fare, several Yellow Cabs would position themselves in a blockade formation to harass the La Salle taxi driver. At least eight Yellow Cabs continuously circled the building "like sparrows," and each time one of them pulled into the vacant spot reserved for Hotel La Salle taxi pick-ups, the driver would stop briefly, asserting his presence in enemy territory before continuing on his loop.

When a hotel guest wanted a cab, the doormen at the Hotel La Salle used a whistle to hail the La Salle taxis. Recognizing this, the Yellow Cab drivers acquired their own whistles, blowing them every few seconds to confuse and irritate their rivals. When a Hotel La Salle taxi would respond to the phantom call, a Yellow Cab would then take its place in the cab stand line. These antics created such a spectacle that a crowd of people exiting the theaters for the evening gathered on the sidewalk to spectate this spontaneous version of a free street show. Eventually, an extra detail of police arrived to control the crowds and subdue the drivers. In the end, one Yellow Cab driver was arrested for parking on the streetcar tracks.

When Hotel La Salle manager Ernest J. Stevens heard about the incident, he was furious. The following day, he threatened to sue for an injunction against all Shaw-owned taxis and livery vehicles, while simultaneously praising his employees for their restraint during the incident. That same day at Yellow Cab, Shaw and Hertz took out ad space in the *Tribune* for an open letter to the public, in which they declared that their company had "no desire to monopolize the taxicab business in Chicago" but instead wanted their "fair share of it":

> The law gives no one a monopoly and we feel that all taxicabs should not only be equal under the law, but have equal opportunity for securing business in the streets of the city. . . . The recent unfortunate condition in La Salle Street was not of our seeking. We admit that . . . the situation got beyond the control of everybody concerned. As soon as we learned of the undue zeal of our employees, which caused inconvenience to the public, we ordered the improper tactics stopped. We have notified our employees that any driver violating the law will have to take the consequences personally. Our company will not stand back of any man who does things that the law and good taste say he should not do.

Despite the ad's reassurances, the Yellow Cab drivers themselves appear to have still harbored a fair amount of zeal, and when interviewed by reporters, they publicly predicted the war would continue for a long time.

The animosity that brewed between the Yellow Cab drivers and the Hotel La Salle drivers continued to escalate throughout January and into February. On January 29, two Yellow Cab drivers threw a brick through the windshield of a Hotel La Salle cab and were promptly arrested. The following day, a fistfight between Yellow Cab drivers and Hotel La Salle cab drivers injured one man. By February 1, the clashes between the drivers had become so frequent that the Chicago Police Department stationed a detail of police at four separate locations throughout the city—the Bismarck Hotel, the Hotel Sherman, the Hotel La Salle, and the Denman garage in East Garfield Park—to prevent further fighting. At least temporarily, this police presence seemed to quell the violence.

CONTESTED CONGESTION: THE FIGHT OVER CAB STANDS

That spring, perhaps unexpectedly, drivers for the sparring cab companies found themselves united by a common enemy: City Hall. By 1917, Chicago's city streets had reached a new height of congestion. Automobiles now dominated, but they still shared the road with livestock, pedestrians, and Chicago's extensive electric streetcar system, one of the largest in the country. This frequently led to dangerous conditions as cars zipped in and out of streetcar traffic, or parked along curbs on sections of the tracks, preventing the streetcars from moving forward. There were almost thirteen hundred taxis operating on the city's streets by this time, all vying for space at one of just twenty-four public cab stands, which could accommodate a total of no more than about 160 taxis throughout the downtown area.

Because of this, the blocks with designated cab stands became completely flooded with idling taxis. The public cab stand in front of City Hall on Randolph and Wabash was a particularly congested area, with cabs from the Hotel La Salle and Yellow Cab often occupying the parking along the entire block, which enraged some members of the public and the City Council. "Such a thing might be all right in Podunk or Oskaloosa, where everything on wheels ties up in front of the courthouse. . . . But it won't do here," a writer for the *Chicago Eagle* bemoaned.

Some of the aldermen were ready to act. On Tuesday, March 13, the City Council passed two parking ordinances intended to "solve" traffic congestion in the Loop. The first prohibited all automobile parking on downtown streets during rush hour, from 7:00 to 10:00 a.m., and from 4:00 to 7:00 p.m. The second ordinance designated "streetcar loading zones," which prohibited all parking within one hundred feet of intersections, effectively limiting parking to just the middle third of every downtown block. A third ordinance, increasing the number of designated cab stands in the city from twenty-four to seventy, was defeated by a vote of thirty to twenty, which prompted John Hertz to warn that, "if it is not passed, taxicabs will have to operate [exclusively] out of garages and cause the [affordable] taxi service to end." He chalked up the failure of the cab stand ordinance to "a few aldermen with personal axes to grind." Luckily for Hertz and the other cab companies, those few aldermen had a change of heart. At the next City Council meeting, the cab stand ordinance passed, establishing thirty-one new cab stands downtown and nineteen cab stands in outlying neighborhoods like Washington Park, Woodlawn, Uptown, and Wicker Park. Hertz celebrated the decision in the press, saying that "passage of this ordinance means good service and cheap rates."

The expansion of the cab stands and the huge increase in the number of taxis on the road reflected the public's embrace of this form of transportation, the popularity of which was impossible to ignore by that time. However, that same popularity made some of the cab company owners greedy. "We want to let you in on a secret," a Yellow Cab ad proclaimed in large print on March 21, 1917. In it, Shaw and Hertz alleged that ninety days earlier, late in 1916, they had been approached by leaders of rival livery companies and cab companies to make a quiet agreement to simultaneously raise rates, in effect creating an illegal price-fixing campaign:

> Ninety days ago, the Shaw Livery and Yellow Cab were asked to help form a combination of . . . companies to create a trust and increase the rates. . . . When we refused to join this combination, or have anything to do with it, the others went ahead regardless and raised their rates.

It was true that the Atlas Cab Company had briefly raised their rates in January, but their leadership blamed fluctuating gasoline rates for the change, and lowered them again several weeks later. Nevertheless, in the ad, Shaw and Hertz went on to claim the moral high ground, proudly proclaiming that Yellow Cab executives were simply "not that kind of businessman." They did not admit it in the press, but Yellow Cab's increased competition from the Hotel La Salle taxis in 1917 was surely on their minds when they made the decision not to raise rates.

Even America's entry into World War I in April of 1917 could not dampen Chicago's enthusiasm for taxis, though that event did serve to quiet the competitive sniping among the rival taxi drivers, at least temporarily, as many young men began to enlist, or be drafted into military service. For the time being at least, a grudging truce inspired by patriotic unity brought a halt to the open hostilities between cab drivers on the street.

MERGERS: YELLOW CAB ACQUIRES PARMELEE

Despite the additional competition posed by the Hotel La Salle cab fleet, Yellow Cab continued to thrive. In July, Shaw and Hertz negotiated with Charles McCulloch, manager of the Parmelee Transfer Company, to acquire the taxi arm of Parmelee's business. The Parmelee Company was one of the oldest livery and baggage handling companies in the city. For many years, they had enjoyed exclusive cab stand rights at all of the city's train stations, due to agreements they had made with the railroads dating back to the 1850s. Parmelee's transition from horse-powered livery to automobile taxis happened concurrently with Shaw Livery's rise in the auto livery business. However, unlike Shaw Livery, Parmelee had incurred the wrath of many Chicago residents when it claimed it was not beholden to city rules and regulations, because all of its cab stands operated on private railroad property. After the City Council passed the first regulations lowering the maximum rates allowed to be charged, Parmelee continued to charge exorbitantly high rates, emboldened by their exclusive rights at train stations.

However, the City Council's expansion of the cab stands in 1917 finally busted Parmelee's stranglehold on the railroad terminal business, allowing other cabs a chance to pick up fares at train stations as well. Because of this, Shaw and Hertz spied an opportunity: They made an offer to relieve the Parmelee Transfer Company of its beleaguered, unpopular, and now toothless taxi division, keeping McCulloch on as manager and offering him a position on the Walden W. Shaw Board of Directors. He agreed. (The Parmelee Transfer Company retained ownership of its baggage transfer and omnibus service.) After acquiring the Parmelee taxi business, Shaw and Hertz retired the Parmelee cars and replaced them with more than two hundred Yellow Cabs and additional Shaw Livery touring cars, increasing the Shaw Corporation's total number of vehicles on the street to more than eight hundred. It was a remarkable accomplishment, considering the two men had begun Shaw Livery just a decade earlier with a total of ten cars. The Parmelee acquisition was another bold business move, and one which paid off successfully.

A KNOCKOUT ROUND OVER SIGNAGE AND STANDS

After a subdued summer, tensions between the cab drivers flared again in the fall. Yellow Cab's growing size and influence in the city continued to chafe the drivers for the small, independent cab companies. In September of 1917, the sergeant in charge of the Chicago Police Department's Vehicle Bureau issued an order requiring all taxis to remove any signs from the front of the cars advertising a rate of 20 cents per mile, on the basis that the signs were misleading to the public. (The current rates at the time, as set by city ordinance, were 25 cents for the first half mile and 20 cents per half mile after that.) The Independent Taxi Drivers' Association considered this new police order an enraging injustice. They decried the city's perceived favoritism of the Yellow Cab Company, which had painted a large mural on the east wall of its Motor Row garage advertising the 20-cent-per-mile rate. Although requiring the independent taxi drivers to remove the signage from their cars, the police evidently took no umbrage with the mural, angering the independents.

On November 10, a "riotous mob" of seven taxi drivers got into a brawl while vying for fares in front of the Blackstone Theater at final curtain call that evening. Responding to the altercation, a policeman arrested one of the drivers, firing his gun into the air to scatter the remaining offenders. In a twist of irony, just a few days earlier, Shaw and Hertz had run a Yellow Cab ad extolling the company's "New Class of Driver":

The Yellow Cab has created and developed an entirely new class of cab-drivers. They are as far from the old bandit and roughneck style of cab men as the Yellow Cabs are from the old style of ill-smelling vehicles. They are men of good positions—men of ambition—men with families to support who regard their work as elevating rather than degrading. They are healthy, strong, vigorous and brave. They are careful, painstaking, courteous and accommodating.

As this latest incident demonstrated, however, even the "new class of driver" was also occasionally prone to getting into fistfights on the street to secure a taxi fare.

Later that month, the fight over cab stands escalated again when another bill came up for a vote before the Committee on Local Transportation in the City Council. The new bill proposed to further expand the number of cab stands, adding another twenty-three. More importantly, it would eliminate the practice of allowing the city's hotels and clubs to maintain private cab stands. As a result, Manager Stevens of the Hotel La Salle, as well as representatives from several other hotels in the Loop, vigorously opposed the ordinance. On November 21, they packed into a committee meeting, uninvited, and demanded to be heard. One by one, they aired their complaints: first a representative from the Palmer House, then the Windsor-Clifton, then the Congress Hotel, and finally the Hotel La Salle. When he rose to address the aldermen, however, Stevens miscalculated his statement, slyly accusing the aldermen of favoritism toward Yellow Cab when he announced that, "No alderman rides free in our cabs." The insinuation that aldermen did ride free in Yellow Cabs, and therefore bestowed favoritism on Shaw and Hertz's company, was not lost on the City Council members.

"You can't talk that way here!" one alderman shouted, red-faced and outraged. "That's an insult," another concurred. "We are not asking those stiffs for anything." The hearing devolved into a screaming match, as the committee chairman rapped helplessly for order for several minutes. When the room finally quieted down again, the chairman addressed Stevens: "Mr. Stevens, your remark was uncalled for. By inference, you have insulted every member of the City Council. You owe the committee an apology." Chastened, Stevens apologized.

The hotels weren't the only organizations opposed to the new ordinance. "The chauffeurs' union is against this measure," Alderman Kennedy declared, speaking for the independent drivers. "You're trying to give a monopoly to Shaw and Yellow Cab," he continued. Kennedy argued that although the cab stands were intended to provide equal opportunity to all of the cab companies, Yellow Cab unfairly flexed its power by overwhelming the cab stands with Yellows, thereby preventing any of the other cab companies from claiming a spot. After the histrionics of the hearing, the City Council decided to return the measure to the committee for further review.

Yellow vs. Red: Imitation or Flattery

By the time 1918 dawned, with America now deeply involved in World War I and shrouded in a wartime reality, it was hard to ignore Yellow Cab's ongoing success. Since debuting three years earlier as a "new kind of cab company," Yellow Cab had dominated the streets of Chicago. The company's business model was so successful that Shaw and Hertz had begun to franchise it to several other cities throughout the United States. Kansas City, St. Louis, Detroit, and Newark, New Jersey, boasted Yellow Cab franchises. In Chicago, nearly a thousand Yellow Cabs plied the streets for fares, and every one of those cars was built by the Yellow Cab Manufacturing Company. At the close of the previous year, the Walden W. Shaw Corporation had reported gross earnings of nearly $1 million, or more than $21 million in today's money.

Competitors could not help but take notice of Yellow Cab's success. Stevens's introduction of the Hotel La Salle cab fleet was one of the first significant attempts to steal business away from Yellow Cab in Chicago. Then, on January 5, 1918, Shaw and Hertz filed a lawsuit against the upstart Red Cab Company for trademark infringement. They alleged that Red Cab logos copied Yellow Cab's, which had been adapted from the earlier Shaw Livery logos and featured the familiar "Y" shape often associated with the city of Chicago (representing the shape of the Chicago River), contained inside a circular belt with a buckle. They sought twenty injunctions to prevent Red Cabs from using the logo.

This lawsuit most likely ignited animosity between the taxi drivers. The day before Hertz and Shaw filed it, guests of the Hotel Brevoort, a modest hotel not far from the Hotel La Salle, were driven out of the lobby by a horrible smell: Another stinkbomb had been thrown in the Taxi War. "It seems to be the old trouble between the [union] taxi drivers and the Shaw Company," the manager of the Hotel Brevoort told a reporter for the *Chicago Tribune*. Once again, the conflicts went unresolved.

COME ONE, COME ALL: TAXI SERVICE FOR A VAST CITY

In terms of square miles, Chicago is an enormous city. To the east is Lake Michigan, an inland sea that orients the city and stretches well beyond the visible horizon, providing a calming panorama to the otherwise urban visual plane. But to the north, south, and west, there has never been anything to restrict the city's development—only miles and miles and miles of Illinois prairie. In the last quarter of the nineteenth century, after the devastating Chicago Fire, the city began rebuilding and sprawling in all three directions. Today, a person can drive down Western Avenue, one of the few north-south surface streets that traverses the city's entire length, entering the city limits at Howard Street in Rogers Park, and drive for an impressive twenty-five miles before exiting the city limits again at Western and 119th Street.

By the end of 1917, the city covered almost two hundred square miles, and was second only to New York City in total area. Because of this, Chicago has always been a city of neighborhoods, and of distinctive microregional identities: South Siders who almost never traveled north of the Loop were mirrored by North Siders who never made it south of 12th Street. Ambitiously, Yellow Cab aimed for a business model in which it could send a taxi to any request within the vast city limits in ten minutes or less, and would drop off a passenger anywhere in the city and even as far as the suburbs of Oak Park and Evanston. To accomplish this, the sheer size of Chicago demanded a rapid increase in the number of taxis, and people who could drive them.

This amazing growth lured many people to work for the cab companies. And more than many other industries at the time, the cab industry in Chicago offered opportunities to marginalized Chicagoans, including Black people, Jews, and even women. In fact, in October of 1917, facing a labor shortage of working-age men due to World War I mobilization, Yellow Cab had hired 150 Black women to work as car washers on the night shift in the main garage, a move that was so unusual for the era that it warranted several column inches and three photos in the *Chicago Tribune*. Singing the praises of his new employees, the Yellow Cab garage night manager said, "They are 100 per cent more efficient than men.

. . . They waste no time, they are quick and accurate, and they turn a clean car out every three minutes."

As it remains to this day, Chicago's South Side was the center of the universe to thousands of people. In fact, in many ways, the South Side of Chicago in the 1910s served as a microcosm of the city as a whole. Chicago's "old money" elites still occupied grand homes in South Side neighborhoods like the Prairie District, South Shore, Kenwood, Jackson Park Highlands, and Oakland. The commercial area of Motor Row stretched along Michigan Avenue from the Loop south to 26th Street. The University of Chicago was about to enter its third decade in Hyde Park, and that neighborhood and the surrounding areas still retained the air of international glamour bestowed upon them as the site of the wildly successful World's Columbian Exhibition twenty-five years earlier. And along South State Street, from 22nd Street moving south, the heart of Black Chicago was attracting more and more residents every year.

By 1918, at the dawn of the Jazz Age, the South Side had become the epicenter of the jazz scene in Chicago, due to this rapidly rising population of Black residents, many of them recent arrivals from New Orleans. As the city's factories and industries began to attract more and more Black migrants from the southern states, an area that would come to be known as Chicago's "Black Belt" formed along this narrow length of South State Street, due to restrictive housing practices in many other areas of the city. In the years that led up to World War I, the entertainment district of this neighborhood was known as "The Stroll," a "Black Bohemia of crowded streets where cabarets and pool halls, vaudeville theaters, dance palaces and chop suey parlors provided the backdrop for fast-paced nightlife," according to Stanford historian Margaret Moos Pick.

This "fast-paced" nightlife encouraged the rise of a specific type of club known as a "Black-and-tan cabaret." Black-and-tans, as they were called, catered to the musical tastes of the Black community, but welcomed patrons of all colors, a distinct departure from the segregationist practices in most of the city at that time. In these Black-and-tans, according to historian William Howland Kenney, the "Sporting Set" gathered: dapper sons of wealthy families, politicians, artists, actors, immigrants, and Black Belt regulars, often drinking and dancing shoulder to shoulder. These cabarets became some of the first and only integrated spaces in Chicago. Because of this—and because of the frequent presence of gambling, prostitution, and, after the passage of the Volstead Act in 1919, illegal liquor—the Black-and-tans maintained an air of illicit excitement.

The Entertainers' Café was one of the early Black-and-tans in the city. Located on the southeast corner of 35th and Indiana Avenue, along a stretch of 35th Street that was home to other famous Black-and-tans like the Apex Club, the Sunset Café, and Dreamland, the Entertainers Café opened by 1913, and spotlighted performances of ragtime, vaudeville, and eventually jazz music. Like many of the Black-and-tans, nightly entertainment might feature "female impersonators" as well as music—with a "come one, come all" mentality, Black-and-tans were some of the earliest LGBTQ-friendly establishments in the city as well, while still maintaining a certain respectability. (In 1920, Yellow Cab would hire the Entertainers' Jazz Band to perform for its company parties, which took place over three nights in the Chicago Coliseum.)

At 9:00 p.m. on March 19, 1918, two taxi drivers got into a fistfight in front of the Entertainers' Café. A few hours later, perhaps seeking vengeance or attempting to assert dominance at the curb, six men converged on the same spot and got into a fight the *Tribune* described as a "free-for-all." As the blows landed, a taxi suddenly drove by and two shots rang out, one hitting the owner of a nearby bar, and one hitting a manager of the Entertainers' Café in the finger. The taxi sped off. As incidents like this demonstrate, the feuds between taxi drivers were not limited to the lucrative corners near expensive hotels and clubs in the Loop. Taxi War–related violence touched many neighborhoods throughout the city and affected the rich and working class, the Chicago resident and the visitor, and Black people as well as white.

TWENTY-FIVE SHOTS

Well into that year, the battles on the street continued. Eighteen months after the Hotel La Salle introduced its own line of cabs, the skirmishes between the Hotel La Salle cabs and other taxi drivers raged at the cab stand in front of the hotel. In June, the trouble kicked up again, this time taking the form of an "intense rivalry among the taxi drivers who park their machines in front of the hotel," according to the *Collyer's Eye*. The weekly sports journal went on to report that "some of the drivers are accused of having tried to wreck the cars driven by their rivals."

In response to this, when Hotel La Salle manager Stevens saw Yellow Cab drivers breaking city ordinances in front of his hotel, he called the police on his competition. On June 30, a policeman arrested four taxi drivers at the Hotel La Salle cab stand on charges of "soliciting business away from a machine, failure to possess a valid city chauffeur's license and blockading traffic." This was essentially a battle waged over regulatory compliance. But just a few days later, the incident expanded.

Henry Jacobsen was an experienced driver for Yellow Cab who had already seen his share of conflict on the job. The previous year, he had been robbed of his cash kitty by two thieves posing as taxi patrons. They got away with a total of $12. Perhaps because of this incident, Jacobsen carried a gun in his taxi. On the evening of July 7, 1918, Jacobsen picked up a fare on the city's South Side—two women and a man climbed into the back of his cab. He was driving near Halsted and 26th Street when a Red Cab with six men inside of it pulled up alongside him. One of them took out a revolver and started shooting at Jacobsen. He pulled out his own gun and returned the shots one-handed, while speeding with the other hand toward Yellow Cab's main garage a mile and a half away. The Red Cab pursued, continuing to fire on Jacobsen. He returned their fire as his passengers in the backseat screamed and ducked for cover. Jacobsen later estimated that about twenty-five shots were exchanged in the incident. Despite this, no one was hurt.

Sergeant William Kennedy of the Chicago Police Department had been assigned to guard the Yellow Cab garage, a precaution deemed necessary due to the recurring violence between rival drivers. Jacobsen pulled into the garage, still pursued by the men in the Red Cab, who pulled in after him. Jacobsen yelled for the policeman, who managed to arrest three of the six men before the Red Cab escaped again. Kennedy handcuffed the three men and put them in the custody of a nearby policeman named Thomas Howard, before commandeering another car to attempt to pursue the Red Cab. While Kennedy was out searching for the Red Cab, Howard began to transport the three men in his custody to the nearest police station, but one of them made a run for it. In an attempt to detain the escaping prisoner, Howard pulled out his weapon and shot the man, hitting him in the wrist. Despite this, the man broke free from Howard and made it to his home on West 31st Street, where he was arrested again a short time later.

With the rivalry between Yellow Cab drivers and Red Cab drivers now at a crescendo, these incidents of violence between them began to punctuate the streets of the city more frequently. On August 28, several drivers from the two companies engaged in a fistfight brawl at Madison and Dearborn Streets, over the control of a cab stand there. That fight resulted in the arrest of two men: a Yellow Cab driver and a Red Cab driver, both of whom had been so engaged in pummeling each other that they failed to notice the presence of a policeman as he arrived on the scene.

While the drivers postured to gain the advantage over each other in the streets, Shaw and Hertz took their branding battle to court. On June 4, a circuit court judge had awarded Yellow Cab an injunction against an independent cab driver who attempted to siphon off a portion of Yellow Cab's business by painting his taxi yellow. In his ruling, the judge determined that Yellow Cab had "originated and developed a special service in which the [yellow] color scheme was the determining identification." However, immediately upon the issuance of that ruling, attorneys who represented a group of more than fifty independent cab drivers contested it. A few days later, a different judge sided with the independents and denied that injunction. Shaw and Hertz responded to the temporary setback: "All private [taxi] owners should know that the bars have not been let down. . . . We still rely upon the principle against imitation established by Judge Pinckney in the only permanent injunction case heard and decided." And so the court battles, like the street battles, raged on.

On New Year's Eve, 1918, Shaw and Hertz were inspired to address the issue again. On the holiday that was traditionally one of the busiest days of the year for the cab business, they ran a newspaper ad titled, "Don't Blame the Yellow Cab for What Imitators Do." "Success invites imitation," the ads declared.

We are a success; therefore we are imitated.... These cabs are gotten up and painted to look like Yellow Cabs. They are intended to look like our cabs, and a flock of imitators is trading on our name and reputation. To protect our rights and to protect the public who want to ride in Yellow Cabs, we have been forced to go into the courts. We have obtained over 75 injunctions, restraining the use of imitation cabs. We are pursuing the imitators as fast as they come out, and we intend to continue our pursuit of them.

As 1918 came to a close, the world still at war and the city suddenly gripped in the throes of the deadly Spanish flu pandemic, the problems of the cab industry may have seemed inconsequential to most Chicagoans. They had no way of knowing then how deadly the streets of Chicago would become in the ensuing months, racked by street violence ignited by the sparks of roiling racial tensions; or how the city's transportation infrastructure would come screeching to a halt almost overnight; or that the Taxi Wars would escalate to a new phase, one which left several people dead in its wake.

CHAPTER 4

Pedal to the Metal

The War Escalates (1919)

MACLAY HOYNE HAD NO SYMPATHY FOR CON MEN AND NO PATIENCE for liars. Born on October 12, 1872 to a prominent Chicago family—his great-grandfather was one of the original incorporators of the village of Chicago in 1837, and his grandfather, Thomas Hoyne, was elected mayor in a disputed election in 1876, though the victory was overturned by a Cook County circuit court twenty-eight days later—Maclay Hoyne inherited the family's civic inclinations. In 1912, Hoyne was elected Cook County state's attorney.

He quickly established a reputation as an aggressive and effective prosecutor who unsparingly pursued anyone engaged in crime, illegal greed, graft, or malice. Under his leadership of the state's attorney's office, many a swindler, grifter, and racketeer boss eventually found himself on the stand, facing charges brought by the unflinchingly prosecutorial Hoyne.

Even out of the courtroom, Hoyne could be stubborn and blunt, disinclined to engage in even the smallest social pleasantries with those he determined to be crooked. "I would say you lie, and you know you lie, and you know I know you lie," he once wrote to a politician during an investigation into graft at City Hall. Hoyne's shrewd eyes, which were enhanced by wire-rimmed glasses held up by a prominent, beaked nose, saw through schemers and illegal-advantage-seekers. During his eight years as state's attorney, his office would win more than five thousand convictions on a wide range of cases, indicting everyone from arsonists and illegal wiretappers to crooked policemen.

Because of his strong moral convictions, the anti-corruption Hoyne frequently butted heads with the city's larger-than-life mayor, Republican William Hale "Big Bill" Thompson. Thompson had been sworn in as the forty-first mayor of Chicago on April 26, 1915, just one month after Shaw and Hertz had first announced their new Yellow Cab venture. The former manager of a New Mexico ranch, Thompson earned his nickname not only from his imposing physical size—he was six feet tall with a round stomach, broad shoulders, and square jaw—but also due to his political flamboyance and over-the-top bravado. (He once famously rode into a City Council meeting on horseback, wearing a Stetson hat.) Thompson would go on to serve three nonconsecutive terms as mayor, from 1915 to 1923 and again from 1927 to 1931. His occupation of Chicago's top post ushered in a period of political corruption so flagrant and boldly unapologetic that following his eventual defeat in 1931, the *Chicago Tribune* would write, "For Chicago, Thompson has meant filth, corruption, obscenity, idiocy and bankruptcy. . . . He has given the city an international reputation for moronic buffoonery, barbaric crime, triumphant hoodlumism, unchecked graft, and a dejected citizenship. He nearly ruined the property and completely destroyed the pride of the city. He made Chicago a byword for the collapse of American civilization." Even an early biography, slightly more sympathetic to its subject, described Thompson as "intoxicated by absurd ambitions, corrupted and seduced by flattery."

When Thompson first came up for re-election in the spring of 1919, Hoyne ran against him as an Independent, but found himself lost in a crowded field of competitors. Never one to dwell on his losses, Hoyne turned his attention back to the state's attorney's office. Then, less than two months after losing the mayoral race, Hoyne found himself and his office in an uncomfortable position: caught in the crosshairs of the Taxi Wars, between Ernest J. Stevens and the Hotel La Salle on one side, and Shaw and Hertz at Yellow Cab on the other.

Suing and Counter-Suing: A Battle in the Courts

From the surviving newspaper accounts, it appears this round of feuding between the two organizations started like this: On Thursday, May 22, 1919 (according to later allegations from John Hertz), Yellow Cab drivers arrived at the company's cab stand across from the Hotel La Salle and discovered that their phone line had been intentionally severed. These dedicated phone lines represented an important step forward in Yellow Cab's business model—the company paid for their installation so that the taxi starter at the cab stand could easily stay in touch with the telephone dispatch center at the main Yellow Cab garage. Without the phone line, Yellow Cab was at a significant disadvantage, and the drivers suspected their Hotel La Salle rivals of sabotage. According to Hertz, when his employees confronted the Hotel La Salle drivers about the incident, two Yellow Cab drivers were attacked. This prompted Hertz to lodge a complaint with Jay Abrams, the house detective at the Hotel La Salle, who indicated that the best way to get the attacks to stop was for Hertz to remove the Yellow Cab stand across the street.

In the nights that followed, skirmishes erupted between the feuding drivers. On Friday, May 23, two shift supervisors for Yellow Cab—Abraham Katz and Morris Blumenthal—approached the doorman at the Hotel La Salle, threatening him and eventually "slugging him," according to hotel manager Stevens, who then took his complaints about Katz and Blumenthal to the newly elected sheriff. "I protested to Sheriff Peters and told him he shouldn't give [deputy] commissions to such men," Stevens said. Next, he complained to the chief of police, who advised him to press charges, which he did. Katz and Blumenthal were arrested and hauled into court, but the judge ultimately released them. "In police court, they . . . laughed at us," said Stevens. "That afternoon one of our men was slugged right in front of the hotel." At Yellow Cab, Hertz deflected the accusation. "Stevens is romancing," he told a reporter.

The trip to court had only served to further inflame the tensions. The following Monday, May 26, the bad blood between the Yellow Cab employees and the Hotel La Salle drivers emerged again, resulting in a brawl in front of Yellow Cab's main garage at 21st and Michigan. When the five-man fight subsided, both sides accused the other of instigating it.

Stevens later alleged that paid "sluggers" for Yellow Cab had followed two Hotel La Salle drivers, Joseph Wokral and Jack Finkelstein, down Michigan Avenue to the Yellow Cab garage before forcing them out of their cars. He claimed they then threatened Wokral and Finkelstein with guns and beat them severely. Hertz countered that Wokral and Finkelstein voluntarily appeared at the Yellow Cab garage (possibly seeking revenge for Friday night's incident), and that three Yellow Cab supervisors—Blumenthal again, plus Sheridan "Red" Clinnin and L. Romano—were simply acting within the bounds of their roles as temporary sheriff's deputies when they neutralized the attack.

The next day, Stevens and hotel detective Abrams stormed into Hoyne's office, demanding the Cook County state's attorney open a grand jury inquest into the Taxi Wars. "The Yellows are out to get our drivers," Stevens said. "My men are peaceable. There are 1,500 drivers in the Loop, and if desperadoes are to operate, it will resolve itself into a real gunman's war." Stevens could have no way of knowing how prophetic that statement would turn out to be, though Hoyne remained judicious.

Stevens and Abrams claimed that Yellow Cab was trying to force the Hotel La Salle taxi fleet out of business, "through the maintenance of a coterie of sluggers, who terrorize the La Salle cab drivers." However, Shaw and Hertz, along with Yellow Cab counsel Benjamin Samuels, turned up at Hoyne's office a little later in the day demanding counter-charges against the Hotel La Salle employees, alleging roughly the same complaint against their competitor.

After some deliberation, Hoyne decided not to recommend the case to a grand jury inquest. "I didn't think it was wise to do that," he told a reporter. Instead he advised both sides to press charges against the other through the more traditional channel of the municipal courts. Hoyne assigned two assistant state's attorneys to each represent a side in the municipal court case. "It looks to me like a war for supremacy between two corporations," he declared, adding that he felt "put in the middle."

Following Hoyne's advice, Stevens and Abrams pressed charges against the three Yellow Cab supervisors—Katz, Clinnin, and Romano. When the case came up to be heard before a judge nine days later, however, one of the alleged victims, Finkelstein, failed to appear in court.

Today, there is no way to know whether this indicates that Finkelstein's story was not one he was willing to swear to under oath, or whether Yellow Cab employees were in fact waging a campaign of intimidation so effective that Finkelstein was not willing to risk appearing in court. However, Finkelstein's failure to appear resulted in the judge dropping the charges against all three Yellow Cab employees. Instead, on June 10, Finkelstein personally sued Yellow Cab for $100,000, alleging that he was the victim of a "systematic war of intimidation against the employees of the Hotel La Salle" by Yellow Cab drivers, but his complaints went unanswered. All of the parties involved returned to their jobs, and the incidents left many unhealed wounds.

ABOVE THE LAW

By the time the disagreements between Yellow Cab and the Hotel La Salle had escalated to the attention of the Cook County state's attorney in May, they had simmered for several weeks. One month earlier, sensing the need for a law enforcement presence dedicated specifically to the taxi industry, the police chief had assigned a special liaison officer, Detective Thomas Mangan, to the main Yellow Cab garage on 21st Street.

But Mangan wasn't the only law enforcement presence in the garage. Because taxi drivers were easy targets of robbery and carjacking, and occasionally risked their lives interacting with known criminals who wanted a cab, Hertz and Shaw had approached the Cook County sheriff to negotiate a system of deputizing some Yellow Cab employees to make arrests when they witnessed (or fell victim to) illegal activity in the course of their job duties. The sheriff agreed, and issued sheriff's deputy stars to several Yellow Cab employees, many of whom were supervisors for the company. This practice was not uncommon at the time and dated back at least to the turn of the century, when the sheriff deputized citizens to help quell violence during some of the earliest Teamsters' strikes. However, the practice of deputization was problematic: Often, deputized citizens became tempted to use that power for their own benefit.

At the Hotel La Salle, Stevens alleged that the deputized Yellow Cab drivers used their badges and relative immunity from the law to "terrorize" his employees. He argued that the Yellow Cab drivers implemented these intimidation tactics to scare off their rivals and secure a larger portion of the cab business for themselves. The Hotel La Salle wasn't the only organization to question this practice of deputization. A few months after Hoyne declined to open a grand jury investigation into Stevens's complaints, the Chicago Federation of Labor (CFL) took up the Hotel La Salle's cause. The CFL secretary, E. N. Nockels, made an official complaint to the chief of police, arguing that deputized Yellow Cab employees used their power to intimidate and harass other taxi drivers throughout the city. This time, the chief took the complaint more seriously. The CFL was an extremely powerful force in Chicago in 1919, comprising 245,000 members, or nearly half of the city's total workforce as of 1910. As a result of this sizable membership, the CFL had a powerful sway of influence over elections and appointments to city leadership positions. At a hearing in front of the city officials on July 24, the leader of the committee tasked with investigating the complaint reported that the allegations were "true in substance," and handed over to Samuel Ettelson, the city's corporation counsel, a list of the Yellow Cab drivers who were known to be members of the Yellow Cab "slugging crew," employees who used their sheriff's deputy badges to gain immunity for their actions.

Faced with this incontrovertible evidence from the Chicago Police Department, Ettelson affirmed the drivers' right to carry revolvers for personal protection as deputy sheriffs, but declared that they had "no right to violate the law and make assaults upon any class of citizens." He went on to say, "If they are guilty of acts of that kind, the owners of the individual taxicabs or their attorneys should procure warrants and cause their arrests." While on the surface this seemed like a win for Nockels and the independent taxi drivers, in practice, Ettelson essentially left the onus of prosecution on the potential victims. With no resolution to their complaints, the hearing merely perpetuated a cycle of vengeance and retribution between Yellow Cab employees and their adversaries. It would not be long before this led to more violence.

WHY BECOME A TAXI DRIVER?

Taxi driving during these early days of automobiles was not an easy job. The hours were long, and the cars lacked modern conveniences like power steering or even heat. The drivers sat in an open front section of the car, exposed to the elements during every extreme weather condition Chicago cycled through during the year. As Yellow Cab itself explained in an ad in February of 1920, "If you have never driven a cab, or your own open car, you don't know what it is to sit in that open spot when the mercury is below zero or a howling blizzard is smashing clouds of snow across your face."

On top of these discomforts, taxi driving could be a dangerous profession, as it remains to this day. Simply driving on the busy and uncontrolled streets of Chicago meant that drivers risked collisions with other vehicles, and these collisions occasionally resulted in serious injury and even death. In addition to the high volume of vehicles on the road, drivers had to maneuver around large groups of pedestrians in the city's busiest areas. Transportation historian Paul Barrett described how, in Chicago

> by early 1920s, the motorist and the pedestrian were engaged in an angry and often deadly struggle for mastery of the street. Pedestrians ducked around traffic policemen who tried to hold them back at street corners. They surged across automobile thoroughfares near beaches and mobbed Loop streets during rush hours, blocking all traffic.

Even well-meaning pedestrians, particularly children, frequently failed to anticipate the presence of fast-moving automobiles in the streets, and this, combined with the absence of traffic signals, could lead to tragedy. On several occasions, taxi drivers struck pedestrians who stepped out in front of their cars, or injured themselves making a last-minute adjustment to avoid that grim fate.

There was also the constant threat of robbery—because taxi drivers under Shaw and Hertz's popular new "European system" were required to carry cash in the car, they became easy targets for thieves. And the public-facing nature of the job left cab drivers exposed to all kinds of people, from the drunk and belligerent, to the mentally unstable, to the most dangerous criminals. (In an incident in March of 1919, a union rep from the Chicago Waiters' Union with a fondness for alcohol shot two bullets into the back of a Yellow Cab because he "didn't like Yellow Taxi chauffeurs nohow.")

And yet, despite the dangers of the profession, as well as the challenges of finding able-bodied men of working age during World War I, by May of 1919, Yellow Cab boasted nearly one thousand drivers, and another one thousand support employees, with a waitlist of eager hopefuls who wanted to work for the company. Yellow Cab's ability to attract such a large workforce was bolstered by its unique profit-sharing model, which the company expanded that year. The exact cash amount that an employee received was based on a complicated system of seniority and merits or demerits, depending on behavior. In 1920, some of the highest paid drivers were making more than $60 per week, which translated to an annual income equivalent to around $46,000 today. On top of the available cash bonus, each employee in good standing at the end of the year received a portion of common stock in Yellow Cab equal to between 2.5 percent and 7.5 percent of their commission or salary that year, again based on their behavior, with the possibility of a further year-end stock bonus via a common stock lottery. However, to be eligible to receive their common stock, employees had to prove to the company that they were fiscally responsible by putting at least five dollars per month into a savings account.

This corporate paternalism extended to the employees' health, dental, legal, and sartorial needs as well—Yellow Cab employed an in-house doctor, nurse, dentist, attorney, and even a tailor, whose services the employees were encouraged to make use of, free of charge. There were Yellow Cab lunch rooms, which served hot meals to employees at a sharply discounted rate. (Coffee was provided free of charge to drivers.) There was a Yellow Cab band, made up of musically inclined employees who auditioned for the coveted spaces. Eventually, there was even a "Yellow Cab Camp": forty acres along the shores of the Fox River near Yorkville, Illinois, with fifty family tents that could be reserved by any Yellow Cab employee free of charge during the summer months. "The Yellow Cab Company wants to be your father, mother, uncle, aunt and best friend,"

John Hertz is quoted as telling his employees. "Nothing can happen to you that is not our concern. We have the money and the means to do for you things your father and mother would like to do but can't . . . look upon us as your home." If a driver came down with an illness and required additional medical services, the company paid for home visits by the in-house doctor or nurse, or arranged for hospital stays and procedures. Yellow Cab even worked out an agreement with an obstetrician who provided services to expectant employees or their wives. "When any of [the drivers] succumbs to illness, as of course one will occasionally, despite all precautions, we take him home or to the hospital and *see him through*—doctor's bills, hospital bills, nurse's bills and what not," manager Charlie Gray explained in the company newsletter, the *Taxigram.*

These employee perks were nearly unheard-of at other companies during this era, and the benefits were boosted by Yellow Cab's policy of exclusively promoting from within. "Before new drivers go to work on a cab," Gray wrote, "I call them in and tell them what we expect of them and what we intend to give them in the way of good treatment as employees of this company." He would make it clear to new employees that the company encouraged everyone to attempt to work their way up the company ladder: "Every boss in the operating department started five or six or ten years ago just as these new men are starting, and earned his present position by his energy and ability," Gray explained. New drivers underwent a two-week training course with a company instructor, which included everything from machine handling (how to properly crank the engine, how to apply tire chains in rain and snow) to customer courtesy and safe driving.

But perhaps the most attractive aspect of taxi driving in this era was simply this: The use of automobile taxis as a means of getting around the city was continually growing in public popularity. In a very short period of time, since the first Yellow Cabs appeared on the street in 1915, the taxi had claimed a vital role in urban transportation and in the public imagination. In 1919, stage and screen actor Taylor Holmes starred in the silent film *Taxi*, about a wealthy man who has a reversal of fortune and starts driving a cab, only to eventually work his way up to become vice president of the taxi company, a story eerily similar to that of Gray's at Yellow Cab. The public's embrace of taxi culture only seemed to bode greater and greater growth for the industry. Then, in July of 1919, the taxi's importance in urban life would suddenly come into sharp relief, when Chicago briefly faced a transportation crisis unlike anything it had yet experienced in the twentieth century.

THE RACE RIOTS AND THE PUBLIC TRANSIT STRIKE

Nothing highlighted how dangerous, but also how potentially lucrative, taxi driving could be during this era better than the unlucky confluence of two major events that gripped the city of Chicago simultaneously at the end of July 1919: the deadly Race Riots, and a citywide public transit strike. Racial tensions in the city had been escalating for months, as Black migrants came north to find work and Black veterans returned from service abroad, taking jobs that white, working-class residents unjustly felt should be theirs. A month before these tensions would erupt into dangerous riots, Yellow Cab had reminded its drivers, through the employee newsletter, that the company tolerated no racism. "Attention of drivers is called to the fact they must be courteous to colored people at all times," the reminder read. "Any driver found guilty of incivility on account of a man's color or race will be in serious trouble. This applies particularly to 27th and State, and 35th and State." These were the locations of Yellow Cab stands within the Black Belt, and the company could sense there was trouble brewing on the streets that summer.

In the last week of July, the powder keg began to ignite. For several weeks, the public transit workers' union had been attempting to negotiate an eight-hour workday and a pay raise for their fifteen thousand members, who were responsible for the smooth operation of the city's extensive cable car system, as well as the L. The talks between all of the involved parties—the union-represented employees and their leadership, the owners of the cable car lines and train lines (which were all still privately owned), the mayor and his Public Works Commission, and the governor of Illinois, who had inserted his authority into the situation—went around in circles for several weeks, never approaching anything like an agreement.

The negotiations continued day and night. Then, on Sunday, July 27, in an incident entirely unrelated to the transit strike, a seventeen-year-old Black teenager named Eugene Williams went swimming near a whites-only beach at 29th Street. While in the water, he accidentally drifted across an invisible border in Lake Michigan segregating the "Black" and "white" swimming areas. For this minor transgression, a group of white men picked up rocks and began violently hurling them at Williams in the water. One of the rocks struck Williams in the head and caused him to drown. When the police refused to arrest the man responsible for Williams's murder, the city's barely contained racial tensions flared into overwhelming street violence, with roving gangs of vigilante white men and boys traveling to the Black Belt to take out their aggression, while groups of Black men and boys defended their neighborhoods and similarly sought out white victims in other parts of the city.

At the same time, throughout the devastating first full day of these riots, the transit strike negotiations continued, and finally the governor believed he had brokered a compromise between the transit owners and the union leaders that everyone would agree to. Ignoring the racial violence raging south of downtown, union leaders called a late-night meeting of the membership to vote on the proposed deal. However, during the middle-of-the-night meeting, the union membership voted to defy their own leaders. To the surprise of everyone involved in crafting the compromise, union members refused to accept the agreement and instead opted for an immediate systemwide strike. At 4:00 a.m. on the morning of Tuesday, July 29, every streetcar and L train stopped where it stood, and the drivers and engineers walked off the job into what would go down in history—for reasons entirely unrelated to the strike—as one of Chicago's most violent nights.

The next morning, every person in the city as yet untouched by racial violence awoke to an entirely different but also significant problem—their commute to work was suddenly limited to only a handful of transportation options: the suburban steam trains, private vehicles, their own two legs . . . or a taxi. Taxis traveling between the Loop and the North and West Sides of the city (where the rioting had yet to spread) saw more business than they could handle. The biggest challenge they faced was an utter lack of traffic control, as the vast majority of police, including all of the traffic directors, had been removed from their usual posts and sent to the riot zone. In Chicago prior to the introduction of stoplights, traffic directors played a vitally important role in keeping traffic moving steadily through the busy Loop, and the loss of their service created chaos and gridlock on the streets.

Additionally, taxi service to and from the city's South Side was extremely limited due to the violence. By the afternoon of Tuesday, July 29, Yellow Cab was refusing to route its cabs south of 12th Street to protect the safety of its drivers. A reporter for the *Chicago Tribune*, trying to hail a cab to the Black Belt to report on the violence that afternoon, struck out several times before he successfully hailed a Hotel La Salle taxi to take him on a tour of the riot zone. The driver agreed to the fare despite the fact that he had seen a Yellow Cab that "just came back with bullet holes through the top."

As the violence spilled over into the Loop in the following days, the streets of the business district became scenes of mob-fueled terrorism and open anarchy. Among the many horrifying incidents witnessed by ordinary Chicagoans on those days, there was at least one shooting where a taxi was the intended target. On Wednesday, July 30, people walking on the sidewalk in front of the Clark Street entrance of the Hotel Sherman looked up to see several men standing on the running boards of a moving black limousine. The men opened fire on a Yellow Cab idling in front of the hotel as their limousine turned north on Clark, and then disappeared. No one was hit. Police never determined whether the incident was related to the race riots or the Taxi Wars or some other feud.

The riots raged on for several days while the mayor and the governor engaged in a tense political battle, neither one willing to call out the National Guard and accept the political responsibility of that decision. Finally, the mayor relented. Just after midnight on Thursday, July 31, five assembled regiments of the National Guard, patiently waiting at local armories for the call to action, were ordered to report to the Black Belt. Even this development was a boost to the taxi industry: Commanding officer General Dixon chartered one hundred Yellow Cabs to transport some of the Guardsmen to their designated zones.

As the National Guard worked to restore order to the streets, the transit strike negotiations took a turn for the better. Later that same day, the striking public transit workers voted to accept the governor's amended compromise, and at midnight on Friday, August 1, the first cable cars rolled out of their storage barns and resumed their regular service. By the time the average Chicagoan returned to work the next Monday, the city had calmed once again. The previous week's events had claimed the lives of at least thirty-eight people, injured more than five hundred, and left one thousand people homeless. But at least one industry had come out of the mayhem ahead. Recapping some of the creative transportation solutions the city had devised in response to the public transit strike, the *Chicago Tribune* pointed out that "taxi companies thrived." The Hotel La Salle records revealed that the week of the transit strike, the taxi department grossed its third-highest earnings of 1919.

Expansions, Mergers, and Acquisitions

Even after the transit strike ended, the taxi business showed no signs of slowing down. In August, Yellow Cab celebrated four years of service in Chicago. The onetime experiment of the Shaw Livery company had proved so successful that Shaw and Hertz had decided to retire their original, charge-account-based Shaw Livery cabs for good. On August 15, 1919, the remaining eighty limousine-style Shaw Livery cabs were taken out of commission. Then, at a meeting of the board of directors for Yellow Cab in mid-October of that year, the company leaders raised the suggestion of splitting the taxi side of the business from the cab manufacturing side of the business, offering all existing Yellow Cab shareholders stock in the spinoff company. Since Shaw and Hertz had first added the manufacturing arm of the business in 1916, they had received more and more contracts to build cabs for other cab companies, including the growing number of Yellow Cab franchises throughout the country. The time seemed right to give the manufacturing side of the business a separate identity. Meanwhile, on the taxi side of the business, Shaw and Hertz intended to increase their fleet by an additional three hundred cabs in the first quarter of 1920, bringing the total number of drivers to 1,428.

Around the same time, the Hotel La Salle taxi fleet was also seeing a great deal of success, turning a profit nearly every week of 1919. Because of this, Stevens decided to commission the hotel's preferred architecture firm, Holabird & Roche, to design a South Side cab stand that the hotel would erect on land they had recently acquired near Mandrake Park in the posh Oakwood neighborhood on the city's Near South Side. Constructing this cab stand allowed the Hotel La Salle to boast to the city's wealthy South Siders that they could have a Hotel La Salle taxi at their door in 15 minutes or less. The Hotel La Salle South Side cab stand went into service the week of October 25, 1919, with thirty taxis assigned to the station. For both companies, the new decade just over the horizon promised to be one of great business success, but only one of them would survive to reap the rewards.

Trippel Murder

As Chicago entered the final few weeks of 1919, a pall fell over the mood at the city's restaurants, bars, and cabarets. In late October, the US Congress had passed the Volstead Act, prohibiting the manufacture and sale of alcoholic beverages. Overnight, Chicago's thriving bar scene dried up. Walking around the Loop on October 30, a day after the bill's passage, a reporter for the *Chicago Tribune* described how "gloom pervaded the Loop liquor palaces," and "bartenders walked disconsolately up and down their vacant rooms." To the city's many restaurateurs and bar owners, the future looked bleak. "I don't think many of the places now open will last long," one bar owner complained. "There isn't enough trade to justify the upkeep—nearly everybody is losing money in rent and overhead expense already. We can't keep that up long."

Prohibition would create an incredible boon to Chicago's underworld in the form of illegal rum-running. However, even in the pre-Prohibition era, the city had managed to produce a number of gang bosses, many of whom would go on to either mentor or succumb to (or in some cases, both mentor and then succumb to) the next generation of Prohibition gangsters. Characters like "Big Jim" Colosimo had built criminal networks rooted in gambling, prostitution, and racketeering, while others, like Maurice "Mossy" Enright, took advantage of the city's significant labor struggles to gain their criminal advantage, in what became known as the "labor rackets." This type of racketeering might include extortion of employers using the threat of unlawful strikes, organized work stoppages, picketing, or workplace sabotage. It could also include bribery of employers in exchange for allowing the employer to ignore the established collective bargaining agreement. Enright excelled at this kind of racketeering, which often involved personal threats, physical intimidation, beatings, and the occasional murder.

By the early 1910s, Enright had become an organizer for the American Federation of Labor and a major player in several of the city's powerful labor unions. He was both feared and revered for his illegal and extralegal methods of intimidating employers and squashing his opponents. The Irish-American Enright was also reportedly allied with the Italian-American enforcer Johnny Torrio, Colosimo's nephew and right-hand man. No gangland boss operated alone, and Enright was no exception. He gathered a group of henchmen around him, including one Eugene "Gene" Geary, who cut his teeth as early as 1913 working as a labor slugger for a wide array of Chicago's unions—"changing unions so frequently it was hard to keep track of him . . . his services were to be had by any labor organization that . . . had the funds," according to one newspaper report.

On November 22, 1919, Yellow Cab driver Leonard Trippel was drinking beer in the Cadillac Bar with a friend and former Yellow Cab driver named Patrick Barton. Trippel was originally from the small town of Milton Junction, Wisconsin, and he had served twenty-two months overseas in the US military during World War I. Now back in Chicago, he lived in Woodlawn, a middle-class neighborhood on the city's South Side, and resumed his job as a driver for Yellow Cab. The bar where he and Barton were illegally drinking was located just around the corner from the main Yellow Cab garage. It was managed by a man named Blue, who was working alongside two bartenders that night, serving late-night drinks to the night owls who lingered.

Around 2:00 a.m., Gene Geary walked in. It's possible Blue the bartender recognized him and sensed trouble; in addition to being a known member of Enright's gang, Geary had also previously owned the Blatz

Saloon and Gardens near "the Stroll." In that neighborhood, Geary had been arrested several times in conjunction with shootings; in fact, just two years earlier, he was arrested in a shoot-out that took place inside his own saloon. But none of the charges against him ever seemed to stick.

According to witness accounts and newspaper reports, that November night, Geary spotted Trippel in Blue's bar. "There's the big [expletive] I had a fight with the other night," he said. Overhearing this, Trippel's buddy Barton attempted to defuse the situation. Just when it looked like the two men were about to shake hands and walk away, Geary said, "Well, if you want to fight it out, we'll go in the back room." As Geary pulled Trippel toward the center of the room, Barton attempted to help his friend, but Geary's companion John Ganey pointed a gun at him. He could only watch helplessly as Geary shoved the muzzle of a gun into Trippel's abdomen, and shot him twice.

As Trippel slumped to the floor, Geary and Ganey escaped among the confusion, exiting quickly and hopping on a passing streetcar. However, word of the shooting quickly reached the Yellow Cab garage one block away from Blue's Bar, and several Yellow Cab drivers took off in their vehicles after the streetcar. Catching up to it, they positioned their cars on the tracks to block its path, holding Geary and Ganey until a policeman arrived on the scene and made the arrest. Trippel was rushed to a hospital but died the next morning from his wounds.

The cause of the shooting was never fully determined—during his trial, Geary claimed that he and Trippel were fighting over a woman named Ruth Kirk, and that Trippel had previously threatened to kill him. However, Kirk's testimony corroborating this story was ruled perjury when it turned out she lied about her identity. Another Yellow Cab driver named Herman Markowitz testified that a few nights before the shooting, he had seen Geary kicking and beating Trippel in front of a cigar store, and that Geary had a revolver visibly protruding from his pocket. The night of the shooting, Markowitz said he heard Geary threaten to "get" Trippel.

Between the time Geary killed Trippel in November of 1919, and when he went on trial for the offense in March of 1920 claiming self-defense, Geary's mob boss Mossy Enright was murdered, shot eleven times with a shotgun as he stepped out of his car one February evening. Police tracked down Geary for questioning in the Enright murder. He was out on bond awaiting trial, and organizing workers in the Union Stockyards. Police hoped to gain insight into who might have wanted Enright dead that month, but they struggled to turn up many solid leads.

As a result of Enright's death, Geary's notoriety increased. When he went on trial for Trippel's murder in March, Geary attracted a lot of attention. Despite the defense attorney's weak self-defense argument and the fact that several of the defense witnesses were accused of perjury or found to be generally untrustworthy, a jury took just a few hours to acquit Geary of Trippel's murder.

Although there is no definitive proof that Trippel's murder was anything more than an isolated personal incident, it is true that in the weeks after the shooting, Geary felt he was being pursued by Yellow Cab. Following his unexpected acquittal at trial (Hoyne described it as a "rank miscarriage of justice"), Geary went on to declare that "Yellow Cab was after me and after me hard." It is not difficult to imagine that the incident was related to the ongoing battles between Yellow Cab and the city's unionized cab drivers, with Geary acting on behalf of one of the labor organizations.

Less than three months after he was acquitted of Trippel's murder, Geary was arrested once again for killing a man in a bar. This time, the police determined that Geary had never met the man he killed and that the shooting was "unprovoked." Another Yellow Cab driver had witnessed Geary at the scene of that shooting, telling police, "I recognized him right away . . . I saw he had been drinking and was looking for trouble. I didn't want to get into anything with him, remembering what Trippel got. . . . " This time, a jury would find Geary guilty and sentence him to death. Whatever his true motive for murdering Leonard Trippel in November of 1919, Geary would take it to his grave.

CHAPTER 5

0-to-60

Checker Enters the Fray (1919–1920)

ON DECEMBER 8, 1919, WITH CHRISTMAS JUST A LITTLE MORE THAN two weeks away, shoppers crowded the sidewalks of the Loop, vying for space with businessmen returning from late lunch meetings, delivery-men making their rounds, and women in the latest fashions stepping into and out of the city's stately department stores. Chicago's downtown merchants had filled their shops that year with the best gift items of the era: phonographs, pearl lorgnettes, silk pajamas. At the Klein Loan Bank and jewelry store, Sam Klein and his partner Sam Greenfield had filled their window displays with their most glittering jewelry and their finest watches, hoping to draw in an affluent shopper looking to purchase a gift.

Instead, Klein and Greenfield's ornate window display attracted thieves. Around three o'clock that afternoon, Greenfield stood in the front of the shop, assisting Ben Newmark, a customer who had returned to pick up a repaired watch. Suddenly, three young men walked into the store. The "pimply-faced" leader wore a dark brown overcoat that matched his chestnut hair, and one of his accomplices sported a dark fedora hat. Entering the store, the thieves ordered Greenfield and New-mark to "throw up [their] hands." Herding them into the back of the store with Klein, the three robbers proceeded to clean out the store's window displays as well as its two jewel safes—"taking only the most valuable gems" according to one reporter—and robbing the cash register of around $2,000 in cash and Liberty bonds.

The three thieves then escaped out the front door, carrying trays of gems past stunned shoppers as they climbed into a red-colored taxi to make their getaway. Newmark, Klein, and Greenfield ran out of the shop yelling for help. A policeman patrolling nearby heard them yelling and jumped in a Brown Cab to attempt a pursuit, but the taxi carrying the thieves weaved in and out of the busy Loop traffic until it disappeared from view. The thieves successfully made off with about $30,000 in gems, cash, and Liberty bonds (the equivalent of more than $500,000 today).

Acting on a tip a few days later, the police arrested Isadore Goldberg, night superintendent of the Hotel La Salle taxi fleet, naming him as the leader of the heist. They also arrested several alleged accomplices: Ben Lieberman, George Cohn, and Meyer Cohn. (Despite having the same last name, the two men were unrelated.) The twenty-four-year-old Goldberg was already well-known to the Chicago police: In 1916, he had spent several months serving time for auto theft at the Pontiac Reformatory. After returning to the city and taking a job as a driver with the Hotel La Salle taxi fleet, his name appeared in the police blotter regarding smaller incidents between the rival cab companies. Just two months before the jewel heist, Goldberg had been indicted by a grand jury for robbing a Yellow Cab night superintendent of $39. At the time of his arrest, he was also awaiting trial on a separate charge of exchanging gunfire with a Yellow Cab driver as part of the Taxi Wars.

Following his arrest for the jewel heist, Goldberg was interviewed by representatives from the state's attorney's office, and he wove a complicated tale, which seemed designed to implicate Jay Abrams, the house detective at the Hotel La Salle, in the incident. This testimony may have been retaliatory in nature; it was Abrams who provided information to the police that initially led to Goldberg's arrest. Attempting to cast aspersions on Abrams, Goldberg made accusations of his own. According to the *Tribune*, he described "in great detail" Abrams's "alleged participation in the feud between the La Salle taxi cab chauffeurs and drivers for the Yellow Cab Company," and claimed that Abrams had provided him with a revolver to shoot at Yellow Cab drivers if necessary.

On December 15, a few days after Goldberg's statement to the state's attorney's office, the plot thickened further. Hotel La Salle manager

Ernest J. Stevens was working in his office when he received a visit from an unknown man and woman. The man claimed to be Goldberg's brother-in-law, and demanded that Stevens pay Goldberg's bond to have him released from custody, the price of which stood at $40,000. The man, who said his name was Levy, claimed that "certain high-up officials" at Yellow Cab had offered him the same amount, but only if Goldberg would implicate Abrams in the jewel heist. Stevens declined to pay Goldberg's bond, and instead contacted the Hotel La Salle's corporation counsel to document the odd visit.

When the case came to trial in March of 1920, Stevens was reminded of this visit. Halfway through jury selection, Goldberg's accomplices, the two Cohns, made statements from their jail cells confessing to the jewelry heist, but naming Abrams as the mastermind behind the plan. The Cohns claimed that they had been led by Goldberg to understand that Abrams held ten thousand shares in the Klein Loan Bank and jewelry store, and "wanted it robbed so he could get his money out." They went on to provide details about the planned heist, including the allegation that the revolvers they used for the robbery had been provided by Abrams.

Assistant state's attorney John Lowery immediately doubted the accusations. "The confessions should be regarded with caution," he said. On March 4, Hoyne himself went on the record to address the accusation that Yellow Cab officials may have induced the Cohns to make such an accusation against Abrams. "In justice to the Yellow Cab Company, it is my duty to say that I have no evidence, and that this office has no suspicion, that the concern is in any way involved in any frameup," he told a reporter.

Responding to the accusations against him, Abrams denied owning any stock in the store or having any prior knowledge of the holdup, and claimed that Isadore Goldberg and the Cohns were only implicating him because of the Taxi Wars. "The whole affair against me is a frameup between Goldberg and the officials of the Yellow Cab Company," he insisted. The grand jury agreed that Abrams was innocent of any involvement in the jewel heist and dropped the case against him a few weeks later. Goldberg and the Cohns were found guilty and sentenced to jail time.

A NEW PLAYER ON THE SCENE: ENTER CHECKER

By 1919, the Hotel La Salle taxi department was not the only rival to find itself butting heads with Yellow Cab. That year, some of Chicago's independent taxi drivers were no longer content to let Yellow Cab dominate the market, and so they decided to do something about it. They realized that the number of Yellow Cabs on the road far outnumbered the fleets of any other single entity or organization, and that because of this, the company wielded influence with law enforcement, local politicians, and the powerful Chicago Association of Commerce. The independent drivers felt that the earlier fights over cab stand locations and proper signage had unfairly advantaged Yellow Cab, which flexed its size and power and usually got exactly what it wanted. As a result, many independent taxi drivers felt steamrolled and slighted by Yellow Cab's dominance, complaining that the same set of rules did not apply to all taxis equally and that Yellow Cab was getting preferential treatment from the city in a variety of ways. As early as 1917, the Chicago Federation of Labor had complained that Yellow Cab used its power in the courts "as a bludgeon to batter down the efforts of union chauffeurs to earn a living wage." The independent drivers wanted to tip the scales back in their favor.

So on February 6, 1919, a group of three independent cab drivers, headed by a man named Frank Dilger, had spent $2,500 to incorporate the Checker Taxi Company in Oak Park, immediately west of Chicago's city limits. The company did not have a traditional corporate structure; instead, it was formed as an affiliation of independent drivers. Drivers owned their own cabs, paying an association fee for liability insurance and space for their cabs in a Checker garage. Soon, other independent taxi drivers wanted these benefits as well, and joined the affiliation. During the first year of its existence, Checker added about "three or four cabs a month," according to later estimates by company leadership.

By banding together into this cooperative agreement, Dilger and the other members of the Checker Taxi affiliation were also able to leverage their buying power to purchase new cabs at more affordable rates. Although the Checker-affiliated drivers might have chosen to order purpose-built cabs from the Yellow Cab Manufacturing Company, their anger toward Yellow Cab's tactics in Chicago led them to order a competitor's purpose-built taxi instead: the Commonwealth Mogul, which they then painted in a checkerboard pattern to distinguish their new brand. In fact, the Commonwealth Mogul became so closely identified with the Checker brand that the manufacturing company, the Commonwealth Motor Company, eventually changed the name of the taxi model to the Mogul Checker.

The Commonwealth Motor Company was a direct competitor to Yellow Cab Manufacturing, though it was a much smaller business. The two companies also differed in that Commonwealth did not make the bodies for its vehicles. Instead, it partnered with a Joliet, Illinois–based company called Lomberg Auto Body Manufacturing Company. Both Commonwealth Motors and Lomberg Auto Body struggled financially, despite the contract with Checker Taxi. In 1919, to keep his company afloat and fill the Checker Taxi order, Lomberg Auto Body founder Abe Lomberg made a decision that would affect the cab industry for decades to come. He sought a $15,000 loan from a fellow Russian immigrant who had achieved significant business success in a very short time: Morris Markin.

Markin's story was an almost unbelievable, rags-to-riches, American immigrant story. He was born July 15, 1892 in Smolensk, a small city in western Russia close to what is today the modern border of Belarus. Brown-haired and blue-eyed, Markin was born into a poverty-stricken Jewish family and grew up speaking Yiddish at home. In his youth, Markin worked in a clothing factory, eventually becoming a supervisor of the trouser manufacturer's sewing department. In 1913 at the age of twenty-one, Markin immigrated to the United States, arriving at Ellis Island with $1.65 in his pocket and speaking no English. A story frequently repeated at the time of his death says that an Ellis Island janitor took pity on the helpless new arrival and loaned him the $25 he needed to pay the fees to enter the country. In 1914, Markin arrived in Chicago, where one of his uncles had already established residence.

Two years later, in August of 1916, Markin married a fellow Russian immigrant named Bessie, and their first child, Josephine, was born the following year. Drawing on his experience working in a clothing factory, Markin apprenticed with a Chicago tailor, and proved to be a quick learner. By the time Josephine was born, he had purchased the business from the tailor's widow and earned enough money to bring several of his siblings to the United States. Together, he and one of his brothers opened a clothing factory and received government contracts to provide pants to the US military during World War I. By 1919, Markin's clothing factory was so successful that he felt comfortable loaning Lomberg $15,000 to fulfill the Mogul Checker orders. Markin most likely did not suspect it at the time, but this would prove to be a very pivotal decision in his life. By the mid-1920s, Markin would turn most of his attention and financial investment toward this new industry, and become a key player in Chicago's Taxi Wars.

THE BATTLE OVER CITY LICENSING

The same year that Dilger formed the Checker Taxi affiliation, the City Council passed an ordinance that would change the way cab companies could operate. It was a decision that not only had an outsized effect on Checker Taxi's affiliation-based model, but ultimately came to influence the cab industry well into the next millennium. On December 29, 1919, the City Council had voted to establish a Public Vehicle Licensing Commission within the executive branch of the city government. To carry out the tasks assigned to the new commission, the council had also created a new role within City Hall: the Examiner of Public Motor Vehicle Operators. This person would work with representatives of the Chicago Police Department to "license and inspect public vehicles [and] taximeters," as well as conduct the examinations of all driver's license applicants.

The new ordinances required that, from that point forward, to be considered a legal livery vehicle, all taxis operating on the streets of Chicago had to obtain a cab stand license from the city. The Public Vehicle Licensing Committee would be placed in charge of granting these licenses. To protect public safety, the committee would ensure that "no public vehicle shall be licensed until it has been thoroughly and carefully inspected and examined and found to be in thoroughly safe condition for the transportation of passengers; clean, fit, of good appearance, and well painted and varnished." This meant that before he approved a cab stand license, the examiner had to physically inspect each vehicle for safety and adherence to city regulations, and also confirm that the meters in each cab were functional and accurate. "The commission shall refuse a license to any vehicle found to be unfit or unsuited for public patronage," the ordinance stated. Once a vehicle had passed the inspection, the owner of the taxi would be required to pay a licensing fee of $5 per year to the city, and would then receive an official card signed by the examiner, containing the license number and the name of the "person, firm or organization" that owned the cab.

To further deter "freelance" or "pirate" cabs, the new ordinance also required that the name of the cab owner be painted on the side of the vehicle. At Yellow Cab, all of the cars were owned by the company, and so this prompted Shaw and Hertz to declare in an ad in February, 1920: "We are forced to comply with this ordinance; consequently the doors of Yellow Cabs are being repainted." They went on to register their support of the new rules, saying, "It's an honest man's law and protects us and every responsible cab company and individual owners, because it prevents unscrupulous cab-drivers from pirating on the business."

Not all individual cab owners agreed with this assessment, however. On March 8, 1920, the Independent Auto Taxi Owners' Association filed suit for an injunction to prevent the city from prosecuting taxi drivers who failed to obtain a cab stand license. The independent drivers complained that they were being treated unfairly, and that the commission refused licenses to several applicants simply because their "lamps or wheels are similar in color to that of the Yellow Cab Company." (When refusing to issue the licenses, the members of the commission cited a clause in the new ordinance meant to address the "imitative appearances of taxis.") The drivers of the Independent Auto Taxi Owners' Association also accused one of the members of the commission of being financially invested in the Yellow Cab Company, and claimed that he was using his role as the commission's chairman to deny licenses to Yellow Cab's competitors.

Checker Taxi joined other cab operators in complaining bitterly about the city's licensing practices. Throughout the remainder of the year, Checker Taxi leaders would clash with "certain city officials," who they accused of retaliating against the company on behalf of Yellow Cab. By September, the city would arrest several Checker drivers on charges of operating a taxi without a valid city cab stand license. Outraged, Checker leadership insisted that their taxis had passed the required city inspections and the company had paid all the necessary fees, and yet still the city had denied the cab stand licenses. Checker leaders accused city officials of conspiring with Yellow Cab to try to put its competitors out of business. The city officials countered that they had denied the licenses on the grounds that the Checker taxis were all owned by their individual drivers but featured only the Checker affiliation logo on the side of the cars, not the owners' names, and therefore violated the new city ordinance.

However, Checker leadership and the heads of the other taxi companies strongly suspected a political motive behind the refusal to issue licenses. Checker leadership responded that the cabs were in fact company property, and submitted proof to the city that taxi drivers who signed up with the Checker affiliation were paid in stock of sufficient face value to cover the cost of the car. But the commission remained unpersuaded, and Checker taxis continued to operate without valid cab stand licenses, leading to the arrests. Eventually, a municipal judge would side with Checker, and demand that the city issue the licenses or face contempt. Despite this, the commission continued to refuse to grant the cab stand licenses through the end of 1920.

JOCKEYING FOR POSITION: CHECKER JOINS THE WAR

By May of 1920, a little more than a year after Dilger formed Checker Taxi with a total of three affiliated cabs, Checker's membership had grown to 150 drivers. This growth was so successful that the leadership decided to take the company public, authorizing $200,000 in capital stock and taking over company ownership of some of the cabs in its fleet by offering stock to the drivers in exchange for the company's equity in the cabs. John Hertz would later accuse Checker of employing this business tactic to circumvent the new city ordinance requiring that independent cabs display the name of their owners. "By organizing into these associations, they hoped to dodge the city ordinance which requires each independent to place his name on the door of his cab," he complained.

The Checker leadership proved impervious to Hertz's irritation. Newly empowered following these structural changes, the Checker Taxi

Company made its first serious attempt to siphon off a small but significant portion of Loop taxi fares in July, when they took over the cab stand in front of the DeJonghe Hotel and Restaurant at Monroe and Wabash. The DeJonghe was an old-fashioned, Belle Epoque–era hotel, opened in 1899 by Belgian brothers Charles and Pierre DeJonghe, chefs who had first come to Chicago to serve food to visitors at the World's Columbian Exposition in 1893. After opening their hotel five years later, the hotel's restaurant became a popular dining destination for the city's elite, famous for a rich dish invented there and named after the brothers—Shrimp DeJonghe. By 1920, the DeJonghe Hotel's Victorian Gothic façade and modest size appeared outdated, eclipsed by the larger and more modern hotels like the Hotel La Salle and the Hotel Sherman, but the restaurant remained a beloved Chicago fine-dining experience.

By establishing dominance over the cab stand in front of the DeJonghe Hotel's popular restaurant, Checker Taxi announced its arrival in the Loop in no uncertain terms. Undeterred by Yellow Cab's dominance, the new affiliation of Checker taxis had every intention of stealing business away from the number-one cab company in the city, and they weren't afraid to go after a prime cab stand location to do so. The Yellow Cab drivers recognized this aggression for what it was—a ruthless business ambition that took direct aim at their success—and retaliated. Checker's leadership later alleged that Yellow Cab "immediately took the offensive and opened warfare, blocking our stand, wrecking our cabs and beating up our drivers."

On July 26, the Taxi Wars erupted anew. The trouble began in the Loop, as a large group of taxis idled in front of the theaters, ready to take patrons home for the night. As the Yellow Cabs and Checker Taxis waited, they struggled to secure the best spots to win this lucrative, post-show theater business. According to the *Tribune*, roughly fifty cabs from the two companies "jockeyed for position in a line in front of a Loop theatre," in a scene that must have recalled a similar incident between Yellow Cabs and Hotel La Salle taxis several years earlier. This "jockeying for position" eventually led to a fistfight between drivers from the two companies. As the flood of theater patrons spilled out of the building, however, the skirmishing in the Loop stopped.

Later that night, the real battles between Yellow Cab and Checker Taxi broke out on the city's Near West Side. The two companies held real estate not far from each other: the Checker Taxi garage at Harrison and Racine was located just five blocks directly south of a Yellow Cab branch garage. After the incident in the Loop earlier that night, a Checker taxi "acting as a scout" drove past the Yellow Cab garage, and gunmen inside the car fired at the building as they drove past. Hearing the gunshots, the Yellow Cab employees in the garage responded immediately, jumping in their cars and speeding in formation past the Checker Taxi garage, shooting at the Checker garage in retaliation. The Checker drivers returned fire and took off in pursuit of the Yellow Cabs.

The Associated Press report of the incident elaborated on the tactics used by both companies.

> For hours, the battling drivers played every trick of mobile warfare against each other that they could think of. Strings of Yellow Cabs, in line, rushed past the headquarters of the Checker Company at breakneck speed, emptying revolver broadsides into the latter's offices. Rallying, the . . . checkered cabs of the attacked concern dashed out en masse and ripped into the Yellows for counterattacks.

Individual drivers, racing at high speeds, would pull up directly beside a rival cab and "empty their pistols at each other at close range." Police later determined there were a total of five gun battles over the course of the night. The attacks continued until daybreak on July 27. However, despite the dramatic newspaper descriptions of the incidents, the police reported no casualties and arrested just three drivers.

Then, in the early morning hours of August 5, a twenty-one-year-old Checker driver named Anthony Sugar was standing in the doorway of the company's garage. It is likely that the Checker employees were still on alert for counterattacks following the gun battles of the previous week. Sugar may have been waiting to start his shift or he may have been positioned as a scout, scanning the block for potential trouble. As he looked out over the dark Chicago streets of the Near West Side, an unmarked touring car sped past and a shot rang out, hitting Sugar and severely wounding him. Despite the brazenness of the attack and Sugar's grave wound, the incident remained isolated, with no further escalation that night. The police eventually attributed the incident to the "war of rival taxicab companies." Defying the odds, Sugar survived. Then two days later, newspapers across the country carried a short news item from the wire services reporting that "fighting was resumed . . . between chauffeurs of the Yellow and Checker taxi companies, resulting in the wounding of two men," though no further details were given.

On August 15, more than twenty Yellow Cab employees were working in the company's Monroe Street branch garage when they heard a loud explosion of dynamite, followed by the sound of breaking glass. In the initial aftermath of the explosion, panic ensued. Several windows were broken and one employee was injured by the blast, which just missed the twenty-eight-hundred-gallon, underground gas tanks used to refuel the cabs. Al Weinshank, Yellow Cab's 10th Street garage superintendent, told the police the explosion was most likely the work of "a rival taxicab organization." However, this proved to be the final attack in this round of battles between the two companies. Checker Taxi leaders later attributed the temporary cease-fire to the chief of police "suppress[ing] the trouble."

New Leaders for a New Phase of the War

Though the city of Lake Geneva, Wisconsin, lies just eighty miles northwest of Chicago, its atmosphere could not have been further removed from the Taxi Wars erupting on the streets of Chicago. A bucolic town located on the easternmost point of pristine, spring-fed Geneva Lake, by 1920, Lake Geneva was well established as a summer haven for many of Chicago's wealthiest families: the Wrigleys of chewing gum fame, the meatpacking Swifts, the Drake family whose namesake hotel was being built in downtown Chicago that very year. These elite families used their exceptional means to build luxurious "cottages" on the shores of the lake, where they spent the summer months engaged in a busy social season, climbing aboard their private steam yachts for outings to places like the Lake Geneva Yacht Club and the Lake Geneva Country Club. "In leafy seclusions, their red gables peeking thru the tree tops that line the banks of Lake Geneva, are the summer mansions of many of Chicago's most substantial citizens," wrote the *Lake Geneva Regional News.*

In the summer of 1920, Walden Shaw decided to join them. Shaw purchased Wadsworth Hall, an estate originally built in 1906 for Norman Wait Harris, founder of Chicago's Harris Bank. Even by ostentatious Gilded Age standards, the house the Harrises had commissioned in Lake Geneva was breathtaking. Sited on nearly forty acres of land with eight hundred feet of lake frontage, the house was designed by the noted Boston architectural firm Shepley, Rutan and Coolidge, and contained thirteen bedrooms, a wood-paneled library, a polished terrace, a grand entry hall with soaring forty-foot ceilings, and a formal dining room with a ceiling full of intricate, ornamental plaster piping in the shape of garlands and acanthus leaves. Shaw purchased the estate from Harris's daughter and her husband, and moved his family into the incredibly lavish lake home for the summer season. He renamed the estate "The Stenning," after his grandfather's home in England.

Shaw's decision to purchase an estate in Lake Geneva coincided with another significant change in his life: He was getting out of the taxi business. Since forming Walden W. Shaw Livery fourteen years earlier with his partner John Hertz, Shaw had built not only the largest taxi company in Chicago but also one of the most successful cab manufacturing businesses in the country. Now, it appeared Shaw was ready to remove himself from the increasingly escalating violence of the taxi industry in Chicago. By the end of 1920, he would step down as president of the company, remove himself from the board of directors, and sell his Yellow Cab stock, retiring to spend his summers at the new Lake Geneva estate and his winters in California.

Hertz took over the presidency of Yellow Cab and selected his old friend and longtime Shaw Livery and Yellow Cab employee Charlie Gray to replace him as vice president and general manager. Other corporate changes were under way at Yellow Cab as well. By November of 1920, the board of directors had approved a plan to separate the taxi branch and the manufacturing branch of the company into two individual entities by creating more than fifty thousand new shares of stock in the Yellow Cab Manufacturing Company, pending the approval of the current

Yellow Cab stockholders (and eventually requiring a hearing before the US Supreme Court). In just five short years since producing its first taxi, Yellow Cab Manufacturing had built more than one thousand cabs and shipped them to cities around the world. This rapid success of the cab manufacturing branch meant that from this point forward, the Yellow Cab Manufacturing Company would stand on its own and remain independent from the Yellow Cab taxi business in Chicago. Eventually, Yellow Cab Manufacturing would prove so successful that General Motors would acquire it in 1925.

At the same time that these changes were taking place at Yellow Cab, things were changing behind the scenes at Checker as well. The Checker business model differed from the Yellow Cab business model in that Checker remained an affiliation-based company, which meant that drivers came to the company already owning their own cabs or with plans to purchase their own cabs through Checker's relationship with Commonwealth Motors and Lomberg Auto Body. Because the Checker Taxi Company did not produce its own cabs, this left the drivers frequently indebted to these outside companies that together manufactured the Checker Mogul taxi.

Hoping the Checker orders would be sufficient to buoy his business, Abe Lomberg had approached Morris Markin for a loan in 1919, but by 1920, Lomberg could not keep up with the payments. Markin repossessed the loan by taking over first the Lomberg Auto Body Company and eventually the Commonwealth Motor Company as well, in a complicated business deal executed through questionably legal tactics. He combined the two companies and eventually relocated the plant to Kalamazoo, Michigan. On February 2, 1922, Markin would rename the venture and introduce the Checker Cab Mfg. Co., named after the company's most popular product: the Checker Mogul taxi produced for Chicago's Checker Taxi affiliation. However, throughout the 1920s, the two companies—the Checker Taxi Company of Chicago and the Checker Cab Mfg. Co. of Kalamazoo, Michigan—remained financially separate and did not yet share any leadership. But Markin would soon realize that it was in his new cab manufacturing company's best interests to have control over its primary client, and begin plotting a strategy that would gain him effective control of both companies.

For the time being, however, the Checker Taxi affiliation continued its rapid growth. By the end of 1920, there were around six hundred Checker taxis on the streets of Chicago, and the company leadership decided to purchase a larger building on Madison Street in West Garfield Park to serve as Checker's central garage and offices. By vacating their previous offices, Checker not only gained more space but also benefited by putting nearly five miles between their headquarters and Yellow Cab's West Side garages, the site of the previous summer's dramatic turf war. At the time, Checker's leaders may have hoped they were turning over a new leaf, but this hope would have proved misguided. The Taxi Wars were just getting started.

PART II
REV YOUR ENGINES, 1921–1924

CHAPTER 6

Stay in Your Lane

The First Grand Jury Investigation and the Murder of Thomas A. Skirven Jr. (1921)

CHICAGOANS OPENING THEIR NEWSPAPERS ON SUNDAY MORNING, March 6, 1921, probably did not guess that on page 8A of the *Chicago Tribune* they would find a very direct and politely scathing missive from John Hertz in a two-column Yellow Cab ad titled, "So the Public May Know." "The attacks made on our cabs late at night by members of a so-called taxi-cab company, are not due to 'labor troubles' as has been stated, but to ordinary thuggery and a desire to intimidate our men who are getting the great bulk of the public trade," he wrote. Without ever naming his rival publicly, Hertz made it clear that he considered Checker Taxi drivers the sole instigators in recent street battles, and that Yellow Cab had a long list of supporters on its side, including city law enforcement and the state judiciary branch. Hertz rejected the concept of a Taxi War, arguing that, "Yellow Cab is doing no fighting," and that Yellow Cab drivers were, in fact, "almost powerless to defend ourselves and our property."

Hertz went on to describe the implied Checker drivers as "gangsters and products of the poolrooms" (coded language for thieves and con men) who drove for a "fraudulent" company that did not adhere to the city ordinances. He cited a recent court case in which a coroner's jury had declared Checker's affiliation-based business model "a subterfuge to avoid liability and financial responsibility." He accused Checker drivers of jealousy, claiming that Yellow Cab's "recent decrease in rates has angered them to the point of bombing our stations and attacking our cabs." In concluding this unusual ad, Hertz declared, "We can't indulge in revolver battles in the streets."

In fact, a revolver battle in the street is exactly what inspired the ad. Chicago's Lincoln Park neighborhood in the 1920s was a pleasant, upper-middle-class part of town that attracted those who preferred to live in comfortable homes and modern, full-service apartment buildings close to the amenities of the 450-acre Lincoln Park itself. The sidewalks around the park were full of fashionable families who spent their leisure time strolling through the Lincoln Park Zoo and the Lincoln Park Conservatory, or dining at the popular Café Brauer, an upscale restaurant overlooking the park's South Pond. A postwar building boom was under way in the neighborhood, and smaller, wood-frame homes were rapidly being replaced with soaring, palatial apartment buildings and residential "hotels" that offered the finest linens, silver, and crystal, as well as optional maid service. However, that March, it became clear that even this quiet, genteel neighborhood located miles north of the Loop was not immune to the perils of the Taxi Wars.

The day before Hertz's strongly worded ad ran in the *Tribune*, in the early morning hours of Saturday, March 5, a group of fifteen Yellow Cabs and Checker Taxis sped alongside each other on the otherwise quiet streets that passed through the park, driving erratically as bullets flew in both directions, their sharp sound punctuating the darkness. No one was hit, but following the incident, two drivers from each of the cab companies walked into a nearby police station hurling complaints about the other company's drivers, everyone asserting they were merely defending themselves against the other's aggression.

Following this incident and Hertz's words in the newspapers, the state's attorney's office finally decided to act. When Democrat Maclay Hoyne had served in that role, he had declined to investigate the Taxi Wars on the basis that the incidents constituted a "war for supremacy between two corporations," refusing to allow himself to be "put in the middle." But an election the previous November had introduced a party change at the state's attorney's office: Republican Robert E. Crowe was elected by a margin of more than two hundred thousand votes. And Crowe was never inclined to remove himself from a battle.

The son of Irish immigrants, Crowe was a bright student whose family was politically connected and financially successful enough to send him to Yale Law School. Graduating in 1901, he returned to Chicago and began a rapid rise to public notoriety as an attorney specializing in criminal law. Partnering with his brother Frank, a former assistant state's attorney, and two other Republican attorneys, Crowe formed his own practice and quickly established himself as a bulldog in the courtroom. Describing Crowe, historian Dean Jobb explains that

> Contemporaries described him as "vigorous and quick-tongued," as "blunt, stormy, dangerous,"—a force to be reckoned with. He charged ahead like a prizefighter, attacking opponents with a flurry of verbal punches.

Crowe soon parlayed his courtroom successes into an appointment as an assistant state's attorney. When Republican "Big Bill" Thompson was elected mayor in 1915, Crowe's long-running involvement in the Republican political machine worked to his benefit—Thompson first named Crowe to the city's legal staff and then put him up as a candidate for a seat on the Illinois circuit court. With Thompson as his champion, Crowe was elected to the bench in 1917.

By the time Crowe took over as state's attorney in 1920, he had established himself as both an aggressive prosecutor and a "tough-on-crime" judge. (After introducing a dedicated auto theft court into the city's circuit court system, he personally convicted nine out of every ten defendants.) So when the Taxi Wars hit the streets of Lincoln Park five months after Crowe's election, he did not hesitate to take action. Five days after the Yellow and Checker cab drivers engaged in a late-night shooting chase through the park, Crowe finally did what his predecessor had not—he opened a grand jury investigation into the Taxi Wars and ordered a raid on Checker Taxi's main offices.

On Wednesday night, March 9, perhaps hoping to catch the company's leadership literally sleeping, chief investigator Benjamin Newmark and forty detectives from the state's attorney's office descended upon Checker's West Garfield Park headquarters and began confiscating nearly every file and document in the office, transporting them back to the state's attorney's office for review. Once this task was started, some of the detectives were then dispatched to the streets to stop Checker Taxis on duty, ordering the drivers to report immediately to the state's attorney's office for questioning.

At the heart of Crowe's inquiry was this seemingly simple question: Who owned the taxis of the Checker Taxi Company? The cars featured the distinctive, black-and-white checkerboard paint and the logo of the Checker Taxi Company on the side door. However, if even some of the taxis were still individually owned by the company's drivers, rather than collectively owned by the company, then that would mean that Checker was in fact operating in violation of the city ordinance requiring that every cab identify the name of its owner prominently on the side of the car. These were the ostensible grounds upon which the city's Public Vehicle Licensing Commission continued to refuse to issue cab stand permits to Checker Taxi, a situation which then forced Checker drivers to operate without a valid permit. (The previous month, police had arrested 114 Checker drivers for this very offense.) Checker leadership argued that the company took ownership of the cars when a driver joined the Checker affiliation, by trading them company stock equal to the vehicle's worth. Checker had won three test cases in the municipal courts on these grounds, the judges in all three cases agreeing with Checker's attorneys.

However, when the state attorney general Edward J. Brundage had become involved, he concluded that Checker was in fact *not* the owner of the cabs, and therefore the drivers remained in violation of the ordinance. During the week leading up to the Lincoln Park shootout, Brundage began proceedings to revoke Checker's business charter on the grounds that the company was violating the city ordinances. Checker leaders accused Hertz at Yellow Cab of calling in a political favor from Brundage to ensure this outcome, and on Monday of that week, an unidentified attacker had bombed a Yellow Cab station in Humboldt Park. This round of disagreement culminated in the rolling gun battle through Lincoln

Park at the end of the week, by which point Crowe decided his office could no longer remain idle.

Just one day after the state's attorney's raid on Checker's offices, on Thursday, March 10, 1921, Crowe opened his case before a grand jury. "I am going to stop . . . a reign of terror being inaugurated in this city by any company, association or organization; the throwing of stench bombs, smashing of windows, bombing of homes and places of business and the slugging and shooting of citizens," he announced, adding that the investigation into Checker was just the beginning. Over four days of testimony, members of Crowe's office laid out the state's case, entering into evidence some of the confiscated records, including bills of sale that seemed to undermine Crowe's own argument by proving that the owner-ship of some Checker cars had indeed changed hands from the drivers to the company. Crowe also called to the stand witnesses who had seen the street violence firsthand, including police officers who had been involved in shootings or investigated bombings.

Despite the fact that at least some of the evidence corroborated Checker's claims, the members of the grand jury evidently found Crowe's arguments against Checker compelling. On Tuesday, March 15, the grand jury returned its judgment, finding three Checker officials—President Frank Dilger, Secretary Michael Sokoll, and Treasurer Oscar Ericson—guilty of conspiracy to violate a municipal ordinance, and of defrauding the city of certain licensing fees. In addition, the grand jury indicted seven Checker driver-stockholders for the same crimes.

Far from solving the problem of the street warfare between Yellow Cab and Checker Taxi, the grand jury's judgment only served to add fuel to the fire. Checker's leadership and its drivers accused Hertz and Yellow Cab of exerting unfair political influence in an organized attempt to put Checker out of business. "The hidden flaw in the [Cab Stand Permit Bill] was the tacit understanding by the people administering it that unless you were a Yellow [Cab] driver working for Mr. Hertz, your application was never accepted," wrote the son of a Checker Taxi driver many years later.

Checker was not the only cab company to perceive this discrimina-tion from the city: The week before the grand jury inquest, the Morrison

Hotel Taxi Service Company, the Brown Cab Company, and the Diamond Cab Company were also cited by the city for operating without proper licenses. Assistant Corporation Counsel Carl F. Lund explained that the city was "of the opinion that they are not entitled to have licenses issued to them for the reason that they are not bona fide corporations organized for the purpose of owning and operating taxicabs for hire." But the Checker drivers in particular saw only a conspiracy between Yellow Cab and the city of Chicago to harass Yellow Cab's competitors out of business. Following the indictments, the animosity between the drivers for Yellow Cab and Checker Taxi only intensified, and by the start of the Chicago summer, this bitter sentiment would ignite, ushering in a devastating new phase of the Taxi Wars.

BLOODY NOSES AND BLACK EYES

This time, the trouble began at the Hotel Sherman, site of one of the famous stinkbomb incidents that had marked the earliest skirmishes in the Taxi Wars seven years earlier. On Monday June 6, 1921, the city held a judicial election, the result of a quirk of Illinois politics dating back to 1848, which required (and in fact still requires today) that circuit court judges throughout the state be elected via partisan elections, rather than receive their appointments from the governor or run in nonpartisan elections, as in most other states. That spring of 1921, Mayor Thompson and his closest allies (or "cronies," the term preferred by some reporters) assembled a slate of Thompson-supported challengers in an attempt to unseat the incumbents and gain control of the judicial branch of the county government, thereby removing one of the checks on the mayor's power. This situation required Chicago residents to declare their allegiances. Those people and businesses who were loyal to Thompson were expected to vote for the Thompson slate of judges at the polls. Those people and businesses who were not loyal to Thompson, who in fact felt no warmth whatsoever toward his administration, like the Checker Taxi drivers, instead supported the incumbent judges, known as the "coalition candidates."

Prior to the election, representatives from Checker had met with the chief of police, and they claimed he had told them the police would cease making new arrests of Checker drivers until after the citywide judicial elections. The Checker leadership interpreted this as a veiled warning that the Checker employees should support Mayor Thompson's judicial picks, or face ongoing harassment by the Chicago Police Department. "If this was a hint for the Checker chauffeurs to line up with the Thompson . . . outfit in the judicial election, we ignored it," Checker counsel Leonard J. Grossman later explained. Instead, the Checker Taxi Company had not only publicly declared their support of the coalition candidates, they had gone so far as to host a dinner for the incumbents, inviting one of the leading anti-Thompson judges to speak at the event.

By contrast, John Hertz and Yellow Cab were perceived to be very friendly with the Thompson administration. Because of this, Checker leaders frequently accused the city of favoritism toward Yellow Cab and complained that their own drivers were persecuted by the Public Vehicle Licensing Commission and city government officials for their refusal to support the mayor. However, on the day of the election, the tides turned in Checker's favor when Thompson's slate of judicial challengers was handily defeated, losing by more than one hundred thousand votes. Among the taxi drivers, the Checker drivers had won this round, and in this politically charged atmosphere, the city streets suddenly became a tense playing field once again.

The following evening in front of the Hotel Sherman, a group of Checker Taxis began making a play for dominance at the cab stand in front of the hotel, driving aggressively, cutting off Yellow Cabs, and securing fares out of turn. A large group of spectators gathered to watch, attracted by the dramatic driving and shouting. A detail of police on horseback had to ride onto the sidewalk to restrain the crowds from standing in the street, while other policemen attempted to force the cabs away from the stand. However, this method was ineffective, and the cabs who had not picked up fares merely circled the block and returned to the escalating fray. Someone threw the first punch, and someone else broke the first window of a rival cab, and before the night was over, "several Yellow and Checker chauffeurs received bloody noses, cut lips and blackened eyes," the *Chicago Tribune* reported the next day.

Two Checker drivers were arrested for the assault of a Yellow Cab driver, who was hit over the head with the handle of a car jack. Yellow Cab superintendent Abraham Katz, never one to miss out on a fight, was also arrested on the scene. Eventually, the arrests and the police presence served to quell the altercations—several hours after the incident had begun, the drivers finally dispersed. But the night's battles were just the start of much more serious incidents to come between the drivers for the two companies.

PRELUDE TO A TRAGEDY

Less than twenty-four hours later, the violence started up again in the same spot it had erupted the night before, and this time the police could not contain the violence to a single location. What began as the usual skirmish over cab stand dominance quickly radiated across the city, each incident of violence spurring an escalated retaliation somewhere else in the city. As had happened the night before, disputes at the Hotel Sherman cab stand led to fistfights and smashed car windows, resulting in arrests. Police arrested a Checker driver for "malicious mischief and inciting a riot" when his vehicle struck a Yellow Cab, though the driver contended that he had been rear-ended by another Yellow Cab first, forcing him into the car in front of him. According to later allegations by Hertz, several Yellow Cab drivers had been "slugged" during a brawl. As a result of the melee at the Hotel Sherman again that night, the Checker Taxi Company put all of its drivers on high alert, and told them to "be aware of any other incidents, and to come to the aid of their fellow drivers."

Checker driver Jack Fox heard these warnings, but Fox was a man "who was not easily intimidated." He had been working in the Loop that evening, and knew firsthand about the trouble at the Hotel Sherman. He soon joined it. As he later told the story, he was returning to a downtown cab stand after dropping off a fare when a rival Yellow Cab started speeding toward him from the rear, shooting into his car. Fox hit the gas and pulled a .32-caliber revolver out from under the seat of his cab, where he kept it hidden for personal security. The two cabs began racing side-by-side, heading west on 12th Street, a running gun battle under way as they shot at each other's cars. As they approached Racine

Avenue, a policeman on the corner saw the two cars racing toward him and witnessed Fox firing behind him toward the Yellow Cab. Because of this, the policeman determined that Fox was the aggressor in this street battle and signaled the Yellow Cab to stop and pick him up. He climbed on the cab's running board as they took off in pursuit of Fox, who had turned north. The policeman began shooting at Fox with one hand as he held on to the speeding car with the other. Not realizing the bullets were now coming from a policeman and not the Yellow Cab driver, Fox continued to return fire behind him.

Fox was heading for the safety of a Checker Taxi garage where his best friend, Abe Schwartz, worked as the night manager. Making a hard turn into the garage and slamming on the brakes, Fox fled the vehicle and ran into the building. Pulling up just seconds behind him, the police officer jumped off the running board of the Yellow Cab and ran toward the garage in pursuit. At the door, Schwartz blocked the policeman's path, informing the officer that he was on private property and did not have permission to search the premises. As Schwartz stalled the policeman, Fox ran out the back door and escaped. The policeman arrested Schwartz for obstruction of justice and took him to the Maxwell Street station for questioning. When Fox eventually learned that Schwartz had been arrested and was being questioned, he decided to lay low for a few days, and quietly left town for South Bend, Indiana.

Fox's brother Philip, however, stayed in the city. And his night was just getting started. The two brothers shared the Dodge touring car they drove for Checker, each taking a twelve-hour shift. They had been close since childhood, when their family emigrated from the Galician region of what is today Poland and Ukraine, and settled in a predominantly Jewish neighborhood in Chicago. It was a tough place, an area surrounded by enclaves of other immigrant groups who were loudly anti-Semitic. As children, the Fox brothers frequently got into fights with boys from the Italian and Polish settlements nearby and grew up into "hardened combatants," earning the nickname the "Rough Boys."

The night that his brother got into the running gun fight, Philip Fox was only twenty-one years old. Just the previous month, he had received divorce papers from his wife after a youthful, misguided marriage that had lasted just three months. Much later, Philip Fox's son would remember him as "aggressive, industrious and very fastidious in his habits and appearance," and would describe him as a man "with a chip on his shoulder." Fox's brother was already in trouble that night because of the Taxi Wars. Before the next sunrise, Philip Fox would find himself at the center of a murder investigation.

THE MURDER OF THOMAS A. SKIRVEN JR.

The incidents between Yellow Cab and Checker Taxi that night continued to multiply. In an area of the city then known as the Rialto district, another Checker driver was sitting in his taxi when a Yellow Cab drove by and shot four bullets into his car; he was unhurt. Checker driver Harry Rosenthal experienced a similar assault on the city's Near South Side when a large, unmarked touring car sped past him and opened fire, missing Rosenthal but leaving his cab "riddled with bullets." Not long afterward, a similar touring car fired on police standing a few blocks away. The police returned fire but no one was injured in the exchange. In the Black Belt, a Checker driver was surrounded by four Yellow Cabs who forced his car into the curb, smashing his wheels and windows. Yet another Checker driver said five Yellow Cab drivers attacked him, smashing all the windows in his cab.

Around 1:00 a.m., the violence finally resulted in tragedy. Yellow Cab driver Thomas A. Skirven Jr. stood in front of a Yellow Cab garage on the city's West Side. By this point in the night, nearly every taxi driver in the city must have heard about the fights, the broken windows, the raw aggression, and the shootings, even if they had not experienced any trouble themselves. Skirven was chatting with a few colleagues, all of them keeping an eye out for attacks, when without any warning, an unmarked touring car sped east past the garage, throwing out a deafening hail of bullets. There were at least three gunmen in the car, and they unloaded around twenty-five bullets into the building, one of which struck Skirven on the left side of his chest, above his heart. He was rushed to St. Anthony's Hospital, where he was pronounced dead. Skirven left behind a wife, a three-year-old son named Arthur, and seventeen-month-old twins, Julia and William.

Learning of the cold-blooded murder of one of his drivers, Hertz was enraged. An hour later, around 2:00 a.m., he issued a statement to the press announcing that he would offer a $5,000 reward for the arrest and conviction of Skirven's murderers. "We have gone just as far with the murderous methods of the Checker Taxi Company as we intend to," he declared. "From now on, it is going to be a fight to the finish." Even as news of the reward spread, a Yellow Cab driver in Logan Square was shot in the foot, one of the final acts of violence for the night.

Involuntary Confessions

"Driver Slain in Taxi War; $5,000 Reward" read the front-page headline in the *Chicago Tribune* the next morning. Not long after the early edition of the paper arrived on people's doorsteps, Detective Thomas Mangan was out knocking on Philip Fox's door. Mangan arrested Fox for suspicion of involvement in the murder of Thomas Skirven and led him out of his apartment, heading toward the office of Cook County state's attorney Robert E. Crowe.

"What this for?" Fox asked him. "Is this about that shooting over on Twelfth Street?"

"What do you know about it?" Mangan asked.

"Only what I read in the paper this morning," Fox replied. Mangan didn't believe him.

About the same time that Mangan was arresting Fox, an officer was sent to arrest another Checker driver named Morris Stuben, a close friend of both Philip Fox and his brother Jack. Philip Fox and Morris Stuben were arrested without a warrant and brought to the state's attorney's office. There, they were interrogated separately, both by police and by Yellow Cab corporate counsel. For several hours, the men were brought in and out of a dark room, and physically intimidated. A subsequent trial found that Fox was "beaten, kicked, vilified and threatened with further violence if he did not confess." Eventually, the police officers conducting the interrogations resorted to threatening his life. "Come clean, you little son of a bitch, or I'll throw you out the window," one of them said, kneeing Fox in the stomach. The physical abuse continued with the other officer kicking him in the shins and punching him in the head. Fox was again interrogated by Yellow Cab corporate counsel, who asked, "Do you know anything about it now?" Fox finally capitulated and told the Yellow Cab attorney he'd say anything he wanted to hear if the torture would stop. At 3:00 a.m. on June 10, Fox signed a confession, implicating himself along with Morris Stuben and four others as the gunmen in the car.

Appearing before a judge at a hearing later that same day, Fox vigorously denied his confession, saying that he was beaten, threatened, and "given the third degree" by employees of Crowe's office. Fox displayed severe emotional distress in the courtroom. "Look at my lips," he told the judge, showing off injuries. "Look at my shirt. They tore off all my buttons. Look at my hair. They kept slugging and beating me. I cried for mercy. They would not let me sleep." Stuben accused the interrogators of similar treatment. The judge ultimately sympathized with Fox and Stuben, and ordered them to be removed from the custody of the state's attorney's office and turned over to the sheriff's department instead. (To this day, Fox's case appears in law textbooks demonstrating the legal issue between voluntary and involuntary confessions.)

Despite the weak evidence and tainted confession, the newspapers reported the arrests of Fox and Stuben (and their eventual convictions) as a kind of closure to the incident, perhaps as an attempt to assure the taxi-hailing public that they were no longer in danger from murderous gangs committing targeted street violence. However, multiple incidents on the night of Skirven's murder had indeed put the public in danger. And the City Council took notice of this.

The same day Fox stood in court denying his confession, two aldermen prepared and presented a resolution empowering the chief of police to revoke the cab stand permits of any taxi driver found to be involved in the Taxi Wars. The council unanimously passed the resolution. "Any taxi drivers of either faction who are found fighting will lose their permits immediately," the chief of police said. "The taking of the law into their own hands . . . must stop." The resolution also allowed the police to search drivers and revoke their permit if they were discovered to be carrying a "revolver or other deadly weapon."

The following day, the City Council's local transportation committee opened an inquiry into the Taxi Wars, and summoned the heads of every taxi company in the city to appear before them to answer questions. Over several sessions, the cab company leaders testified about the street battles, some of which had been witnessed firsthand by members of the City Council. Each company hurled accusations at the other and blamed the problems on rival drivers.

"All of the Checker drivers own their own cabs and most of them are mortgaged to the hilt to avoid financial responsibility," Hertz wrote in a public response. "Some of these Checker drivers are products of low pool-rooms—some of them are members of criminal gangs and have criminal records. Others are dismissed employees of the Yellow Cab Company who were discharged for dishonesty and unreliability." Michael Sokoll had taken over as president of the Checker Taxi Company; he testified before the City Council committee, countering that, "The Yellow Cab Company for seven years has been trying to drive other companies out of business through the hiring of sluggers." Yellow Cab general counsel Samuels denied the accusation. "Time and time again, our chauffeurs have been assaulted and their cars damaged by the chauffeurs for the Checker concern," he said.

That same week, police arrested more than fifty Checker drivers for operating their cabs without valid cab stand permits. A handful of drivers for the Diamond Cab Company were arrested on similar charges. "Police officers look on and laugh while the Yellow chauffeurs wreck our cars and intimidate our drivers," Checker's Sokoll further alleged. "Why, a sergeant of police rides around in the Yellow Company's slugger car! His name is Thomas Mangan." At this accusation, the chief of police corrected Sokoll. "Mangan is not assigned to the Yellow Cab Company," he explained. "He is doing regular police work."

However, it appeared that Mangan remained tasked on special assignment to the Taxi Wars—it was Mangan who arrested Fox at his home the morning after Skirven's murder. Sokoll called Mangan's integrity into question: "He told me that if he caught me in the Loop when there was any trouble, he would lock me up and frame on me so they would throw the key away," he told the aldermen.

After listening to this acrimonious testimony from the warring cab companies over several days, the committee members decided to draft a new ordinance concerning taxi rules and regulations, in the hope that these would prevent further outbreaks of gun violence and murder among cab drivers on the streets. The new ordinances said:

- Each cab must file a $10,000 bond with the city or carry that same amount of accident liability insurance.

- Drivers found with "revolvers, blackjacks or other weapons" would have their licenses immediately revoked with no path toward restoration.

- Cab stand privileges required a valid cab stand permit, available only to the "bona fide legal owner" of the cab.

- Drivers convicted of a crime in the past two years were ineligible for a license.

With the passage of these ordinances on June 28, and the arrest of Fox and Stuben for Skirven's murder less than three weeks earlier, Yellow Cab and Checker came to a grudging truce.

UNRESOLVED CONFLICTS

With Sokoll now at the helm of Checker Taxi, the company seemed to begin to acknowledge that its affiliation-based business model did not in fact comply with the new city ordinances. The attorney general's office announced in July that, to come into compliance and become eligible for cab stand permits, Checker Taxi would need to begin a process of corporate reorganization, bringing the ownership of all of the cabs under the corporation's control. Checker corporate counsel Leonard Grossman appeared before a judge shortly after the announcement was made, and he indicated that Checker would in fact attempt to complete the corporate reorganization before September to comply with the new ordinances.

However, this did not happen. Instead, when the grace period offered by the judge ran out in September, the police began aggressively stopping and inspecting Checker Taxis for compliance with the new ordinances. In the nearly three-week period between September 20, 1921 and October 8, 1921, police arrested between fifteen and fifty Checker cab drivers every night for driving without a cab stand permit. Representing Checker, Grossman again appeared in court, seeking a judge to compel the city to grant cab stand permits to Checker cabs without the corporate restructuring. Despite the fact that Checker had not altered its business model, Grossman continued to argue that Checker offered drivers stock in the amount of the vehicle's worth, and that this should constitute sufficient ownership. This time, Checker had the support of a representative from the attorney general's office, who testified in another hearing that Checker Taxi had shown sufficient good faith in complying with the AG's requirements, and that further proceedings regarding the issue would not be necessary.

"This thing has . . . been but a campaign of annoyance and persecution by city officials who are inspired by other sources," Checker president Sokoll complained. "We have done everything in our power to secure these licenses. The city refuses to grant them, and yet arrests us for not having them." Sokoll blamed the situation on a conspiracy between the mayor's office, the police department, the licensing commission, and the Yellow Cab Company, who he said would like to see Checker and its cabs out of business and off the streets.

Following Skirven's murder and the arrest of Fox and Stuben, however, John Hertz and Yellow Cab appear to have moved on from the feud with Checker. In July at the Hotel Sherman (where the most recent flare of street battles had begun just a few weeks earlier), he had entertained representatives from the National Association of Taxicab Owners, an eighteen-month-old organization of which Hertz was a founding member. There, under Hertz's urging, cab company owners from around the country agreed to campaign their respective cities to adopt taxi regulations similar to Chicago's newly passed cab ordinances. They also unanimously joined the National Safety Council and established a committee to promote a "safety drive," based on the success of an internal program Gray and Hertz had piloted at Yellow Cab over the past few months which had reduced accidents by 50 percent.

Hertz followed up these successes by announcing that, beginning on October 1, Yellow Cab would cut its rates for the third time that year, reflecting the stabilizing economy following the uncertainty of the war years. Hertz lowered Yellow Cab rates to 20 cents for the first mile, a full 50 percent less than they had been at the start of the year. Demand for cabs steadily increased; by the beginning of November, Yellow Cab's gross earnings had increased by 10 percent.

Yellow Cab's booming business had inspired technological innovations as well. An article in the *Illinois Bell Telephone News* detailed the incredible expansion of the Yellow Cab dispatch center, which by the end of 1921 comprised the largest telephone installation in the world. The system involved more than two hundred phone operators, supervisors, and dispatchers in the company's main garage. Generally, the department received an average of sixty-five hundred calls per day, but on Christmas Day, 1921, they handled an astonishing sixty thousand calls in twelve hours.

Perhaps because of this unqualified success, Hertz appeared unconcerned about Checker's accusations that Yellow Cab was conspiring with the mayor. Shortly after Sokoll and Grossman attempted to sue the city to issue cab stand permits to Checker, Mayor Thompson and other city officials flatly denied any interference in the taxi industry, and the judge ruled that he had no jurisdiction to compel the city to issue the permits. Once again, Checker and the city of Chicago were at an impasse. And Checker's problems were about to get much, much worse.

CHAPTER 7

Shifting Gears

Civil War at Checker Taxi (1922–1924)

ON TUESDAY, SEPTEMBER 26, 1923, CHICAGO WOKE TO A NEW LAND-scape on the city's most iconic thoroughfare. As it does today, the multi-lane boulevard of Michigan Avenue in the 1920s (still known more accurately then as Michigan Boulevard) gave drivers, passengers, and pedestrians a front-row seat to some of the most imposing, impressive, and well-recognized landmarks of downtown Chicago, from the Beaux Arts–style London Guarantee Building, to the neoclassical Chicago Public Library topped with its ornate Tiffany dome, to the larger-than-life lions regally watching over traffic in front of the Art Institute of Chicago, to the expansive greenspace of Grant Park. On this particular morning, drivers and pedestrians in the vicinity of Michigan Avenue also saw a vision of the future: the city's first stoplights.

From the Chicago River at the north end to 22nd Street on the south end, at every point where Michigan Avenue intersected with another street, the South Park Commission had installed the city's very first stoplight traffic control system. At 7:20 a.m. that morning, after a slow buildup of public excitement and speculation about the project over the previous months but with little fanfare or commemoration of the moment, the city put the first section of the system into use, between Randolph and 7th Streets. For the very first time in Chicago, everyone saw the famous red, yellow, and green lights indicating whether or not it was their turn to pass through the intersections. Whether those drivers, passengers, pedestrians, and bystanders were curious or annoyed by the new contraptions, whether they were trepidatious or eager to be the first to encounter the system, everyone present that morning witnessed something historic: the birth of the future of city traffic.

The system was designed by the National Signal Company, which had overseen its installation over the previous month. The upfront costs for the new stoplight system were footed entirely by one company: Yellow Cab. The system included twenty-one freestanding stoplights, roughly the size of a lamppost, situated in the dead center of the intersections. In addition to this, there were three larger control towers, each roughly the height of a three-story building, which stood in the middle of Michigan Avenue's intersections with Jackson Boulevard, 12th Street, and 16th Street. Hertz and the city leaders hoped this revolutionary new invention would speed the flow of traffic and improve the safety of pedestrians and vehicles alike. Notably, the stoplight colors had not yet codified in their current order: These first stoplights put the yellow at the top, green in the middle and red on the bottom. Inside each stoplight, an electrical box connected the light to the programmed electrical system, with manual overrides available if necessary. The timing of the lights ranged from twenty-five seconds to sixty seconds, the result of an intensive traffic study the South Park Commission had conducted over the previous six weeks.

Perhaps unsurprisingly, the transition from the traffic free-for-all that had previously prevailed on Michigan Avenue (what one opinion writer of the era referred to as the "usual jam and hurly-burly") to the new electric stoplight system did not go entirely smoothly that first day. Taxis, limousines, delivery trucks, buses, private cars, and pedestrians would all have to learn to adjust to the new rules that came with the installation of the traffic signals, which at first included a prohibition on left turns during rush hour. One frustrated husband (described by a reporter as an "erstwhile pompous man in a limousine") complained that first day that there was no way for his driver to get from the southbound lanes of Michigan Avenue to the Art Institute, where he was scheduled to pick up his wife. By the afternoon rush hour, the gridlock was so severe that one reporter spent over an hour trying to drive up Michigan

Avenue between 12th Street and the Tribune Tower, a distance of about one-and-a-half miles. But Hertz remained undeterred by the hiccups the first day, expressing optimism on the effect the stoplights would have on the city's traffic problems. "I am gratified to learn that the lights are working," he said. "I feel confident that the system will prove so successful on the boulevard that it will be extended into the Loop, and into the outlying points of traffic congestion."

Since the previous summer when he had entertained executives from the National Taxicab Owners' Association and presented to them his company's pilot program on safety, Hertz had continued to investigate methods by which he could improve his company's safety record while maximizing its profits. The primary solution he had landed on was one that would have long-reaching effects in Chicago and around the world: traffic signals. "There is practically no limit to the amount we would be willing to pay for the complete regulation of traffic and for the safeguarding of life from traffic accidents [in Chicago]," he had declared.

Hertz had run the numbers to see what the congestion from unregulated or poorly regulated traffic was costing his company: By his calculations, every Yellow Cab passed through the Loop an average of fifteen times a day, and lost an average of ten minutes each time due to traffic congestion. Using Yellow Cab's hourly rate of $3 per hour as a baseline, he calculated that the traffic-related slowdowns were costing each cab $7 per day, which correlated to 30 percent of its earning capacity. Hertz was eager to work with the city to find a solution to the antiquated and frequently ineffective practice of posting traffic-control policemen with whistles at the Loop's busy intersections. "Watch the crowds at any Loop intersection," Hertz went on. "See them sweep over the curb and dash into the street when the traffic whistle has been blown against them."

So on April 22, 1922, Hertz had approached the South Park Board Commission and submitted a proposal: Yellow Cab would pay for the installation of a traffic signal system on Michigan Avenue. Similar traffic signals had already been installed on Fifth Avenue in New York City, as well as other busy intersections in Cleveland and Detroit. Those systems were manually operated, with a small room constructed in the center of an intersection to serve as a perch for the man operating the traffic signal.

People who had seen these in use in other cities marveled at how completely drivers obeyed the signals and how the regulation allowed traffic to move "like clockwork." The South Park Commission took Hertz's proposal under advisement and began investigating the feasibility of automated traffic signal towers for Chicago.

By March of 1923, the commission had approved Hertz's proposal, and the National Signal Company began constructing the three towers and twenty-one stoplights. Hertz agreed to donate the system to the city at a cost of up to $60,000, with the caveat that the city would repay his investment if it was successful. Hertz hoped that the experiment would streamline the traffic on Michigan Avenue and encourage the city to invest in the installation of more traffic lights throughout the Loop. According to the terms of Hertz's donation, if the city deemed the installation of the traffic lights a success, then they agreed to reimburse him for the cost of his donation after two years. By most accounts, though that first day of operation in September proved to be a challenging one, by the second day of the stoplight system (following a few amendments to the rules regarding left turns), traffic policemen were lauding its success at controlling traffic congestion. Hertz's prediction of the unequivocal success of a stoplight system in Chicago very quickly appeared to be coming true.

CHANGES AT CHECKER

While Hertz and Yellow Cab focused on issues of safety and traffic congestion, significant changes were underway at Checker Taxi. After the numerous legal battles and street fights of 1921, it appeared that Checker had opted to embrace a new tactic to gain legitimacy from the city to receive their cab stand permits and continue operating legally, thereby expanding their business. So around the same time that Hertz was first suggesting the idea of a stoplight system to the South Park Commission, Checker Taxi announced a corporate restructuring and reorganization. Corporation counsel Leonard Grossman left the company to found his own taxi company, the Black and White Cab Company. On February 27, 1922, new leaders at Checker took out an ad in the newspaper announcing "its complete reorganization into a million-dollar company." The corporate restructuring brought with it a new president, Clifford J. Gordon, as well as a new secretary and treasurer. The same newspaper ad that announced the changes also boasted of two new Checker garages, one at the city's popular Riverview Park amusement park and one at California and Van Buren, to better serve the city's West Side. "With this reorganization," the ad proclaimed, "and the changes and additions in personnel and equipment, the Checker Taxi company is better fitted than ever to serve the public."

However, behind the scenes, this corporate reorganization was not unfolding smoothly. On May 24, just three months after the company took out this ad declaring its fitness to serve, David Ostran, a member of the Checker Taxi board of directors, filed a petition for injunction against the company in Cook County circuit court. Ostran accused Gordon and the new Checker leadership of conspiring with certain other members of the board of directors to get their way through the threat of physical harm. Ostran claimed they had employed "twelve persons, commonly described as 'gunmen,' who are known as 'superintendents,' to intimidate the stockholders." In this case, the stockholders were also the drivers, and Ostran's complaint alleged that the presence of these enforcers effectively strong-armed any dissenters among the drivers. He accused this group of men of forming a "clique of control" within the company, holding secret meetings from which they barred any members who disagreed with them. Ostran claimed he was motivated to file his petition when this "clique" removed him from the board of directors for his refusal to support their ideas.

The group in power, Ostran declared, "intends to impair the assets of the corporation, ruin its credit and standing, so that a rival corporation may obtain control of the Checker Taxi company at a low price." Ostran further suspected that "unknown bidders" had promised the current president and his supporters a large payout if they could successfully tank the company. Like many of the twelve hundred Checker drivers, Ostran was a member of the International Brotherhood of Teamsters union. So in the weeks following his removal from the board of directors, he sought help from his union, in the form of protection and additional strength to oppose those who had removed him. From that moment on, the union—at that time headed by its business agent, Timothy F. Neary—became a key player in the internal struggle unfolding at Checker.

At their best, unions in 1920s Chicago could provide a platform for workers to band together and advocate in their own interest against powerful and wealthy employers who otherwise had no inherent incentive to consider the interests of the labor force. At their worst, unions could devolve into gangs where those in power abused their positions to enact a specific agenda through psychological and physical intimidation of the membership. By the 1920s, as they had for decades before that, unions in Chicago could wield an immense amount of power through both legal and extralegal methods. In fact, the common practice of hiring paid enforcers (or "sluggers" in the parlance of the era) to intimidate, threaten, beat, and control those members who refused to align with the union's agenda only increased following the start of Prohibition in January of 1920, as Chicago's Mob bosses took up labor racketeering as a way to launder the vast amounts of money they were making through the trafficking of illegal liquor. In the case of Checker Taxi, Neary's iron-fisted leadership of the International Brotherhood of Teamsters, aided by muscle from union-friendly gangsters, initially gave him unchecked power over the Checker drivers. Neary's enemies within the company would eventually describe him as a "virtual dictator."

At the time that Ostran filed his petition against the Checker leadership, the attorney general's office had run out of patience with Checker Taxi as well. After declaring the previous autumn that his office felt Checker was showing "sufficient good faith" in complying with their demands, Attorney General Brundage had since filed proceedings against the company, seeking to revoke their business charter on the grounds that Checker Taxi leaders had made false statements to the secretary of state and had generally misused their charter. If a judge sided with the attorney general's office, Brundage could order the immediate dissolution of the company.

However, despite Ostran's accusations and the complaints from the attorney general's office, the judge ultimately ruled in favor of Checker Taxi, granting the company the legal right to exist as a corporation. To appease the attorney general, the judge imposed a fine of $1,000 against

Checker for failure to hold a proper stockholders' meeting when expanding the company the previous autumn. In explaining his decision to uphold Checker's business charter, the judge explained that the company was by that time a "growing concern" of more than one thousand employees and that, at least since the previous autumn, Checker had begun to operate as a "bona fide corporation of use and benefit to the community." For the time being, Checker Taxi was saved. But as Ostran's petition hinted, a storm of internal strife was forming within the company, which would soon lead to some of the most harrowing and lethal events of the Taxi Wars.

MORRIS MARKIN AND THE NEW "CHECKER CAB"

Despite Ostran's initial assertion that an internal faction inside the board of directors was intent on devaluing the company for their own financial gain, Checker continued to grow in size and market share. This meant the company needed more cabs for their fleet, and Morris Markin was eager to provide them. After taking over the Commonwealth Motor Company and the Lomberg Auto Body Company when those two concerns could not repay the loans he had given them, Markin had consolidated the two companies into the Checker Cab Mfg. Co. in February of 1922, and updated the design of the former "Checker Mogul" taxi model, renaming it the "Checker Cab (Model C)." These new Checker cabs and the cabs produced by the Yellow Cab Mfg. Co. were the only two models of purpose-built cabs available on the market at that time, putting them in direct competition with each other.

A few months later, in July of 1922, Markin had announced that the production of the new Checker cabs was set to begin on September 1. "Having closely watched the performance of the Mogul Cab through millions of miles of service in the fleet of the powerful Checker Taxi Company of Chicago, as well as in the service of its other national users, we know that the Checker Cab now being built is as humanly perfect as a man-made machine can be, and in this production, only the highest standard of engineering and manufacturing will be tolerated," Markin boasted in a letter announcing the new company. Orders for the updated Checker cabs started rolling in, and by the following April, Markin had made the decision to move the manufacturing plant out of Joliet, relocating to Kalamazoo, Michigan, where a large, skilled workforce of automakers was readily available. By doing this, Markin began his journey from clothing manufacturer to taxi manufacturer, one which would have long-reaching consequences.

However, in pursuing this path, Markin made enemies. In March of 1923, Markin's former debtor Abe Lomberg accused him of manipulating the stock of the new Checker Cab Mfg. Co. to "freeze out" Lomberg's shares in the company. Lomberg claimed that his shares were worth more than $112,000 (nearly $1 million in today's money), and that Markin refused to issue him equivalent stock certificates in the newly organized company.

Two months later, due to a separate complaint, a judge found Markin and Checker Cab Mfg. Co. secretary Michael Glassberg guilty of perjury and conspiracy to violate Illinois's "Blue Sky" law, a safeguard intended to prevent securities fraud. And around the same time that the judge found fault with Markin's company, John Hertz and the Yellow Cab Manufacturing Company sought an injunction against Markin and Checker Cab Mfg. Co. for design infringement, accusing the new Checker cabs of featuring a shutter design unique to Yellow Cabs. A court would eventually rule in Checker's favor on the matter. But it was clear that Markin was now playing a version of business politics that elicited the rancor of many people. He would soon up the ante.

The Murder of Frank Sexton

At the same time at Checker Taxi, things had only gotten more and more tense. As Ostran's lawsuit indicated, as early as 1922, internal conflicts raged as two factions within Checker Taxi fought to gain control of the now million-dollar company. On one side of the conflict were the men siding with the gangster-affiliated union, a group which included Ostran. On the other was a group of drivers loyal to a still-secret sect within the company opposed to Neary and the unionists.

By 1923, this jockeying for power had spilled over into the streets. Because Checker had begun as an affiliation-based company, each driver initially came into the company owning his own cab, and was then offered company stock in the amount of the cab's worth. This made each Checker driver a shareholder in the company, which meant that they each had one vote at the annual shareholders' meeting in all decisions regarding the corporate leadership. On June 19, 1923, the Checker Taxi Company was scheduled to hold their shareholders' meeting and corporate elections. That day, each company shareholder, including almost all of the drivers, could walk into the Broadway Armory, a large brick building in the city's Edgewater neighborhood resembling an eighteenth-century fort, and cast a vote to determine who would lead the company. The outcome of the election would determine the new president, vice president, secretary, and treasurer of the company, as well as the board of directors, and, therefore by extension, control of the company. If a shareholder could not be present to cast his vote that day, he could sign over his vote to another shareholder through the use of a proxy form, which empowered the designated proxy person to cast a vote on the shareholder's behalf.

As the president of Checker Cab Mfg. Co., a separate and unaffiliated business entity, Morris Markin was not a shareholder in Checker Taxi and could not vote. But he realized that there were many advantages to ensuring that the leadership at his largest client was friendly to his own interests—if he could get Checker Taxi leadership to sign an exclusive deal to buy taxis from his cab manufacturing company, he stood to make a large sum of money. As yet, however, Markin had not had any luck getting the current Checker leaders to agree to this. By his own admission, he had butted heads with the unionists.

And so, Markin had devised a plan: to establish his own secret cabal among the Checker Taxi drivers, and then to aggressively pursue anyone who was not inclined to support this inner circle. Markin chose Emanuel "Manny" Goldstein as an ally in this scheme. Little is known about Goldstein. A photo of him from the era shows a wiry and nervous-looking man in his late forties, wearing old-fashioned, black wire-rimmed glasses and sporting a small, trimmed mustache. Like Markin, Goldstein was Jewish. He lived in a working-class immigrant neighborhood called Ukrainian Village with his wife, Yanka, just eight blocks east of where Markin lived, and had been working as a cab driver for at least five years, starting out working for a small company called Emery Motor Livery before transitioning to Checker.

It is unclear why Markin chose Goldstein as his preferred candidate for president of the company at that moment. But according to later allegations, Markin directed those drivers who were loyal to him at Checker Taxi to aggressively support Goldstein's candidacy for president of the company in the upcoming election. Markin's tactics were allegedly so aggressive that he printed proxy forms and sent members of that inner circle out to the streets to persuade holdout unionists by any means necessary—including intimidation tactics, threats, violence, and bribery—to sign over their proxy votes, ensuring a win for Goldstein.

Publicly, Markin denied any direct involvement, making a statement through his attorney, John Prendergast: "Mr. Markin has no interest in the present fight, other than that he has advised some of the drivers how they can wrest control of the company from the union men," he declared. He then added, "Of course, he also is anxious to see the union ousted, because they have been fighting [Checker Cab Mfg. Co.]." Markin and his attorney painted the unionists as the aggressors in this fight, arguing that the union had its sights set on controlling Checker Taxi at all costs. Markin accused the union leaders of providing their own paid sluggers from among the city's gangs to threaten, beat, and intimidate those who refused to align themselves with the union. As the elections approached, the stage was set for a conflict.

The violence erupted on June 3, 1923. A Checker driver was standing outside the main Checker Taxi garage in West Garfield Park when two cars drove past and opened fire, racing off into the darkness. The driver was uninjured, but he estimated a total of about seven men had fired on him from the cars and attributed the attack to recent "trouble with some of the men" that had made him temporarily quit driving. He did not give a clue as to which side of the internal conflict he aligned himself. Then, two days later, six men engaged in a "slugging and pistol battle" at an intersection two-and-a-half miles southwest of the first incident. When the smoke cleared, a known union slugger and Checker superintendent named Robert "Happy" McDonald was wounded by a bullet to the leg. Another Checker driver asserted that McDonald and three other union enforcers had been the instigators. He said they approached him while he had a passenger in his cab and "attempted to make him pay his union dues," but when he declined, they opened fire as the passenger cowered in the backseat. The reference to "union dues" may have been a coded message referencing which side of the Checker civil war they expected the driver to join. Arriving on the scene, police arrested two of the unionists as they attempted to flee in a car.

These incidents proved merely a prologue. On Wednesday night, June 6, Checker drivers John Rose and Max Raifman approached the intersection of Robey and Division Streets in Wicker Park, where a group of fifteen men stood on the sidewalk, many of them union-aligned Checker drivers. Under questioning, Rose and Raifman later claimed they had been sent by Markin as "proxy gatherers" to persuade the men in the meeting to sign over their votes to drivers loyal to Markin and Goldstein. As Rose and Raifman approached the group, they were met by Frank Sexton, a Checker Taxi road supervisor and a known union slugger. At twenty-five, Sexton was fair-haired and full-lipped, his face retaining the look of an innocent schoolboy. However, Sexton's role as union muscle demanded a toughness and a familiarity with danger. When Rose and Raifman spotted him approaching them, a gun battle ensued. No one could say who fired the first shot, but Sexton and Rose each shot twice, and Sexton collapsed to the sidewalk, mortally wounded.

Rose and Raifman confessed to the killing but claimed that they had acted in self-defense. Police arrested them and brought them in for questioning, and as the drivers told their story to police, Markin's alleged role in Checker Taxi's internal battles began to emerge for the first time. Rose and Raifman claimed that a group of "several businessmen and lawyers"—police initially withheld Markin's name from reporters—had entered into a conspiracy to gain control of Checker Taxi through an orchestrated "reign of terror" among its drivers. For several days before Sexton's murder, Rose and Raifman said, they had been compelled to convince holdout drivers to sign over their proxy votes to members of Markin's inner circle.

Hearing these serious allegations from Rose and Raifman, Robert E. Crowe and the state's attorney's office got involved once again.

Members of Crowe's office interviewed the men about the nature of the alleged conspiracy and the people involved in it, and went on to name several people for police to bring in for questioning. These included five unnamed attorneys as well as Emil R. Carlson, secretary of Markin's Checker Cab Mfg. Co., and Morris Markin himself. Crowe's office now suspected that Markin was attempting a hostile takeover of the Checker Taxi Company, his largest client, by pressuring, threatening, or bribing more than 50 percent of the driver-shareholders to sign over their votes to proxies who would vote as he dictated at the Checker elections, which were scheduled to take place in two weeks' time.

As assistant state's attorneys were interviewing Rose and Raifman into the middle of the night, and preparing to issue a summons for Markin to appear for questioning, the stakes escalated further. Early in the morning of Friday, June 8, Markin and his family—including his wife, Bessie, and their two young daughters, Shirley and Josephine—were sleeping in their home, just south of the sprawling Humboldt Park, when they were awoken by a deafening explosion that shook the whole house, waking neighbors several blocks away. Markin and his wife were thrown from their bed by the force of a bomb exploding at their front door. Witnesses later said the bomb had been thrown from the window of a passing car. Following the attack, Markin, Carlson, and Goldstein went into hiding, and for several days police could not find Markin to bring him in for questioning by the state's attorneys.

The next day, the editorial board of the *Chicago Tribune* lamented the increasing violence on the city's streets due to the internal war at Checker, writing,

> There is no safety in war. If cab drivers are capable of turning loose a fusillade of revolver shots against each other in the course of some conspiracy, they are capable of wounding or killing their innocent passengers in such a battle.

Crowe was equally livid, and declared he would put his entire office on the case of the internal war at Checker if necessary. "One man has been murdered and many have been beaten and shot during the last week," he declared. "It must stop or I will order the arrest of every man operating a cab on the streets of Chicago." Crowe's office was already off to a good start; that day alone, his office had ordered squads of police to investigate common meeting places of Checker drivers for evidence of criminal conspiracy or activity, and police arrested forty men in those raids.

The Violent Run-Up to the Checker Elections

The crux of these incidents lay in the rapidly approaching company shareholders' election. As the meeting date got closer, Max Parker, Oscar Lavin, and Walter Morris—three Checker driver-shareholders representing the unionists, or the "majority shareholders" as they identified themselves—filed a petition in court on Monday, June 11, seeking the appointment of a special commissioner to preside over the election, to ensure a fair outcome and prevent physical assaults. The drivers filing the petition charged that they were being pressured to vote in line with the "ruling minority" and that drivers who attempted to protest these bully tactics were badly beaten or "hauled before a 'trial board' and severely penalized."

The complaint further alleged that any of these "majority shareholders" who attempted to oppose the bully clique were attacked by a "flying squadron" of sluggers who threatened to kill them. As a result, without court-ordered protection, Parker, Lavin, and Morris feared that they would be "routed by sluggers" if they showed up to vote at the election the following week. The editorial board of the *Chicago Tribune* eventually noted that it was rare for union-backed employees during this time to turn to the police for protection, and lauded what they hoped would be the beginning of a new relationship between labor and law enforcement. However, the request revealed just how rancorous and dangerous the internal tensions at Checker had become.

A judge sided with Parker, Lavin, and Morris and ordered that sheriff's deputies be present at the Checker shareholder elections to search everyone entering the building for "firearms and knives with blades longer than two inches." On Tuesday, June 19, Checker employees on both sides of the conflict filed into the Broadway Armory, everyone submitting to the weapons search before they could take their seats inside, where a former assistant state's attorney was present to oversee the election and ensure a fair outcome. However, before the voting could begin, during the initial business of the meeting, a problem arose regarding the verification of corporate records. Until the matter was settled, the vote would have to be postponed. This may have been a stalling tactic on the part of Markin's inner circle, as their preferred candidate for president, Emanuel Goldstein, remained in hiding after the incidents of the previous two weeks.

INTIMIDATION AND PERJURY

For the next several months, with Goldstein in hiding, Checker Taxi managed to maintain an unusually low profile. Following the continuance of the election, the unionists had declared victory. For the time being at least, Markin's loyalists kept quiet, perhaps waiting for the date of the rescheduled election before planning their next move. However, in October, Rose and Raifman were scheduled to appear in court for the June murder of Frank Sexton. A few days before the trial, Goldstein quietly returned to Chicago with the intention to appear as a witness for the defense. Before the trial opened on October 9, Goldstein was finally back in his home in Chicago when two men knocked on his door and lured him into his front vestibule, where they beat him "nearly unconscious" before escaping into the night. In light of this witness tampering incident, Rose and Raifman's attorneys requested the trial be postponed.

Less than two weeks later, another associate of Markin's, the assistant sales director at Checker Cab Mfg. Co., was attending the annual convention of the National Association of Taxicab Owners at the Hotel Sherman when he was lured into an alley just north of the hotel by a telephone call from someone impersonating a policeman. Markin's colleague arrived in the alley only to face two assailants, who knocked him down, beat him, and kicked him before fleeing the scene. This made him the second ally of Markin's to be physically assaulted that month.

While his associates were facing threats and violence in Chicago that fall, Markin himself was preparing to head to New York, where in early November he appeared before Judge Cohalan of the state supreme court on the matter of the copyright infringement alleged by Hertz and the Yellow Cab Manufacturing Company. The judge was evidently unmoved by Markin's arguments. Instead, he ordered Markin arrested for bribery and perjury when it was determined that, to bolster his case, Markin had bribed three Checker drivers in Chicago to lie to the judge and swear to forged affidavits. Markin was arrested but quickly released on a $10,000 bond.

Then, on December 21, 1923, Emanuel Goldstein was brutally assaulted once again, this time in the Cook County Courthouse. Around 9:10 a.m., he walked into the courtroom to file a new motion in a pending court case that he had recently brought against the International Brotherhood of Teamsters. In the hallway outside the courtroom, union slugger Happy McDonald and two other men grabbed Goldstein and pushed him into a small bathroom just outside the courtroom door. As he called for help, they beat him so ferociously that they knocked out his front teeth. Hearing his screams, court bailiffs ran into the bathroom to find Goldstein bleeding on the floor and McDonald reclining against the wall, as the other two attackers ran down the hallway.

Despite the vicious attack, the hearing began at 10:00 a.m. as planned. Goldstein stood toothless and bloodied beside his attorney, who requested that McDonald be held in contempt of court for behavior "clearly intended to obstruct the proper administration of justice." Under oath, McDonald denied participating in the attack, a statement so absurd under the circumstances that Goldstein's lawyer argued his statement amounted to perjury. The judge agreed, and ordered McDonald to serve sixty days in jail for contempt of court.

Mass Shooting at Checker Headquarters

Finally on January 29, 1924, after a delay of more than six months, the Checker Taxi shareholder elections finally proceeded, guarded by thirty sheriff's deputies, who again searched participants for weapons. After all the violence and bloodshed between the two warring factions within the company over the previous months—including the accusations of coercion, bribery, and physical violence in the service of "proxy gathering"—once the votes were tallied that day, Goldstein emerged the winner and was officially declared the president of Checker Taxi. Joseph Wokral (formerly of the Hotel La Salle taxi fleet, where he was involved in at least one violent incident between drivers for the Hotel La Salle and Yellow Cab) was voted in as vice president, and Samuel Amsel as treasurer. For the time being at least, the unionists found themselves outorganized, outmuscled, and outvoted.

This should have come as no surprise, perhaps, given that less than two weeks earlier, on January 17, a nineteen-year-old woman named Pearl Barkan was walking on Division Street past Hermann's drugstore when she heard a deafening sound: a bomb detonating in Brown & Koppel's restaurant and pool hall across the street. The explosion toppled pie cases and brought plaster raining down inside the restaurant, the force blowing out the front window of the building and sending debris flying in every direction. Forty yards from the blast site, Barkan was struck by flying glass and shards of wood. She collapsed on the icy sidewalk and was rushed to a hospital, where she later died from her wounds, an innocent victim of the Checker civil war.

Police were well acquainted with Brown & Koppel's as a hangout for Checker Taxi drivers—it had been the scene of several past incidents related to the Taxi Wars. Following the blast, they questioned more than forty Checker drivers and officials. Through this questioning, they determined that the bomb had been intended as a warning to the unionists. It was a percussive announcement that they were expected to vote for Goldstein, a dire warning for which an innocent young woman named Pearl Barkan gave her life.

However, though Goldstein's election win proved a temporary setback, the unionists at Checker had no intention of accepting defeat graciously. Instead, they stayed quiet and plotted their response. In an attempt to ensure a peaceful transition of leadership, the chief of police had assigned two patrolmen to guard the Checker offices on West Madison Street following the election, where they remained for several weeks. Despite this, Goldstein said that he received mail and telephone threats from union leader Neary during the changeover. Then on Friday, February 8, 1924, after Goldstein and the new leadership had moved into their offices and officially taken over the day-to-day management of the company, the guard detail was removed. As soon as the police were off the premises, Amsel received a phone call in his office from someone he identified as "a union official." The voice on the other end of the line sent him a warning, saying, "I'm going to take a crack at that place." A few hours later, four armed men arrived at the Checker offices and forced all of the Checker drivers present to line up against a wall, while they delivered a "a forceful lecture" and further threatened the men by displaying their weapons. They left without further incident but warned they would return the following day.

At 10:40 a.m. on Saturday morning, these unionists made good on their promise. A large Studebaker pulled up in front of the Checker headquarters and several men entered the building. Amsel was in the main office when two of them appeared and demanded to see Goldstein, the newly elected president, who was fortuitously off the premises at a meeting with the chief of police to negotiate for an extended period of police protection. Amsel told them to wait. Instead, they went back outside to get their accomplices who were waiting in the car, and the group headed for the main garage door entrance.

Pulling out their guns, the group opened fire and forced open the garage door. Inside the building, Checker employees ducked for cover as glass shattered around them and smoke from the guns filled the room. Switchboard operators screamed, mechanics lunged for cover, a bookkeeper locked himself in a closet, and two clerks hid in the company's walk-in vault. Wokral hid in his office when the shooting started, and Amsel retreated to his inner office and locked the door. In the unionists' failed attempts to find the newly elected president, they exchanged gunfire with a handful of armed Checker employees before escaping again, jumping on the running board of their car and continuing to fire indiscriminately as the driver slowly pulled away in the smoke and confusion.

The Murders of Israel Rappart and Leo Gistenson

When the police arrived on the scene, they found three victims of the shooting. Hearing the commotion, a Checker driver had emerged from a cafe across the street to see what was happening and was hit in the ankle by a stray bullet as the attackers retreated. Inside the building, two guards were shot: Leo Gistenson suffered gunshot wounds to the head, chest, and abdomen, and Israel Rappart lay dead just outside of Amsel's office. The twenty-seven-year-old Rappart had been hired just the night before as a private security guard, presumably to replace the police guard detail the company leadership had lost just that morning. He was on the job less than two hours when he was murdered. Gistenson, another private guard, died later that night from his wounds.

Investigating the incident, police called in witnesses to the Marquette police station and to the state's attorney's office to give statements. Prendergast, Markin's attorney now acting as Checker's counsel, issued a forceful statement in the days following the attack. "Other thugs and sluggers trying to wreck our legitimate business are on the Checker pay roll, placed there by [union leader] Neary," he claimed. "The new management has not yet had time to eliminate them, but we will. This shooting calls for a showdown and we are going to see if we can be protected from the onslaught of lawless persons." Prendergast went so far as to seek a contempt-of-court ruling against Neary for violating a judge's injunction restraining union officials and former cab company officials from interfering with the actions of the new management.

THE TRUTH WITHOUT FEAR OR FAVOR: INVESTIGATION FROM THE STATE'S ATTORNEY

Immediately after the shooting, State's Attorney Crowe opened yet another investigation into the war at Checker, assigning five of his assistants to investigate the incident in an attempt to "get the truth without fear or favor." One of the first people they interviewed was Neary, who voluntarily arrived at their offices eager to share his side of the story, claiming he had nothing to do with the shooting at the Checker offices. The state's attorneys must have believed his story, because he was questioned and released, along with two other officials from his organization. Neary and his union officials may have started to regret their alliance with gangsters, who it appeared now wielded more power and decision-making authority within the union than Neary himself.

Next, Crowe's assistants called in new Checker vice president Joseph Wokral and one of the garage superintendents, questioning them for hours, beginning in the afternoon of February 11 and continuing through the night and into the early morning hours. Based on these interviews, as well as the coroner's inquest into Rappart's and Gistenson's murders, Crowe's office issued arrest warrants for six union-affiliated gangsters: Dave Ostran, Daniel "Danny" Stanton, John "Jack" Cherbo, and Mitters "Button" Foley—known as "The Four Horsemen"—as well as "Big Jim" Mogley and his brother Sydney. Stanton and Foley were known members of the South Side Sheldon gang. Mogley was one of the men accused of being in the assailants' car the night that Thomas Skirven was murdered in 1921, and was out on bail at the time of the incident. Ostran was the former director of Checker Taxi whose 1922 court petition first hinted at the internal war that would come to consume the company. The most famous member of this group, Danny Stanton, was a known racketeer and a well-connected captain of a South Side bootlegging gang, fiercely loyal to Chicago gangster Johnny Torrio (and eventually to his successor, Al Capone).

Less than five days after Neary voluntarily appeared in Crowe's office to assert his innocence in the shooting, he placed all eleven hundred Checker drivers on the union's "unfair" list, essentially kicking them out of the union and disavowing all connection with them. "About the first thing the new officials of the Checker Taxicab Company did when they assumed office was to hire a gang of gunmen and sluggers," he declared. "We gave the Checker drivers ample time to repudiate the actions of officials of their company. When they sat idly by, we believed it best to sever all connections with them." The message Neary sent was clear: Those drivers who wanted to maintain their membership in the International Brotherhood of Teamsters would have to quit driving for Checker. This decision was made easier for some of them when the new Checker leadership began cleaning house, dismissing those who had openly opposed Goldstein's candidacy.

By February 20, five of the six men wanted for the murders of Rappart and Gistenson—all except Sydney Mogley—were in police custody, and Crowe assigned two assistant prosecutors and twenty police detectives to patrol the streets to maintain a "forced peace" in this current battle of the Taxi Wars. For the moment, other dramas consumed the streets of Chicago, and the internal war at Checker Taxi died down, roiling just beneath the surface, ready to spill over again in a few short months' time.

CHAPTER 8

Crank It Up

The Civil War at Checker Continues (1924)

TWO MONTHS AFTER THE DRAMATIC SHOOTING AT CHECKER HEAD-
quarters, and more than nine months after the murder of Frank Sexton,
that tragic event which gave both police and the state's attorney's office
the first indication of the deadly war raging at the company, the two men
who had confessed to Sexton's murder appeared before Judge Hosea
W. Wells in the Cook County Courthouse. It was the ninth time they
had made appearances in court for this charge, traveling with their attorneys to the imposing stone building on Clark Street, the tapping of their
shoes echoing along the marble floor outside the solemn courtrooms.
Each of the eight previous appearances had resulted in postponement of
their trials—sometimes at the judge's request to accommodate an overfull
docket, sometimes at the request of the attorneys. (In at least one memorable instance, this request for postponement was due to the physical
assault of one of the witnesses, newly elected Checker Taxi president
Emanuel Goldstein.)

On April 22, 1924, "Smilin' Jack" Rose and Max Raifman stood
before a judge for the ninth time. Once again, rather than hearing the
case, Judge Wells issued a continuance and postponed the trial. The dead
man's father, Patrick Sexton, watched from the back of the room as the
two men who had confessed to murdering his son were told once again
that they were free to leave the courtroom. Everyone present—reporters
and family members, police detectives, and potential witnesses—had to

accept that no justice would be delivered that day. Slipping into the hall-way after the judge issued the ninth set of continuances, Patrick Sexton watched Rose and Raifman exit the courtroom, his hand curled around a gun he had carried with him to the courthouse that day. When he saw his son's murderers walking down the hall toward him, he may have inter-preted their body language threateningly. (They "started to rush at me," he later claimed.) Or he may have simply run out of patience, tired of waiting for the justice system to mete out punishment to his son's alleged killers. Unconcerned by the crowd of bystanders milling nearby and pass-ing through, Sexton shot two bullets down the hall, missing Raifman but striking Rose in the chest.

As Rose collapsed onto a bench, mortally wounded, Sexton imme-diately gave himself up to a police sergeant. "Now I'm satisfied," some of the people closest to the shooting swore they heard Sexton mutter as he watched Rose bleeding to death on the courthouse bench. Police moved quickly to arrest him. Ten days later, Raifman returned to the courthouse for the postponed trial, where he was found not guilty of Frank Sexton's murder by reason of self-defense. By that time, Rose had died from Pat-rick Sexton's gunshot wounds: Vigilante justice was the only form of jus-tice served to either of the men who confessed to Frank Sexton's murder.

PREMIER JOINS THE FRAY

After taking control of Checker Taxi in the early part of 1924, Markin's inner circle—Goldstein, Wokral, Amsel, and Prendergast among them—had moved quickly to remove any dissenters, and Neary and the union officials had perhaps intentionally aided their efforts by making it clear that any drivers who wished to maintain their union membership in the International Brotherhood of Teamsters would have to leave Checker. Over the summer of 1924, some of these ousted union drivers started working instead for a newly formed Chicago cab company: Premier Cab.

The first few Premier Cabs, built by the Premier Motor Company of Indianapolis, appeared on the streets of Chicago in May of 1924. Over the summer, the company continued to add around thirty-five cabs per month to its initial fleet. By September, Premier Cab had adopted the tagline "The Taxicab of Distinction," taking out an ad in the newspaper announcing that each cab was driven by a "Premier driver" and backed by a reputable insurance company, a claim which appears to have been entirely untrue. The ad boasted that "each of these men is a qualified union driver who has had five years' intensive driving experience, and comes with a clean record." It went on to explain that the company had established dedicated Premier cab stands around the city. What the ad did not state, but perhaps implied, was that these drivers with their five years of experience came mostly from the Checker Taxi Company.

In November, Premier Cab announced that former superintendent of schools Peter A. Mortenson had been named president of the company. Mortenson's elevation to the position may have been an attempt to lend legitimacy to the enterprise, something Premier was noticeably lacking: At least one newspaper suggested that some of the financial backing to start the new cab company had come from "organized labor" in the wake of the war at Checker. Rumors swirled that at least some of the first Premier drivers were recruited by "the leader of one of the city's killer gangs" from his network of criminal underlings. Although Mortenson had been named president, he exerted no control over the company and in fact knew very little about its operation—his presidency was nominal. Instead, those unnamed men who had started the company used Mortenson's reputation and connections to solicit additional investors through aggressive tactics. Stock salesmen knocked on the doors of schoolteachers, unskilled tradesmen, and Mortenson's contacts throughout the Swedish-American community, and applied high-pressure sales tactics to cajole and coerce them into buying shares in Premier Cab, sometimes in amounts as little as two or three shares at a time. Whether these average Chicagoans handed over their money willingly—lured by comparisons to large, successful companies like the Ford Motor Company and dazzled by the promise of big money to be made—or under coercion, most of them would never see that money again.

Despite the establishment of Premier Cab and the exodus from Checker of many of the union-affiliated drivers, tensions at Checker Taxi had still not entirely calmed. In April, one month before Premier Cab debuted on Chicago's streets, two Checker employees were fined $600 for attacking and severely beating a rival cab driver. Then, late on the night of

Saturday, May 3, a bomb exploded at the main Checker garage, "partially wreck[ing]" the building, according to newspapers. Due to the late hour of the explosion, there were only three people on site and there were no injuries. Police determined the bomb had been thrown from the nearby tracks of the L train. When they questioned Goldstein about who he thought might be responsible, he gave them the names of the men who had been arrested for the murders of Israel Rappart and Leo Gistenson the previous winter, indicating that he blamed the same unionists for the bombing that he had fingered for the murders. Police investigated the bombing but did not arrest anyone.

RED MCLAUGHLIN AND THE HIT ON "LEFTY" WRIGHT

Two months later, on July 9, the internal war at Checker created even more bloodshed. Just after 9:00 p.m., Joseph "Lefty" Wright, the acting general superintendent of Checker Taxi—and assistant to the Checker general manager and former Lincoln Park policeman Harry Morley—was chatting with a colleague at a Checker garage at the corner of May and Harrison Streets when a figure appeared in the doorway. The man wore a gray hat pulled down low over his eyes, and as he stepped into the doorway, he pulled out a gun and fired three shots at Wright, fleeing as Wright collapsed with a bullet in his thigh. Wright was rushed to a nearby hospital. As he was prepped for surgery to remove the bullet, police questioned him but found him initially reluctant to name his attacker. "Sure, I know who shot me, but what in hell's the use of telling you fellows?" he told them. "I'll take care of that guy myself."

In fact, his alleged attacker, Eugene "Red" McLaughlin, may have had similar thoughts on his mind. McLaughlin was an independent gangster, active on the city's hardscrabble West Side. The youngest of three brothers born to Irish immigrant parents, McLaughlin ran into trouble with the law from a young age, when he loosely allied himself with West Side "hijacker, gunman and extortionist" Ted Newberry. (Newberry had briefly worked as a Checker Taxi superintendent as well.) At the time of the attack on Wright, Red McLaughlin had been released from the Joliet Penitentiary for only a few days, having served a three-year sentence for robbery. He was just sixteen years old when he first entered prison.

Now nineteen, his stint at Joliet had done little to reform his behavior. With the attack on Wright, he was already on his way to becoming one of the most notorious independent gangsters of the 1920s, described many years later by a grifter and fellow criminal as "the toughest guy in Chicago." His name would eventually appear on the "Public Enemies" list compiled by the Wickersham Commission, a national commission investigating organized crime during the Prohibition era.

His motivation to attack Wright that July night was not immediately clear, but it appears his intention was to kill rather than wound his victim, and he had fallen short of that goal. Wright later told police that McLaughlin had followed him to the hospital and climbed up a fire escape to the third-floor window of Wright's hospital room in an attempt to finish the grim task. Wright claimed that on several occasions he had seen his attacker, McLaughlin, peering in the window at him as he lay in bed recovering from surgery. Wright assumed McLaughlin was looking for an opportune moment to shoot him a final time. "If he hadn't tried to get me while I was down and on my back, I wouldn't have squealed," Wright declared to police. "I'd have squared matters myself."

On July 20, police arrested Red McLaughlin at his home (notably not on the third-floor fire escape of the hospital). Despite the obvious parole violation, McLaughlin was released on bond awaiting trial. Confusingly, police arrested six other people in conjunction with the attack on Wright: McLaughlin's accomplices and fellow Newberry gang members George "Reggie" Moran and David Goldblatt, as well as Checker president Emanuel Goldstein, Checker vice president Wokral and treasurer Samuel Amsel, as well as Wright himself. (How Wright could be arrested for shooting himself is unclear.)

Then on August 12, Checker Taxi leadership held a board of directors' meeting in their new general offices near the Loop. To prevent violence at that meeting, Goldstein requested a special police guard presence, and the meeting itself proceeded uneventfully. However, after the meeting ended and the guard detail left the premises, Checker general manager (and Wright's boss) Harry Morley was walking out of the building with one of the drivers when a gray car pulled up to the curb and a hail of bullets erupted from the window. Morley was shot in the head and the driver in the leg. Both survived.

The next day, police found the gray car with bullets and shell casings still littering the floor, parked in front of West Side gangster Ted Newberry's house. When they arrested Newberry and questioned him, he claimed that he had loaned the car the night before to three men: McLaughlin, Moran, and Goldblatt. Police re-arrested Red McLaughlin one week later. Then, the already complicated plot thickened further in the early morning hours of September 14, when a former Checker employee named Neil K. Porter was shot in the head during an incident at a gas station that initially appeared to be a robbery. However, when the police found the car driven by the alleged "robbers," they discovered a jacket inside it that appeared to belong to Morley. Further investigation revealed that Porter had been dismissed from Checker five weeks earlier, just after Morley was shot. When police confronted Porter about who might have shot him at that gas station, he claimed the attack came on the orders of "an official of the company" as part of the internal Checker war.

No one outside the company quite knew what to make of the deadly power struggle going on at Checker Taxi. On September 24, a judge heard the case regarding the attack on Wright, and ultimately found insufficient evidence against all seven defendants, acquitting the Checker leadership, as well as McLaughlin, Moran, and Goldblatt in Wright's attack. Just a few days before the judge heard that case, two empty Checker cabs parked on the South Side were bombed by unknown assailants in a span of twenty-four hours, in one case "demolishing the machine and breaking windows in several nearby houses." Police attributed the bombs to "union troubles" but could not make any further headway on the cases.

ACCUSATION OF FRAUD: MARKIN AND THE BLUE SKY LAWS
The day before a judge in Chicago declared insufficient evidence to convict anyone of Wright's murder, Markin stood in front of Judge Cohalan at the New York State Supreme Court for a second time, to defend himself against the charges of bribery and conspiracy that had arisen out of the copyright infringement case in the same court the previous year.

He and Checker Cab Mfg. Co. secretary Emil R. Carlson pleaded their case before the judge, who after hearing the evidence and testimony, ultimately decided to dismiss the charges. It was a welcome outcome for Markin.

Just a few months earlier, in April, he and Checker Cab Mfg. Co. treasurer Michael Glassberg had also stood trial in Chicago, accused of violating a new state statute known as the "Blue Sky" law. The booming stock market of the 1920s created an environment that was ripe for fraud. Brokers, brokerage houses, investment advisers, and corporate leaders all had monetary incentive to alternately inflate or deflate a company's value, depending on the situation. An investor looking for information on a specific company's stock could only hope that the person presenting the information was telling the truth, and many of them weren't. As more and more people began to invest in the stock market during this era, swindles and fraud became commonplace occurrences.

"Blue Sky" laws—supposedly given that name because one early supporter claimed that many of the men selling securities in this era were so dishonest they would "sell building lots in the blue sky"—were a collection of laws implemented by several states to attempt to regulate these abuses and to protect the public from fraudulent investments. Illinois's Blue Sky Law had not been on the books very long, and when Markin and Glassberg stood trial for violating it, no one in the state of Illinois had yet been convicted of such a crime. That was about to change. The jury hearing the case did not come to their decision easily—they had to be sequestered overnight and continue their deliberation in the morning—but on April 25, 1924, they found Markin and Glassberg guilty of falsifying a financial document filed with the secretary of state, and a judge sentenced them to thirty days in Cook County Jail and fined them $2,000 each. Glassberg served his sentence, but Markin successfully deferred his jail time.

THE BEAR RAID

While the contentious battles continued to rage at Checker, its rival Yellow Cab went through a strong period of growth and expansion, as John Hertz turned his attention to further transportation endeavors. As early as 1919, Hertz had stepped away from the day-to-day operations of the company, leaving the management of the taxi business to his second-in-command, Charlie Gray. Instead, Hertz focused his attention on the bigger picture of the company's financial management and business growth. Among his accomplishments in this role, Hertz had expanded the employee stock program and formed a motorbus manufacturing division of the company called the Chicago Motor Coach Company. Then, in the first quarter of 1924, he took Yellow Cab public on the New York Stock Exchange, a decision that ultimately opened the company up to a new form of attack.

Yellow Cab was unquestionably thriving. Each month, Hertz and Gray tasked their communications department with the composition of a new Yellow Cab ad to run in the local newspapers, extolling the huge strides the company had made since debuting its service in 1915. On July 29, 1924, the Yellow Cab ad proudly announced "Yellow Cab Celebrates its Ninth Birthday," and went on to list the company's many accomplishments. "We have rescued the people from the dismal traditions of the cab trade and driven the roughneck driver to the woods," the ad read. "We have built a great cab system and cab service and set an example which the whole world is trying to follow. We have covered Chicago to its limits, like a blanket, and created a fine body of 6,000 industrious, courteous, efficient and honest drivers—something that never previously existed." Another Yellow Cab ad later that year implored the reader to "Think back 9 years!" and went on to describe the experience of riding in a freelance taxi of that earlier era. "You stood in the rain, looking for a cab to take you home," it read. "There were only a few straggling 'cabs' in existence. When you finally got one, it was dirty and driven by a roving chap who was under no one's supervision . . . controlled only by his impulses."

Yellow Cab's boosterism of their own virtues and accomplishments was not unearned. In less than a decade, Hertz had scaled up the initial forty-five cabs to nearly two thousand, along the way developing a system for acquisition, maintenance, cleaning, dispatching, driving, and fare collection that was so efficient and carefully considered that it rivaled Henry Ford's famous assembly line in Detroit. On top of this, the company pioneered the widespread use of employee stock options and dividends, which were provided to every employee, men and women, Black and white, no matter what their role in the company, once they met the minimum employment period and kept their record free of demerits. In addition, Yellow Cab provided a bevy of ancillary benefits to all of its employees—vacation time, dental care, medical care, free tailoring services, free legal services, a company restaurant, subsidized groceries and clothing items, life insurance, and an early form of accident or illness insurance, among others. The company sent buntings to every employee who had a baby, sent their in-house doctor to the homes of any employee who had a sick family member, sent flowers to every funeral when an employee experienced a loss in his or her immediate family. The company newsletter, the *Taxigram*, was filled with news items about employees—employment anniversaries, wedding anniversaries, engagements, marriages—as well as letters of thanks from employees and their grateful family members who benefited from these groundbreaking employment perks. One memorable story in the *Taxigram* tells the tale of Georgia Kendrick, the mother of Corinne Margate, a Yellow Cab employee who passed away from an infection. The item in the newsletter describes how Kendrick, who had been born into slavery, took a train to Chicago to lay her daughter's remains to rest, and was able to thrive in a new city thanks to the life insurance provided by the company.

While Yellow Cab provided more and more of these unprecedented perks to its employees, the company's profits were up from the previous year and showed no sign of slowing down. Similarly, Yellow Cab Manufacturing Company was making more cabs than ever, which translated to more profit than ever before. By all conventional metrics, in 1924, Yellow Cab was an unequivocal financial success. However, beginning that spring, Hertz began to notice a troubling trend: The value of Yellow Cab's public stock was slipping, despite the continued financial success of the company. A similar fate seemed to befall the stock of the Yellow Cab Manufacturing Company as well. Hertz decided to investigate. While on a business trip to New York City in March of 1924, he met with a well-connected friend and Yellow Cab investor named Walter Howey, the editor of William Randolph Hearst's *Boston American* newspaper. Howey and Hertz evaluated Yellow Cab's stock trading patterns.

Together, they came to the conclusion that a group of New York investors was deliberately trying to force down the Yellow Cab stock, an aggressive stock market attack that was known as a "bear raid." Howey and Hertz traced the suspicious trading to the New York office of Block, Maloney and Co., and from that information, they suspected that the driving force behind the bear raid originated with Morris Markin and the Checker Cab Mfg. Co.

To stem the tide of the falling shares, Howey arranged a meeting between Hertz, Yellow Cab board of directors' vice president Charles McCulloch, and a savvy Boston banker, investor, and trader: Joe Kennedy. (Several decades later, Kennedy's name would become familiar to all Americans when his son, John Fitzgerald Kennedy, became the president of the United States.) Hertz and Kennedy met at New York's famed Waldorf Astoria Hotel. At that time, the hotel was a hub of luxury and social status, still housed in what had originally been two rival Belle Epoque–era hotels on the site of the modern-day Empire State Building. At the meeting, Hertz explained to Kennedy he had devised a solution to save the value of the Yellow Cab shares: Hertz wanted to buy back as much of the stock as he could to prevent it from collapsing. But to do that, he needed capital, and he asked Kennedy to use his personal fortune to assist him in this endeavor. However, Kennedy had a better idea: Rather than buy back the stock to stabilize the prices, Kennedy suggested they intentionally create volatility in the share prices, in the hopes that the raiders would get nervous and abandon their attack. The key, Kennedy believed, was to feign the appearance that multiple traders were buying and selling large blocks of shares in transactions originating across the country.

Hertz decided to go along with this scheme, and he gave Kennedy control of all of the shares he currently held, plus additional capital secured from Chicago friends including William Wrigley Jr. (another member of the Yellow Cab board of directors), for a total of around $5 million, or more than $86 million today. Kennedy booked a suite of rooms at the Waldorf Astoria, installing multiple phone lines and a ticker tape machine so he could monitor the markets in real time. For the next month, Kennedy used these rooms as his battle headquarters, spending the majority of the day on the phone to brokers across the country, ordering them to either buy or sell Yellow Cab stock as a reaction to the daily behavior of other investors. According to Kennedy biographer Ted Schwartz, "Each day, Joe took a sheet of paper and wrote out a pattern of buy-and-sell orders that seemed random in nature but was designed to confuse the short sellers." One day, Kennedy might flood the market with Yellow shares only to purchase them all back at the end of the day. That pattern might be repeated the next day, or instead he might choose to do the reverse: buying shares in the morning and selling them off at the end of the day. Kennedy's ultimate goal was to spook the raiders into permanently selling their shares. It was a bold approach, and one that had never before been attempted at this scale.

Kennedy's plan succeeded. By the middle of May 1924, the values of Yellow Cab's shares had returned to their pre-raid amounts. Hertz rewarded Kennedy handsomely for his role in the solution, giving him a sizeable cash payment, Yellow Cab stock, and an invitation to become an early partner investor in a new business idea that Hertz was nearly ready to reveal to the world: rental cars.

On September 28, 1924, Hertz took out an ad in the *San Antonio Express*, announcing the formation of the Hertz Drive-Ur-Self Corporation. For the past two years, he had been researching the market for what would become the rental car industry. He had determined that the most important element to the success of such an endeavor was to manufacture a purpose-built vehicle that could blend in with other private automobiles, and to organize agencies that could then rent those vehicles to private citizens. By the summer of 1924, Hertz had quietly opened a handful of "Drive-It-Yourself" stations in Chicago and Louisville, Kentucky, where he tested the new service and found it to be extremely profitable. Hertz was now ready to take his rental car concept to a national audience. In exchange for Kennedy's work fighting off the bear raid that spring, Hertz invited him to become an early investor in the new business. For his part, Hertz was soured by his experience on the stock market. "I knew something about the taxicab business, but I knew nothing of the ways of Wall Street," he later told B. C. Forbes. "I have now reached the conclusion, however, that the best thing to do is to attend strictly to taking care of business and to leave the stock to take care of itself."

DEAD IN A DITCH

On November 22, 1924, Chicago detectives received a call from the police in the suburb of Aurora, about forty miles west of the Loop. In a ditch on the side of a highway, police had discovered the body of John "Jack" Cherbo, a known union slugger. Cherbo was one of the men who, along with several accomplices including West Side gangster Danny Stanton, had been accused and later acquitted of the murders of Israel Rappart and Leo Gistenson during the attack on the Checker Taxi garage earlier in the year.

When police arrived on the scene, they discovered that Cherbo had been shot once in the back of the head, execution-style. His body had then been dumped from an automobile onto the side of the road. Police investigating the murder determined Cherbo had most likely been killed by a rival gang member, "probably in revenge for the part the police contend he played . . . in the course of the Checker war."

Given Cherbo's affiliation with Stanton, who was fiercely loyal to Johnny Torrio, it's impossible to know exactly why he met his grim fate. But if the detectives' suspicions were correct, that meant that Cherbo's allegiances in the Checker Taxi civil war ultimately led to his murder. It also implied that the "rival gangster" the police suspected of murdering him must have been loyal to the current Checker leadership of Markin's inner circle. And if Cherbo's fellow accomplices also suspected Markin's allies in his murder, it would have put that group—Goldstein, Wokral, Amsel, and corporate counsel Prendergast among them—at high risk of retaliation.

Three weeks later, on Saturday night, December 14, Prendergast was driving home from the Checker Taxi offices downtown to Wheaton, the northwest suburb where he lived. He had been working late hours for the past several weeks. This troubled his wife, who sat up worrying about him for most of the evening. Finally, she received a call from her husband, telling her that he was about to leave the office and head home. He never made it.

At 5:00 a.m. on Sunday morning, December 15, a pedestrian found Prendergast's car crashed at the bottom of a steep embankment on the River Road in Schiller Park, a suburb northwest of the city. When police arrived to investigate, Prendergast's body was found inside the car, which appeared to have broken through a heavy wooden barrier and tumbled thirty feet down the embankment. Police hypothesized that Prendergast had turned hard on the sharp curve to avoid a collision with an oncoming vehicle, or that he had been blinded by the glare of oncoming headlights and missed the road. (In what amounted to a weak argument, Prendergast's brother, a former state representative, attributed the incident to a missing streetlight.)

At the coroner's inquest later that day, the jury agreed to rule Prendergast's death an accident, which meant that police conducted no further investigation into the incident. No one seems to have asked, for example, why exactly Prendergast was driving on the River Road in Schiller Park in the middle of the night, rather than taking a more direct route home from the Loop to Wheaton. The curve where Prendergast's car tumbled over the barrier represents the only section of the River Road in this area with a steep embankment. For no more than one block, the Des Plaines River is significantly lower than the road, before the topography evens out again and becomes the familiar flat land of Illinois. Today, there is a heavy concrete barrier and metal guardrails at that intersection to prevent a plunge like the one that claimed Prendergast's life.

A deeper investigation into Prendergast's affairs would also have revealed that, in 1924 alone, he had been charged with participating in a violent assault against a plaintiff and sued for embezzlement by the president of the Chicago, Palatine and Wauconda Railroad, in addition to his high-profile role in the ongoing battles at Checker Taxi. However, because the coroner's inquest ruled his death an accident, Prendergast's family was free to quickly bury him following a Catholic service the next day, laying to rest not only their husband and father, but also any further questions into his untimely death.

Walden W. Shaw, cofounder of Shaw Livery and the Yellow Cab Company, circa 1920s. *(Courtesy of the Rasin family)*

John D. Hertz, cofounder of Shaw Livery and the Yellow Cab Company, circa 1920. *(From* The Yellow Cab Factory News, *Vol. II, no. 21, June 10, 1921)*

A Shaw Livery cab is parked in front of the Chicago Athletic Association on Michigan Avenue in this photo circa 1910. *(From the Chicago History Museum, ICHi-000358; Kaufmann, Weimer & Fabry Co., photographers)*

A driver stands beside an original Shaw Livery cab. A sign in the window identifies the circa-1911 Thomas Flyer as "The Daddy of All Yellow Cabs." *(Courtesy of Michael Angelich)*

Yellow Cab's main garage at 57 E. 21st Street, described at the time it was built (in 1916) as one of the largest in the country. *(From* Illinois Bell Telephone News, *Vol. 12, 1922)*

The ad that appeared in the *Chicago Tribune* of August 2, 1915, announcing the debut of Yellow Cab on the streets of Chicago. *(From newspapers.com)*

Charles Wellington "Charlie" Gray, circa 1925. A lifelong friend of John D. Hertz, Gray began as a Shaw Livery employee in 1909 and eventually became president of Yellow Cab in 1926. His 1927 death in a freak riding incident sent shock waves through the company. *(From the author's collection)*

A brochure (circa 1917) for the Hotel La Salle's new taxi service. (*From the Chicago History Museum, DN-0080242*)

A vintage postcard (circa 1917) of the northeast corner of State and Madison Streets in the Loop, identifying the area as "the busiest corner in the world." Two first-generation Yellow Cabs are visible among the traffic. *(From the author's collection)*

In this photo from an early safety campaign (circa 1919), a driver stops his Yellow Cab on the cable car tracks to avoid hitting a pedestrian. *(From* The Taxigram, *Vol. IV, no. 19, March 10, 1921)*

At the Yellow Cab Manufacturing Company in 1920, employees install electrical systems into newly built Yellow Cabs. *(From* The Yellow Cab Factory News, *Vol. II, no. 25, September 1, 1921)*

A view of the Yellow Cab telephone dispatch center inside the main garage, which by the end of 1921 comprised the largest telephone installation in the world. *(From* Illinois Bell Telephone News, *Vol. 12, 1922)*

Thomas A. Skirven Jr., Yellow Cab driver murdered in 1921 as part of the Taxi Wars. *(From* The Taxigram, *Vol. IV, no. 23, June 20, 1921)*

Morris Markin, founder of Checker Cab Mfg. Co. and important player in the battle for control of Checker Taxi. *(Courtesy of Michael Angelich)*

MANUFACTURING CORPORATION

Standard Fleet Unit of Checker Taxi Co., Chicago Operating Over 750 Cabs.

We are also well fortified in our knowledge of cab maintenance and operation, and will welcome any opportunity to discuss these vital factors with alert operators who may desire to check their present system of costs, etc.

The writer wants to thank our many esteemed friends for the excellent reception accorded our informal announcement of incorporation, made some months ago. In this connection it is very gratifying to say that our initial three month production of Checker Cabs was sold out shortly following our first showing of one at that time.

Our new plant is now being occupied, and new business will be booked for this commencing September 1st.

You have the writers personal pledge that it will be our constant concern and ambition to make our product and counsel contribute in every possible way to your success and prosperity.

Respectfully yours,

CHECKER CAB MANUFACTURING CORPORATION,

Morris M. Markin

President.

MANUFACTURING CORPORATION

A 1922 letter to the trade announcing the debut of the new Checker Mogul cab, produced by the Checker Cab Mfg. Co. *(From the* National Taxicab and Motorbus Journal, *Vol. 2, no. 8, August 1922)*

This view of State Street looking north from Madison in 1922 demonstrates the traffic chaos of the streets in the Loop, with cable cars, horse-drawn vehicles, trucks, automobiles, and pedestrians all competing for dominance. *(From the Chicago History Museum, ICHi-076206; Kaufmann & Fabry Co., photographer)*

In this photo from 1926, a new stoplight is visible in the center of the intersection of 20th Street and Michigan Avenue on Motor Row just one block north of the main Yellow Cab garage. *(From the Chicago History Museum, DN-0081454,* Chicago Sun-Times/Chicago Daily News *collection)*

English politician Captain Oswald Mosley and his wife, Lady Cynthia, stand in front of a Checker Taxi in 1926. *(From the Chicago History Museum, DN-0080242,* Chicago Sun-Times/Chicago Daily News *collection)*

Yellow Cab drivers pause during their shifts, remove their hats, and stand at attention at 2:30 p.m. on December 27, 1927, to pay their respects to Yellow Cab president Charlie Gray, killed in a freak riding incident two days earlier. *(From* The Taxigram, *Vol. 9, no. 1, January 1921)*

(From left to right) President Bob McLaughlin, Vice President Harry Gordon, Treasurer Barney Mitchell, and Secretary Max Raifman of Checker Taxi pose for a photo circa 1928. For several years, the group ruled Checker Taxi through violence and intimidation while demanding kickbacks from car dealers, oil companies, and taximeter manufacturers. *(From the author's collection)*

PART III
STEP ON IT, 1925–1932

CHAPTER 9

In the Driver's Seat

The Battle for Dominance (1925–1926)

SATURDAY, JANUARY 24, 1925, BEGAN WITH AN ECLIPSE. AT 7:31 A.M.,
just one minute after sunrise in Chicago, the moon began its slow arc for
dominance of the sky, and by 8:00 a.m., the sun was almost completely
obscured. Unfortunately, Chicagoans hoping to witness the celestial event
from their front yards or back porches were sorely disappointed: The January sky that day was full of clouds and industrial smoke that hid the
solar eclipse from view. If he could have seen the mighty sun yielding its
power to the moon that morning, Johnny Torrio may have interpreted it
as a very bad omen.

Torrio, leader of the most powerful South Side bootlegging and vice
racket, was a man who wielded an enormous amount of influence in the
gangland hierarchy of 1920s Chicago. But there was one person who still
held power over him: his wife, Anna. That afternoon, Anna convinced
him to join her on a shopping trip to the Loop. Leaving their home in
the tony Jackson Park Highlands neighborhood that morning, Torrio
nervously scanned the streets for any sign of trouble. Just two weeks earlier, he had returned from an extended trip out of the city, necessitated
by his decision to attend the November wake of one of his biggest gangland rivals, Dean O'Banion. O'Banion had been murdered in the North
Side flower shop he used as a headquarters, most likely by a man that
Torrio had hired. After the wake, O'Banion's successor, Hymie Weiss,

immediately declared war upon Torrio and his associates, and put a price on Torrio's head.

Realizing the danger he was in, Torrio fled the city, presumably hoping his absence would allow Weiss to cool his temper and call off the hit. Torrio traveled to several popular vacation spots—Hot Springs, Arkansas; New Orleans; Havana; the Bahamas; Palm Beach; and St. Petersburg—being careful never to remain in one location long enough for any of Weiss's men to catch up with him. While Torrio was out of the city, Weiss and several other men had instead opened fire upon a car they believed contained Torrio's second-in-command, Al Capone, but Capone had stepped into a nearby restaurant just minutes earlier. His driver was wounded in the attack instead. Shortly after that attempt on Capone's life, Torrio returned to Chicago and found that Weiss was still waiting for him.

That cloudy January day of the solar eclipse, Torrio and his wife returned from the Loop around 4:30 p.m. The driver of their borrowed Lincoln sedan parked in front of their home and the couple got out of the car. Anna Torrio walked into the house, but as Johnny Torrio unloaded the couples' newly purchased items from the car, two men emerged from a gray Cadillac parked around the corner, one armed with a shotgun and the other with an automatic pistol. They surrounded the car and began shooting at Torrio. The initial shots missed their target, hitting the car and smashing the windows and tires. A bullet struck the driver as he put the car into gear and sped away. Torrio dropped his packages and fled toward the house, but before he could reach the front door, his assailants fired on him again, and this time he was struck by five bullets—in the arm, the jaw, the abdomen, and the chest. Torrio collapsed in front of the house, and the men quickly disappeared. A nearby motorcycle policeman arrived on the scene and hailed a taxi to rush Torrio to the nearby Jackson Park Hospital (reporters failed to mention the cab company). Torrio remained in the hospital for three weeks, under armed guard and round-the-clock protection arranged by Capone.

Though seriously wounded, Torrio survived his injuries. The next month, still recovering from the attack, Torrio appeared in federal court on charges of violating Prohibition laws. A judge sentenced him to nine months in the Lake County Jail in north suburban Waukegan, a sentence he opted to begin serving immediately, perhaps preferring the relative safety of jail to his home. By March, Torrio had summoned Capone to his luxuriously decorated cell. There, he announced that he was transferring all of his gangland assets to Capone, including his claim to a percentage of the profits of countless breweries, distilleries, brothels, gambling houses, and cabarets. These assets were rumored to be worth several million dollars, but Johnny Torrio was getting out. Al Capone was now in charge.

By the beginning of 1925, Chicago had been living under the veil of Prohibition for nearly five years, and in that time, the city had seen its street violence escalate exponentially. Criminalizing alcohol had done little to curb the public's demand for it. Instead, the temperance laws had merely created a fertile underground system of illegal rum-running, dominated by speakeasies, bootleggers, and racketeers, and ruled by a handful of powerful gang bosses: Torrio on the South Side, as well as the Genna brothers and the O'Donnell brothers on the West Side, and O'Banion and George C. "Bugs" Moran on the North Side. By the mid-1920s, the street violence of the Taxi Wars was dwarfed by the violent acts committed in the service of illegal booze. Chicagoans lived in a city where contract murders like the attempted hit on Torrio, as well as gun battles and drive-by shootings, regularly happened in full view with little regard for public safety. It was increasingly difficult for the average person, or even those police detectives who remained incorruptible, to disentangle the complicated underlying motives for the violence.

Mayor Thompson, Chicago's first Prohibition-era mayor, made little attempt to crack down on the city's underground operators; instead, by most accounts, he preferred to work the system to his own benefit. This did not sit well with Chicago voters, and in 1923, the city had elected a new, reform-minded mayor, Democrat William E. Dever. Dever had served as an alderman and a municipal court judge. Once he was elected mayor, Dever focused the power of his office on the strict enforcement of law and order in the city, coming down hard on bootleggers as well as those engaged in vice and prostitution. However, Dever's zeal for the law had unintended consequences: He forced the underworld gangs to pursue even more aggressive methods to gain an edge over their competitors. As a result, Dever's "Beer Wars" ushered in a period of intense gang warfare that would come to define Chicago's image for the next hundred years, with Capone serving as the city's flag-bearer across the world.

By contrast, the Taxi Wars had ebbed and flowed on the city's streets for nearly a decade at that point, the cast of characters evolving in concert with the taxi industry itself. While there had always been some overlap between the Taxi Wars and the activities of the general criminal underworld, the incidents related to the civil war at Checker Taxi (including gangland-style executions) ushered in a new phase of the conflict, one which shared much in common with the deadly bootlegger gang wars unfolding simultaneously across the city.

NEW GANG IN CHARGE

In January 1925, the Checker Taxi Company held its annual meeting, which included another election. This was the first shareholders' election since Goldstein had been elected president the previous year, among much contention with Neary and the union. In the intervening twelve months, many of those drivers who had opposed the takeover of the company by Morris Markin's inner circle had decamped to the Premier Cab Company, left the taxi industry altogether, or struck out on their own as independents. So when the 1925 elections rolled around, it was perhaps inevitable that Goldstein's second-in-command, Joseph Wokral, would be elected the new president of Checker Taxi. Another familiar name appeared on the ballot, ostensibly maintaining his allegiance to the ruling party: Max Raifman. Acquitted of Frank Sexton's murder, Raifman was cited in varying news stories following the elections as a member of the company's leadership team, though his official role seemed to shift each time his name was mentioned. But the most surprising name on the 1925 ballot was that of Robert E. "Bob" McLaughlin, brother of union-affiliated gangster Red McLaughlin. He was voted in as the new secretary of the company.

McLaughlin's presence on the leadership team with Markin's proxies may have revealed an uneasy alliance between the two warring parties. It may have represented a coup brewing within the Checker ranks. Or it may have been a clever con on the part of the gangster-affiliated McLaughlins to wrest away power from Markin's men. For the new president, Joseph Wokral, it was an election that would have grave consequences. Eventually, Wokral's uneasy alliance with Bob McLaughlin would prove his undoing.

One Thousand Saturday Night Shoppers in a Panic

The deaths of Jack Cherbo and John Prendergast in the final months of 1924 had done nothing to end the internal tensions at Checker Taxi. If anything, it's likely that these two tragedies—one ruled an execution-style murder, the other ruled an accident—merely inflamed Checker's battles further. Around the time of the election, on January 18, 1925, a Checker Taxi driver was standing on the running board of his taxi, parked at the intersection of La Salle and Jackson in the Loop. It was close to midnight, and downtown Chicago was characteristically quiet for that time of night, just a handful of pedestrians making their way along the city sidewalks.

Suddenly, the driver saw a large touring car full of men about to pull up alongside his taxi. An arm emerged from the window of the touring car and threw a small item about the size of a cigarette under the cab. Sensing danger, the driver leaped from his running board onto the sidewalk as a bomb of "terrific force" exploded beneath his cab, destroying his vehicle and smashing the plate-glass windows of the nearby La Salle Grill, the deafening sound of the explosion echoing throughout the Loop. He survived the blast. Police in the vicinity attempted to chase the touring car on foot, but it escaped into the night.

In fact, that was the second such bombing of the evening. Two hours earlier on the city's South Side, in a busy area of the Englewood neighborhood, witnesses had seen a car with a similar description: "a dirty touring car with its curtains drawn," according to one eyewitness. Someone in the passenger seat had thrown a bomb at a parked Checker Taxi. The resulting explosion was so forceful that it blew a hole in the pavement, lifting the car into the air and wrecking it, and smashing store windows within a two-block radius of the blast. A reporter for the *Tribune* dramatically claimed that the South Side bomb "threw 1,000 Saturday night shoppers into a panic."

In that incident, the taxi driver was just a few feet away from his vehicle when he saw the projectile thrown from the window of the passing car. He dove to the pavement and covered his face, unhurt by the blast. But another bystander named John Gronenewegen was not so lucky; he was hit by flying debris and required medical treatment for cuts to his hands and head. "It's a wonder twenty people weren't killed," a witness to the explosion told a reporter.

When police investigated these bombings that had occurred two hours apart, they concluded that the motive for both was rooted in the factional disputes of the Checker Taxi civil war, but they remained unclear as to the precipitating cause, and were not able to identify or arrest the bombers. Despite the best attempts of the current Checker leadership to remove all of the unionists from the company, it appears there still raged within the company a battle royale, one which could endanger the average pedestrian, shopper, or cab patron at any time.

Kidnapped and Shot

A few months after Wokral's election, on April 13, a Checker driver and member of the Checker board of directors named David Loewenberg was standing near his taxi at a busy, six-way intersection northwest of the Loop, when he was approached by a large touring car, not unlike the one from which bombs had been thrown in January. This time, however, the men in the car did not throw a bomb. Instead, three masked men emerged from the car and forced Loewenberg at gunpoint into their vehicle; he complied, and the car drove away. Several miles later, the masked men stopped near an alley and threw Loewenberg out of the car with four bullets in his body.

As Loewenberg lay in serious condition at the hospital, police questioned him and determined that he knew his assailants and could identify them. Following that interview, police first questioned current Checker officer Max Raifman, and then began searching for Red McLaughlin. Both men had been implicated in separate, previous attacks related to Checker's internal war: Raifman in the murder of unionist Frank Sexton, and McLaughlin in the attack on Checker supervisor Lefty Wright. Loewenberg, the latest victim in the civil war, survived his wounds, but police did not identify a motive or find sufficient cause to arrest either of the accused men for his attack.

That same week, several more taxis were bombed. And three days after Loewenberg's kidnapping and assault, a twenty-one-year-old, independent cab driver was found dead in a puddle under a Baltimore and Ohio Railway viaduct. Detectives determined he had been shot through the head and then run over, his body remaining there until it was discovered by two boys. People who lived nearby told a reporter that they had heard five gunshots, but nobody came forward to identify the assailants. Police remained stumped as to the motive. Then, just as quickly as this round of violence had started, it died down again.

TAXI WAR WITHOUT CASUALTIES

The taxi industry of 1925 was very different than it had been just five years earlier. Each year, a bevy of smaller cab companies came and went, unable to siphon enough business from Yellow Cab and Checker Taxi to survive. Even Ernest J. Stevens and the Hotel La Salle—the institution that was at one time a key player in the Taxi Wars—had quietly exited the taxi business. As early as 1920, Hotel La Salle taxis had found it difficult to compete financially, and the hotel's taxicab department, which had been the source of so much animosity and friction on the streets of Chicago less than a decade earlier, had been operating consistently in the red. In July of 1922, Stevens had sent a letter to the city indicating that the Hotel La Salle was "very anxious" to sell their South Side cab station to the Sinclair Oil Refining Company for use as a gas station. Not long after that, Stevens sold the hotel's fleet of Willys-Knight and Stearns-Knight taxis and leased out the hotel fleet's spot at the Hotel La Salle cab stand. Around January of 1925, at the same time that Joseph Wokral was elected president of Checker Taxi, the De Luxe Cab Company had taken over the Hotel La Salle cab stand, the site of so many previous Taxi War battles.

Almost as soon as De Luxe took over, tensions had flared once again at the northwest corner of La Salle and Madison. On February 24, 1925, following a dinner dance in the Hotel La Salle's ballroom, hotel guests and dance attendees walked out the door hoping to hail a cab, and instead found drivers from the Premier Cab Company and De Luxe Cab Company engaged in a "taxi war without casualties," according to a writer for the *Waukegan News-Sun*. Once again, the drivers were arguing over the lucrative turf outside the upscale hotel. By the time people started pouring onto the sidewalk, the disagreement had escalated beyond mere angry words. Drivers from the opposing companies got into their cabs and "crashed head-on into each other, backed away and rammed into each other again." Stevens called the police, who arrived and ordered all of the cabs to leave the stand. A road supervisor for De Luxe ignored the command and was arrested on the spot. One by one, the rest of the cabs left the block, having resolved none of their disagreements. It was a scene that recalled earlier battles on the same site between Yellow Cab and the hotel's own taxis. The players may have changed, but the fight remained the same.

BURNED CABS AND BRICK-BROKEN WINDSHIELDS

Six months after they took over the cab stand at the Hotel La Salle, on July 14, 1925, De Luxe became the latest cab company to fall victim to bankruptcy, hobbled by insurance claims against its drivers. In the wake of the bankruptcy, Stevens and the Hotel La Salle management agreed to allow the union gangster-affiliated Premier Cab Company to occupy the former terrain of the De Luxe cabs at the hotel's cab stand. It was a decision that did not sit well with some of the Yellow Cab drivers. Two days later, they attempted to oust the Premier cabs from the stand and claim the space themselves.

The Premier drivers fought back and managed to repel the Yellow Cabs. Then, seeking retaliation, they drove the short distance to the Hotel Sherman, where Yellow Cab maintained a taxi stand, and muscled their way onto Yellow Cab's turf. Eventually, the squabble over the cab stands turned violent. Around noon, drivers from both companies engaged in a fistfight brawl dramatic enough to attract a crowd of spectators. Passersby stopped to watch, and shocked hotel guests emerged from the stylish lobby to gawk at the melee unfolding before them. A riot call went out to the nearest police station and a squadron of mounted Chicago police arrived to quell the fight, carrying billy clubs and pistols. They arrested five Premier drivers and two Yellow Cab drivers.

Trying to end this round of fighting, the chief of police ordered all cabs out of the Loop unless they were carrying a passenger or returning to their own garages. However, two nights later, the war spilled over to the West Side, when combatants burned one cab and threw bricks through the windshield of two others in the northwest-side neighborhood of Bucktown. Witnesses told police that three Premier Cabs, displaying no license plates and each carrying four to five men as well as a plentiful supply of bricks and gasoline, pulled up beside three Yellow Cabs. The Premier drivers ordered the Yellow Cab drivers out of their cars at gunpoint (a "wild west display of revolvers" according to the *Chicago Tribune*) and then proceeded to hurl bricks at the empty cabs. Before they left, some of the Premier drivers poured gasoline on one of the cabs and set it ablaze.

Hearing about the renewal of violence between Yellow Cab drivers and Premier Cab drivers, Mayor Dever became irate. "The present taxi drivers' war must stop, and stop immediately," he declared on Sunday, July 19. "We will see whether the taximen control and own the streets, or the people. . . . The latest incident, the burning of a cab on the northwest side, is about the limit." Two squads of police detectives were assigned to the Loop with instructions to arrest any and all cab drivers involved in disputes, with further orders that any cab drivers acting belligerently toward police should be thrown in jail overnight.

THE VIOLENCE OF VENGEANCE

Following Dever's stern warning, the animosity between the cab companies remained stable for the rest of the summer. The Taxi Wars dropped out of the daily newspapers, as readers instead absorbed stories about events like the "trial of the century," the Scopes Monkey Trial in Tennessee, and the ongoing battles between federal Prohibition agents and rum-runners like Capone closer to home. That autumn, however, the Taxi Wars claimed yet another victim. On September 11, 1925, a West Side gangster named Robert "Pudgy" Stamm was released on bail for a gun charge when he got into an altercation with a group of Checker drivers in a pool hall on the West Side of the city. Pulling out a gun, Stamm killed one driver and wounded another with a bullet to the leg. When witnesses were questioned by police, the stories varied: The drivers claimed that they only approached Stamm when they saw that he had just "administered a beating" to another Checker driver. Stamm countered that the group had threatened him first, and that in self-defense, he pulled out his gun and shot toward the crowd.

At the trial, Stamm's lawyers bolstered his self-defense argument when they claimed that he had made enemies of the Checker Taxi drivers prior to the incident. A few months earlier, he had testified against Checker drivers Philip Fox and Morris Stuben, who were accused of the 1921 murder of Yellow Cab driver Thomas Skirven. Fox and Stuben's trial had been delayed many times, and when it had finally proceeded in June of 1925, Stamm had appeared as one of the key prosecution witnesses, fingering the two men for the murder. His testimony must have been compelling. After deliberating for just forty minutes, a jury had found Stuben and Fox guilty of murdering Skirven, and a judge had sentenced them to life in prison.

On the day that Stamm shot the two Checker drivers in front of the pool hall, his attorneys argued, the group had attacked him for his role in that trial, and he had acted in self-defense. Lending credence to this interpretation was the fact that, two days after the shooting, Stamm walked into the police station and surrendered himself to police, saying he "would feel safer in a cell than on the streets or at home." A jury ultimately convicted Stamm of manslaughter for killing the Checker driver in the pool hall.

Wokral's Trials

Wokral had been president of Checker Taxi for less than a year. But in November of 1925, a Checker stockholder had filed a formal legal complaint against him, as well as Raifman, McLaughlin, and the new treasurer Barney Mitchell, accusing them of defrauding him of $5,000 in company stock. The judge held the men to a grand jury on charges of conspiracy to defraud, and set their bail at $15,000 each. A month earlier, during a preliminary hearing of the case, the judge discovered Wokral, Mitchell, and Raifman carrying revolvers into his courtroom, and fined them for the infraction. The three men had presumably hoped to use the guns to intimidate the plaintiff. If so, the intimidation was nearly successful; the day before the trial, the stockholder attempted to withdraw his complaint, but the judge would not permit the withdrawal.

Then, as the holiday season descended on the city once again, the annual Checker Taxi stockholders' meeting loomed ahead. On December 31, 1925, an attorney appeared before another judge with a familiar request, which revealed that the internal battles at Checker remained unresolved: He wanted the judge to assign a protection force of deputy sheriffs to oversee the meeting, which was scheduled to take place in two weeks. The attorney's request demanded the judge name a "master of chancery" (a senior official representing the court) to oversee the election. The complaint also specifically named Wokral, Raifman, and McLaughlin, seeking an injunction restraining them from hiring gunmen or other sluggers to attend the meeting or interfere with company business in any way.

The judge conceded to these requests and named Brigadier General John V. Clinnin as the master of chancery, overseeing a team of deputy sheriffs to ensure order at the January 1926 shareholders' meeting. The judge's choice of Clinnin may have been intentional—Clinnin's brother, Sheridan "Red" Clinnin, was a Yellow Cab supervisor. It was, therefore, unlikely that Clinnin had ties to either faction within Checker Taxi. With Clinnin and the deputies overseeing the election, the January meeting ultimately proceeded without incident. When the ballots were counted, the name that emerged as president of the company was that of Robert E. "Bob" McLaughlin. (Vice president Harry Gordon, secretary Max Raifman, and treasurer Bernard "Barney" Mitchell rounded out the new officers.) Wokral was ousted as president, and he did not take the news lightly.

Premier's Collapse

Checker Taxi was not the only cab company to face significant internal challenges during this period of escalated violence throughout the city.

By the spring of 1926, Premier Cab was facing a crisis. The new taxi company had begun as a refuge for union drivers who had run afoul of the Markin-backed management at Checker Taxi. However, before Premier Cab could celebrate its second anniversary in Chicago, on April 8, 1926, the Illinois Securities Commission halted all sales of Premier stock, on the basis that the company had failed to comply with state regulations governing stock sales. Two months later, the financial straits of Premier Cab reached a point of no return.

On Sunday, July 5, vacationers at Cedar Lake, Indiana—a popular summer resort destination located forty miles south of Chicago—contemplated the end of their Independence Day weekend activities and began to pack up their cars for the return to the city. A federal official in Chicago, enjoying the last few hours of his summer vacation, found his lakeside serenity interrupted when he noticed a conspicuous caravan of forty-seven empty Premier cabs driving south past his cottage. The scene was repeated in Danville, Illinois, the next day, when residents reported seeing twenty-eight empty Premier Cabs pass through town, headed in the general direction of Indianapolis, where the Premier Cab manufacturing factory was located.

Two days later, on July 8, a federal judge arrived at his office in downtown Chicago at the unusually early hour of 6:00 a.m. and issued an immediate bankruptcy order against Premier Cab, naming former US deputy marshal Samuel Howard as the federal receiver in charge of the case. The judge issued the bankruptcy order when it was determined that most, if not all, of the seven hundred Premier cabs on the streets of Chicago were heavily mortgaged, and that even the meters inside the cabs "carried mortgages of a face value in excess of their true value." Just a little more than a year after its formation, the company was under water financially, and those average Chicagoans who had been convinced to invest in Premier Cab over the preceding months stood to lose around $1 million collectively, or more than $16 million today. Following the judge's bankruptcy order, it was Howard's job to salvage what he could of the company's assets, in an attempt to begin to repay the company's debts.

As soon as the bankruptcy order went into effect early that Wednesday morning, Howard was ready. He had spent the previous days devising a plan with Chicago police and federal authorities to set up a city-wide operation to seize and repossess any remaining cabs before the Premier drivers realized the company had dissolved. However, Howard's mission appears to have been thwarted by an informant, who must have tipped off the Premier leadership. Rather than let Howard seize the cabs, Premier leaders had arranged the exodus of many of the fleet's taxis over the Fourth of July weekend, leading to the caravans of empty Premier cabs observed throughout the rural countryside. Not knowing this, Howard organized Detective Bureau "zone squads" in every section of the city, and placed officers on high alert for Premier cabs. These squads stopped any remaining Premier cabs they spotted, and escorted them to the nearest Premier garage, where federal officials were waiting to check in the cabs as newly seized government property. It was officially the end for Premier Cab in Chicago.

THE INSURANCE WARS

In addition to the heavily mortgaged cabs and taximeters, the Premier Cab Company's downfall hinged on the large number of damage suits that had been filed against the company during its not-quite-two-years on the road. Then as now, accident and damage claims were a huge part of the financial map of a taxi company, and there were not yet any enforceable regulations that required cabs to carry additional insurance. That was about to change.

Two years earlier, the city had implemented a new regulation on the taxi industry that required each taxi to carry at least $2,500 of insurance coverage, "to insure responsibility for payment of claims in case of accident and liability." To comply with this rule, the large insurance companies charged taxi owners an annual fee of between $350 and $600 per cab. This was admittedly an exorbitant sum of money in an era when the average national salary was around $450 per year. As a result, the insurance regulation placed a high burden on the independent drivers and smaller taxi companies, and many of them questioned the legality of the rule or simply failed to comply. For two years, the police declined to enforce the regulation as the smaller operators pursued a series of court challenges against it, eventually taking their complaints to the highest law in the state. By the time Premier Cab collapsed in the summer of 1926, the fate of the insurance regulation rested with the Illinois state supreme court. Premier was not the only Chicago cab company to implode under financial strain caused by the insurance regulations that year: Four other Chicago cab companies had also declared bankruptcy, including Red Cab. However, the regulation's supporters argued that the rule's enforcement could have provided financial protection to Premier's investors, as well as the average Chicagoan who traveled in taxis.

By mid-August, the state supreme court had ruled that the insurance regulations—intended to "protect the claims of the public against taxicab concerns by insuring their financial stability"—were in fact legal and enforceable. Upon hearing that the court had ruled in favor of the regulation, Checker Taxi and one of the independent cab companies filed an appeal to the US Supreme Court and sought an injunction barring the city from enforcing the law against them while the suit was pending. However, the chief of police was unmoved by their appeals. Following a meeting with the city's corporation counsel, he announced that, beginning on September 15, the police would strictly enforce the insurance regulation against all taxis.

Hearing this news, the smaller cab companies and independent operators once again turned to the Goliath in their midst and accused Yellow Cab of campaigning for the enforcement of the law, relying on their deep pockets as a way of putting its competitors out of business. Yellow Cab counsel Benjamin Samuels vehemently denied these accusations. "During the past ten years, no less than twenty taxi cab companies in this city have gone into bankruptcy through their inability to pay damage claims," he told one reporter for *Collyer's Eye*. "In fairness to the public, the law should be enforced, assuring passengers in cabs protection against loss of life and injury while using these methods of conveyance." Or, more accurately, against the financial burden associated with loss of life and injury.

Samuels further denied that Yellow Cab exerted any of its influence to prevent insurance companies from issuing coverage to its competitors. "The reports that our corporation is standing in the way of other companies contracting with surety [insurance] companies for their bonds is pure bosh," he declared. "The whole matter in a nutshell is that many of the companies operating on a 'shoe string' are unable to meet the requirement, which would force them to pay their claims. If these companies cannot meet the requirements of the law, then they have no business operating." Like Premier Cab, many of them did, in fact, fail.

THE FIRST ATTACK ON JOSEPH WOKRAL

Premier Cab had folded after less than two years in business. With its collapse, several of the former union drivers originally ousted from Checker Taxi were free to realign themselves with their former employer, which was now under new management: With Bob McLaughlin now serving as the Checker president, the union drivers felt safe to return. Those allies of Morris Markin's who had expelled them in the first place suddenly found the tables had turned.

In October of 1926, one of those men, ousted Checker president Joseph Wokral, left his apartment on the city's West Side and headed downtown. Wokral had close-cropped, dark, wavy hair and wide-set brown eyes, and like many men of the era, he wore a Charlie Chaplin–style mustache. He had arranged to meet three other ousted Checker officials at the Great Northern Hotel. They were meeting in secret to plot a strategy to regain control of the company from the "thugs" and "gangsters" who had usurped it at the last shareholders' meeting, including Bob McLaughlin and his gangster brother Red. At the hotel, Wokral and his supporters began to discuss their options. Should they pursue legal action? Could they safely campaign against the McLaughlins at the coming shareholders' meeting?

The answer came more swiftly than they could have guessed. While their meeting unfolded, the telephone rang, and a friend on the line warned them that the McLaughlins were on the street waiting to ambush the group when they left the hotel. Wokral and his allies stayed put and called the police instead, who arrived and found Bob and Red McLaughlin at the entrance to the hotel with sawed-off shotguns concealed in their coats. A search of the second entrance turned up two accomplices, also current Checker Taxi officials, carrying similar weapons. The police arrested all of them, as well as a fifth accomplice waiting in a car with a Thompson submachine gun. The police put all five of the men in jail pending a hearing in front of Judge John H. Lyle.

The next day, when Wokral heard that the case had been assigned to Lyle, he hurried to the judge's home to beg for his help. Coming to the door, Judge Lyle determined Wokral was there to plead his case. "Anything you have to say must be said in court," he warned.

"I didn't know that coming here was wrong," Wokral intoned. "I've got to have help. They're going to kill me . . . and no one is going to stop them."

Like many Chicagoans, Wokral believed that several of the judges at the time were corrupt, fearful of ruling against the city's violent gangsters and willing to take money or favors on the side to hand down light sentences. But Lyle had a reputation for fairness. Known as the "nemesis of gangsters," he could not be bribed, threatened, or otherwise corrupted. Wokral respected Lyle and hoped that the judge would consider the position he was in.

"Mr. Wokral, if you are in the right, you will get justice in my court," Judge Lyle assured him, and turned to walk back into the house.

"If those fellows go free, I'll be a dead man in thirty days," Wokral warned after him, his voice trembling.

Judge Lyle cut no corners in hearing the case, listening to evidence laid out on both sides in what he later described in his memoirs as a "lengthy hearing." At the conclusion of the hearing, he found all five men guilty on felony charges and ordered them held to the grand jury on bonds totaling $1 million. Under ordinary circumstances, following the judge's ruling, all five men would have been transferred back to jail. However, Checker attorney and former alderman Edgar O. Cook used his political connections to immediately appeal the verdict to a higher court, and the higher-court judge nullified Judge Lyle's ruling within the hour. That judge ordered the men released on just $10,000 bonds. The McLaughlin brothers and their accomplices went free.

A few nights later, on Saturday, October 23, 1926, Wokral and his wife, Irene, were asleep in their modest home, a first-floor apartment in a six-flat building in the Austin neighborhood, when they were awakened by the sound of something heavy hitting one of their windows. It turned out to be a bomb, thrown at the Wokrals' window from a passing car. Despite hitting the window, the object failed to break the glass and instead bounced back on the sidewalk, where it exploded with such force that it broke every window in the six-flat building, as well as the windows in several neighboring buildings. Wokral and his wife escaped injury.

Police investigating the incident summoned Checker Taxi vice president Harry Gordon for questioning but ultimately released him. Officially, the bombing remained unsolved, though Wokral surely suspected the McLaughlins. And yet if he did suspect the brothers of trying to intimidate him out of the company, Wokral refused to let them win. Following the bombing, he and his wife relocated to a different apartment building, while Wokral continued to plot a strategy to regain the presidency of Checker Taxi from the McLaughlin brothers.

THE MURDER OF JOSEPH WOKRAL

At around 9:00 p.m. on Thursday, December 9, 1926, Wokral stepped out of a building in West Garfield Park, on a tree-lined residential street of modest, newly built, brick-and-stone two-flat buildings. Wokral had been visiting Benjamin Bernstein, a friend and fellow Russian immigrant. When they parted that evening, Bernstein saw Wokral to the door and watched him walk down the steps and onto the sidewalk. As Wokral passed a large car parked on the narrow street, Bernstein heard the sharp sound of several gunshots and saw his friend collapse to the ground. The car peeled away. Bernstein said the driver of a passing city bus saw the car attempting its getaway and tried to read the license plate number, but the men inside the car shot at the bus driver as well. "I think one bullet hit a bus window," Bernstein later told police.

Wokral was shot in the head, as well as the right leg, the left hand, and the abdomen. Bernstein ran into the house and called the police, who arrived and rushed Wokral to Garfield Park Hospital in critical condition. Before losing consciousness, Wokral fingered Red McLaughlin for the shooting, telling police he saw the gangster in the car. "The McLaughlins knew I was going to run for president," he told them. "They didn't want me to." Wokral died at the hospital, succumbing to his wounds.

Shortly before midnight, the police put out an arrest warrant for Bob and Red McLaughlin, neither of whom could be located. No additional arrests were made for Wokral's murder. A few days later, Irene Wokral laid her husband to rest in Elmhurst's Mount Emblem cemetery, and still police had no one in custody for her husband's murder. Three weeks after the shooting, following an unusually long delay, a coroner's jury announced that Wokral had indeed been murdered by "unidentified persons" and recommended that those people be apprehended, but offered no further help to the investigation.

Bob McLaughlin, for his part, must have quickly convinced police to call off his arrest. Less than a month after Wokral was gunned down on the sidewalk, Bob McLaughlin's name was once again on the ballot for the presidency of Checker Taxi at the annual shareholders' meeting. On the day of the election, McLaughlin's main rival for the position—the man who had begun the previous autumn to attempt to mount a challenge to his reign—rested six feet under the earth in Elmhurst, Illinois.

CHAPTER 10

Running on Fumes

The Beginning of the End (1927)

IN JANUARY OF 1927, BRIGADIER GENERAL CLINNIN WAS BACK AT THE West Side headquarters of Checker Taxi. As had been the case the previous year, a Chicago judge had once again ordered that the company's annual shareholders' election be held under Clinnin's supervision, with the help of ten deputy sheriffs to ensure fair elections and prevent violence. This time, the judge's order came in response to a petition filed by a group of Checker Taxi driver-shareholders who alleged that the union-affiliated current leadership—Bob McLaughlin, Harry Gordon, and Max Raifman among them—had "instituted a reign of intimidation in order to prolong their tenure in office." The drivers petitioning the judge claimed that McLaughlin and his associates had hired fifty gunmen at a rate of $15 per day (taken out of the company treasury), and that those drivers who opposed the leadership found their lives threatened and their taxis impounded.

In the days leading up to the elections, several squads of police swept the neighborhood looking for the alleged gunmen but found none. Clinnin inspected the election books prior to the meeting and found no irregularities. No gunmen appeared at the meeting on January 11, and the election proceeded as planned. McLaughlin, Gordon, and Raifman were overwhelmingly re-elected, by a margin of 100-to-1. At least some of the shareholders must have been thinking of Joseph Wokral's sad fate as they cast their votes.

Despite the warnings, the Checker Taxi shareholders' election had proceeded peacefully. Six weeks later, however, the Democratic and Republican primaries for Chicago's mayoral election did not go as smoothly. The Republican primary marked the return of Mayor Thompson to the ballot, as he ran against challenger Edward R. Litsinger for the Republican Party's nomination to the main ballot in April. Throughout the city, these primaries were marked by intimidation, violence, and illegal acts. On February 23, 1927, a headline in the *Chicago Tribune* declared, "Hoodlums Raid Polls; Election Gunmen Seized." The article described the arrests of two hundred people accused of engaging in "local warfare" at the polls, and detailed several acts of violence, including the shooting of a poll worker. At least one car full of gunmen went from precinct to precinct, holding up election workers and policemen, stealing ballots and ballot boxes. (Among the men arrested for that crime spree was Isadore Goldberg, who had played a small role in the earlier days of the Taxi Wars when his 1919 jewelry theft had laid bare accusations about the then-ongoing battles between Yellow Cab and the Hotel La Salle.) Other election-related crimes that day included the kidnapping of a judge and an election worker, as well as several cases of multiple voting. This was, after all, the era that popularized the phrase, "Welcome to Chicago. Vote early, vote often."

On the mayoral ticket, former mayor "Big Bill" Thompson handily won the Republican nomination; two months later, he was re-elected mayor of Chicago for a third (non-consecutive) term. Seven years into Prohibition, the city was again under Thompson's leadership; the reform-focused and ethics-minded Dever was out. Upon taking office again, despite campaign promises to the contrary, Thompson abandoned most of Dever's attempts at reform and law-and-order. In fact, far from wanting to enforce laws against rum-running, Thompson was himself the owner of a speakeasy, the Fish Fans Club, which was located on a boat in the neutral waters of Lake Michigan to elude any federal Prohibition agents. When he won the mayoral election that spring, Thompson docked the Fish Fans Club at Belmont Harbor and invited his supporters aboard. So many people took him up on this offer that the boat sank, famously inspiring a joke that so much gin was spilled into the harbor that night that it became the "world's largest martini."

"A TRUE STORY THAT RIVALS FICTION"

As these election intrigues unfolded throughout the city, Yellow Cab experienced escalating success. The previous year, John Hertz had accepted an offer to merge the taxi manufacturing branch of the company, Yellow Cab Manufacturing, with the truck manufacturing division of General Motors, in a carefully negotiated deal that resulted in the formation of Yellow Truck and Coach Manufacturing, with Hertz as the chairman of the board of directors. (He had thrown in the Drive-Ur-Self rental car concept as part of the deal.) Then in January of 1926, Hertz had decided to step away as president of the taxi side of the business, Yellow Cab, to focus on the expanding portfolio of Yellow assets. In Hertz's place, the Yellow Cab board of directors had elected a new president of the company: Charlie Gray.

Charmed by a "true story that rivals fiction," newspapers around the country had carried the story of the onetime cab driver who had risen through the ranks to claim the top spot at the country's largest cab company. Gray was described as a former "ace of chauffeurs" who maintained an affection for all of his employees, but especially the drivers who served as the public face of Yellow Cab. The newspaper profiles painted a portrait of Gray, then fifty-one years old, as "very popular with the 6,000 drivers of his company," a president who knew "many hundreds of them by their first names."

In his writing for the *Taxigram* and in public interviews, Gray never mentioned the many challenges of working in the taxi industry during its first two decades. He never hinted at the industry violence he had been compelled to navigate first as a driver, and then a garage supervisor, vice president, and general manager. The closest he came to publicly commenting on the Taxi Wars came in the form of an oblique reference. When asked for his advice on achieving success, Gray said, "Work hard and be 100 percent loyal to the fellows you are working with."

The transfer of the company's presidency from John Hertz to Charlie Gray had been a seamless one, and by Gray's one-year anniversary in office in January of 1927, Yellow Cab boasted twenty-seven hundred cabs on the streets and eight thousand total employees. Ridership was strong: During one particularly bad stretch of winter weather that January, the company averaged one hundred fifty thousand rides per day, more than double its usual service. Gray continued his safety campaign, a passionate pet project dating back to 1919, and hosted a reception at the Bismarck Hotel for five hundred Yellow Cab drivers with the best safety records in the company. At the banquet, drivers were recognized not just for safe driving but for committing acts of heroism while on duty: A driver from the Vincennes Avenue garage had rescued three children from a fire, and another from the Fulton Street garage dragged a drowning woman out of Lake Michigan. The company eventually rewarded sixty-seven of its drivers with gold medals for the feat of driving for the company for more than two years without a single accident.

In addition to its safety campaign and expanding employee roster, Yellow Cab's financial outlook was sunny as well. In February of 1927, the company released a notice to shareholders announcing big financial gains. "While complete figures are not [yet] available, it is believed 1926 earnings have at least equaled and probably exceeded the record made in 1925," it read in part. The report went on to note that "the company has been making great improvements in its equipment . . . during the fall months, 1,000 new limousine model cabs have been added to the fleet." The employees' collective share of the company's dividends in February 1927 totaled $350,000, or nearly $6 million in today's money.

In the beginning of April 1927, the National Association of Taxicab Owners again hosted its annual convention at the Hotel Sherman in Chicago, and among the event's featured speakers was Harvey D. Wood, Yellow Cab's safety director, who explained how the company had reduced its accidents by 30 percent. Twelve years after first debuting in Chicago, Yellow Cab was unquestionably one of the great leaders and innovators in the taxi industry at the national level. And by this time, it was an industry with national relevance. By 1927, taxis had become an indelible part of city life throughout America, and they had thoroughly captured the public's imagination. That spring, moviegoers around the country could see silent films and film shorts with titles like *A Kiss in a Taxi, Taxi, Taxi, Taxi!*, and *The Taxi Dancer*, the latter starring a very young Joan Crawford.

The Arrest of Frisco Dutch

Former Checker Taxi president Joseph Wokral had been murdered in December, and by April of 1927, police were still trying to locate Red McLaughlin, along with his accomplice Robert "Frisco Dutch" Steinhardt. Wokral had fingered the two men as his killers in a deathbed confession. McLaughlin was wanted for questioning related to other crimes as well, including several jewel heists, two cases of kidnap-for-ransom, and at least one case of "hoisting," or holding up other gangsters and stealing their illegally gotten gains. On April 5, police raided the Webster Hotel looking for McLaughlin, but found instead a small arsenal that included a machine gun. They also found four additional possible accomplices, all of whom were arrested. McLaughlin, however, had reportedly fled to Detroit.

Then on Friday, April 29, 1927, a squad of police traveled to the western suburbs and knocked on the door of Mary Weiss, mother of the notorious North Side gang leader Hymie Weiss. Weiss had been killed the previous October on a street in downtown Chicago by a rival gangster, and it is not clear why the police thought they might find Red McLaughlin at the Weiss family home, though McLaughlin was a known associate of the North Side gangsters, and had even dated a North Side gangster's moll named Mary Margaret Collins. Once again, police failed to find McLaughlin, arresting another man instead. Next, the police went to a home in suburban Maywood looking for McLaughlin. He wasn't there either, but police arrested four men at that location and confiscated a shotgun and a machine-gun clip with loaded bullets.

One of the people the police arrested that day was the as-yet-elusive accomplice Frisco Dutch Steinhardt. They arrested him on the testimony of Wokral's wife, Irene, who said that Wokral had told her before he died that McLaughlin and Steinhardt were to blame. After an initial interrogation, the police held Steinhardt to a grand jury for Wokral's murder, and also announced that McLaughlin was now wanted in conjunction with a separate crime: the plot to kidnap the eleven-year-old heiress of the John G. Shedd estate, to ransom her for a hefty sum. (Whether or not Steinhardt was the source of this information is unclear.)

However, when Steinhardt came to trial in the end of June, it took a jury just five minutes of deliberation to acquit him of Wokral's murder. Attorneys for Steinhardt were able to prove that he had been in Detroit on the day of the attack, by presenting hotel records that indicated he had been evicted that day for lack of payment. The judge had also refused to allow Wokral's deathbed confession to his wife into evidence, which must have left the jury wondering what had led the police to arrest Steinhardt in the first place. The gangster known as Frisco Dutch was acquitted, and Red McLaughlin remained at large.

JOHN HERTZ AND LEONA FARMS

For his part, John Hertz had always found ways to work with Mayor Thompson's office, so the return of the occasionally polarizing mayor presented Hertz with ideas and opportunities rather than challenges. And by Mayor Thompson's third inauguration, Hertz was busier than ever. After shepherding Charlie Gray's ascendence to the presidency of Yellow Cab back in 1926, Hertz remained the chairman of the board of directors of Yellow Cab, and he had launched his rental car concept in multiple cities under the official name Hertz U-Drive-It Co. He remained on the board of directors of several other corporations as well, including General Motors.

John and Fannie Hertz split their time between a luxury apartment on Chicago's North Side and a country home about an hour's drive outside the city. In 1920, they had purchased the large farm in Cary, Illinois, northwest of the city, where they built a comfortable manor home and began a well-organized breeding stable for Kentucky thoroughbreds. They named the property Leona Farms. Wherever he lived, Hertz liked to surround himself with friends, and in 1927, Charlie Gray bought a farm nearby so the two families could vacation together at their country homes that summer.

John and Fannie Hertz also decided to spend part of their winters in Miami. They purchased a grand estate on "Millionaire's Row" in Miami Beach in March of 1927, described as "one of the most beautiful in the resort city," and located north of the Firestone estate. (Hertz and Firestone Tire & Rubber Company founder Harvey Firestone had maintained a close business relationship dating back to at least 1919, when Hertz negotiated a deal for Yellow Cab to lease all of its tires from Firestone, an arrangement that lasted for decades.) Taking advantage of the temperate weather and the plentiful horse training facilities in Florida, Hertz shipped twenty of his thoroughbreds to Miami to train throughout the winter season.

In fact, Hertz's horse breeding and training operation was starting to produce top talent. By the start of the 1927 racing season, the Hertz family was ready to debut two promising horses: Reigh Count and the filly Anita Peabody, both of which were owned in Fannie Hertz's name and raced under the colors of the Hertz stables: yellow and black, a nod to Yellow Cab. When the racing season opened in May that year, the two horses maintained a busy exercising and racing schedule, and John and Fannie Hertz often traveled to attend the races.

However, this travel schedule did not prevent Hertz from staying active as a Chicago business leader, and advocating for his business interests closer to home. Following Thompson's election in April, Hertz began working with the city's corporation counsel to promote his plan for the city's acquisition of the motorbus system, bringing buses into the fold as part of the burgeoning public transportation landscape. He was also invited to serve on the executive committee of the Mayor's Advisory Council. In that role, he was instrumental in helping to secure the financial backing to bring one of the biggest boxing matches of the decade to Chicago's Soldier Field: a rematch between Jack Dempsey and Gene Tunney that would go down in history as "the long-count fight." For a man who had once aspired to be a professional boxing manager, this must have felt like a surreal privilege to John Hertz. As an organizer of the match, he had a prominent seat ringside to watch Gene Tunney defeat Jack Dempsey at one of the most highly anticipated sporting events of the year. The day after the bout, Tunney, along with Hertz and the rest of the executive committee, was received as a guest of honor at a luncheon at the Chicago Athletic Association. A newspaper photographer snapped a picture of Hertz grinning at the champion like a proud schoolboy who couldn't believe his luck in life.

Hertz had a lot of reason to smile that day. In the same edition of the newspaper that carried the photograph of the Gene Tunney reception, the sports page also carried a photo of jockey Chick Lang atop the Hertzes' filly Anita Peabody, who had won the prestigious Belmont Futurity Stakes in New York the previous weekend. The filly stunned the crowd and won the race, just beating stable-mate Reigh Count by a nose and nearly breaking the track record in the process. Anita Peabody won a purse of $91,790 for the Hertzes, or more than $1.5 million in today's money. John Hertz was forty-eight years old, a millionaire, pursuing his life's passions and surrounded everywhere he lived by friends and family. It must have felt to Hertz as though he "never saw the sun shinin' so bright, never saw things goin' so right," to quote a popular Irving Berlin song of the era. However, by the end of the year this luck would run out, and tragedy would brush John Hertz.

THE DEATH OF CHARLIE GRAY

Christmas Day, 1927, fell on a Sunday that year. Throughout the city of Chicago, children woke up early, some creeping quietly, some bounding out of bed, eager to see what Santa Claus had left them under the tree. Yellow Cab's president, the fifty-two-year-old Charlie Gray, along with his second wife, Margaret, woke up to an exuberant house alive with the uncontrollable Christmas energy of their six young children. To the outside world, the Grays must have looked like the ideal family of the 1920s: successful businessman Charlie with his beautiful wife, blessed with six children together and an ever-increasing prosperity that had allowed them to move into their impressive home on Bennett Avenue in the dignified Jackson Park Highlands neighborhood just a few years earlier.

Family was extremely important to Gray, and his commitment to prioritizing family applied not just to his own children, but to the families of his many employees as well. Just two months earlier, he had hosted a party in the grand ballroom of the Hotel Sherman for the families of Yellow Cab employees, presiding over a guest list of two thousand people.

When a photographer captured Gray at the party, he was surrounded by children in party hats, holding a little boy on his hip and smiling with genuine joy at the scene around him.

A similar smile must have crossed his face on several occasions that Christmas morning, as he watched his children—twelve-year-old Charlotte, ten-year-old Margaret, nine-year-old Jane, eight-year-old Ruth, seven-year-old John, and five-year-old Betty—play with new Christmas gifts around the tree. Perhaps Charlie Gray reflected on the good fortune that had led him to this place. Perhaps he wondered how much longer that good fortune could last. Perhaps he had reason to wonder.

The Gray family home was located just a few blocks west of the South Shore Country Club, a refined and exclusive club located on the Lake Michigan shoreline, anchored by a palatial clubhouse built a decade earlier and designed in the Mediterranean Revival style by architects Marshall and Fox. Charlie Gray had been a member of the South Shore Country Club since 1924. The club was the social center for the neighborhood, and it was solely the reserve of elite, white, wealthy families who spent their leisure hours engaged in formal dinners, dances, sporting competitions, receptions, and other social events. (As a Jew, even John Hertz was ineligible for membership.) The ballroom at the South Shore Country Club was designed for these grand affairs, and featured ornate, hand-laid mosaic tile in black and white, with green marble columns supporting a soaring ceiling above the enormous room. Floor-to-ceiling arched windows provided stunning views of the lake and the sixty-five-acre parkland surrounding the club, which included trails for horseback riding and a nine-hole golf course.

After a lavish Christmas breakfast prepared by the family's cook, Gray left his children to their new toys and walked a few blocks east to the country club's stables, where he kept a horse. Although the automobile now dominated the city's streets, Gray, like many people in his social class, still kept a horse for pleasure riding and exercise. Every May, the South Shore Country Club hosted a competitive horse show where its members competed for much-coveted trophies in a wide range of categories. Gray liked to ride in the nearby Jackson Park every morning, if the weather allowed. That morning's temperature was on the cusp, with the thermometer hovering around 25 degrees, but Gray decided to brave the cold. He wasn't alone that morning; he had arranged to ride with two companions: his wife's brother, Robert Berg; and Alton N. Huttel, the treasurer of the Yellow Cab Company.

The three men mounted their horses and headed north along the lakefront toward Jackson Park. Their outing that morning may have been an informal business meeting or just a friendly holiday ride. But when the three men on horseback reached a small lagoon south of the Outer Harbor, disaster struck. According to the newspaper accounts, Huttel and Berg didn't witness the incident themselves. They claimed that Charlie Gray had ridden ahead of them, around a bend and out of sight. Or possibly he had fallen behind them. The stories shifted depending on who was telling them.

When Gray next came into their view, Huttel and Berg found him lying on the ground, unconscious. The details are murky. One newspaper claimed the men thought the horse had stumbled, causing the saddle to slide to one side and Gray to fall off backwards, breaking his neck as his horse galloped away. Another claimed he was found on the ground with a head injury, his horse standing patiently beside its fallen rider. Yet another reported that broken reins were to blame and that the horse had reared up, throwing Gray backward and causing him to hit his head on the hard cinder path.

In the moment, there was little time to assess the scene. Huttel and Berg knew that Gray needed immediate medical care, so they hailed a passing bus and enlisted the help of several passengers to load the unconscious Gray on board. The driver rushed them to the Illinois Central Hospital, a private hospital for employees of the Illinois Central railroad, where Berg worked as a clerk. Jackson Park Hospital would have been closer, but perhaps Berg thought the doctors at Illinois Central had more expertise in this kind of injury, or perhaps he wanted to take Gray to a private hospital where it would be easier to control the flow of people and information for a high-profile patient. By the time they reached the hospital, it was too late. Shortly after their arrival, Dr. Emanuel Friend declared Charlie Gray dead of a basal skull fracture. He suffered no other injuries in the alleged accident.

Gray's death came during an unusually quiet period of the Taxi Wars. If the police ever suspected foul play in the untimely death of Yellow Cab's president, no record of an investigation exists. If they were reminded of the difficult-to-explain car accident that took Checker Taxi counsel John Prendergast's life, or the outright murder of former Checker Taxi president Joseph Wokral just one year earlier, they made no overt connections between those tragedies and this one. The only two witnesses to Gray's injury insisted they were not in fact witnesses at all, and could give no definitive account of what had happened. Given the limited evidence available, a hurriedly convened coroner's inquest declared that Gray's death was an accident resulting from a fall from a horse. His brother-in-law and riding companion Robert Berg provided the information for his death certificate.

As word of Gray's death spread throughout the city, several influential people appeared at the hospital to show support, including the chief of police and several other city officials. John Hertz, who had been Gray's closest friend for more than two decades, rushed to the hospital upon hearing the news, but it was too late to say goodbye. "This is a terrible shock to me," Hertz told a reporter as he left the hospital. "Charlie Gray was one of the most kindly men in Chicago and he died without an enemy." An official for the Yellow Cab Company echoed these sentiments. "He took a personal interest in the private troubles of every employee of the company," he told a *Chicago Tribune* reporter. "His office door was never closed. The news of his death has brought sorrow to everyone in the company, from cab driver to directors."

Gray's wife, Margaret, must have wondered what was keeping him so long. Three of the children were still playing around the Christmas tree when the sad news of their father's death reached the house. Hearing that her husband had been killed, Margaret Gray collapsed. She was forty-one years old, the mother of six young children, and now, suddenly, a widow.

At 2:30 p.m. on Tuesday, December 27, every on-duty Yellow Cab in the city of Chicago, wherever it found itself at that moment, pulled to the curb and stopped in its tracks. Drivers got out of their cars, removed their hats, and stood at attention for two minutes, observing a moment of silence for Charlie Gray, the beloved president of the company, who had begun his career in the taxi industry twenty years earlier as a cab driver himself. Gray's funeral had begun thirty minutes earlier at the newly built Bryn Mawr Community Church. John Hertz had ordered that as many drivers as possible be given time off to attend the funeral. The building was filled beyond capacity with people there to mourn Charlie Gray's loss. Sitting in the pews beside the drivers were some of Chicago's most powerful men: State's Attorney Robert Crowe, future mayors Anton Cermak and Edward J. Kelly, Chief of Police Michael Hughes, Alderman John Coughlin, Judges Harry Olson and Francis Borelli, and Dan Ryan, the president of the Cook County Board of Commissioners, among many others.

The church quickly filled with mourners, and still people kept arriving. Eventually, an overflow crowd of around three thousand people was forced to stand outside the church in silence while the service was performed, the city's richest and poorest funeral-goers standing shoulder-to-shoulder in the cold. No preference was given for the seating, which was strictly first-come, first-served. The interior of the church was covered in flowers sent from every corner of the city, so many flowers that the church's portals and altar were completely buried under them, with even more filling the Gray home. The flowers were sent by a wide cross-section of the people who had filled Gray's life: family, friends, neighbors, colleagues, prominent business leaders, members of city government, Yellow Cab drivers and employees from each of the company's garages, "the boys from Valentine's barbershop," the traffic division of the police department, the "old *Inter Ocean* crowd," the Congress Hotel doormen, the Mandel Brothers department store. Even Yellow Cab's taxi industry rival sent condolences: One of the flower arrangements that arrived for the funeral bore the names of the four members of Checker Taxi's current leadership—Bob McLaughlin, Harry Gordon, Max Raifman, and Barney Mitchell. Condolence telegrams had been arriving from all over the world, including one from Mayor Thompson himself. Newspapers carried the story of Charlie Gray's death as far away as Brooklyn, New York, and Victoria, British Columbia.

Gray's devotion to first Shaw Livery and then Yellow Cab had not wavered in twenty years. But his tenure as president of the taxi company lasted just two years. His absence at the helm of the company in the year that followed would deeply affect Hertz. Just slightly more than a year after Gray's death, Hertz would make a drastic decision, one which just a few years earlier would have seemed unthinkable. The loss of his friend and trusted business confidant was just the beginning of a series of events that would eventually put an end to the Taxi Wars, an end that would come at a high, high price.

CHAPTER 11

Hit the Skids

The Final Battles of the War (1927–1928)

SINCE THE MURDER OF JOSEPH WOKRAL IN DECEMBER OF 1926, RED McLaughlin had been living on luck. He was sought by police not just in Chicago, but in Philadelphia as well—for charges stemming from a jewel heist. For more than a year, the gangster had managed to evade arrest. But Red McLaughlin's luck was about to run out.

On March 2, 1928, Red McLaughlin was drinking illegal liquor in the small, Northwoods town of Hayward, Wisconsin. He'd been hiding out nearby for the past four months, using the alias Robert O'Brien and attempting to blend in with the locals in the small town, not entirely successfully. He had managed to keep a reasonably low profile, but eventually boredom led him to the bottle. That day in early March, McLaughlin got drunk and behaved erratically enough to draw the attention of the local sheriff's department. When a sheriff's deputy attempted to arrest him for drunk and disorderly behavior, McLaughlin resisted arrest. He grabbed a monkey wrench and started beating the deputy and another man who was aiding in the arrest. The second man happened to be the mayor of Hayward, Thomas McClaine. When McLaughlin began attacking him, the mayor pulled out his personal pistol and shot McLaughlin at point-blank range in self-defense. McLaughlin was struck in the chest and seriously wounded, the bullet puncturing his lung. The sheriff's deputy arrested him and rushed him to a nearby hospital, where doctors operated to remove the bullet.

McLaughlin remained in the hospital for two weeks while the sheriff sent fingerprints to Chicago police in an attempt to learn the true identity of the man still known there only as "Robert O'Brien." The Chicago Police Department's fingerprinting experts were leaders in this new crime-solving field. They used their cutting-edge skills to match the prints, and sent their findings back to northern Wisconsin. On March 15, the Sawyer County sheriff's department announced that the man they had in custody recovering at the hospital was the notorious gangster Red McLaughlin, and they would send him back to Chicago as soon as he was well enough to travel. The mayor of Hayward, Wisconsin, had done what no Chicago policeman had been able to do: He found and felled the wanted man.

Extradited to Chicago, McLaughlin denied any role in Wokral's murder, and similarly rejected responsibility for the jewel heist for which he was concurrently facing charges. Despite his assertion of innocence, on April 19, a grand jury indicted McLaughlin for Wokral's murder and ordered that he stand trial for both of the crimes he was accused of. Citing his past tendency to jump bond, the judge ordered that he be held without bail. And so McLaughlin sat in jail.

The murder trial began the week of May 7, but it was hastily adjourned and halted when an attorney for the prosecution made statements to the jury that the defense team considered prejudicial. Instead, the following week, the prosecutors chose to try McLaughlin on the separate burglary charge. The evidence against McLaughlin in that case was damning—he was arrested while in the process of choking his burglary victim, a New York jewelry salesman named Walter J. Newman, while attempting to rob him of more than $100,000 worth of gems (or more than $1.7 million today).

Newman acted as the key witness in the trial. Without Newman's testimony, the case against Red McLaughlin in the burglary trial would have most likely been dismissed. This made Newman's position extremely vulnerable. In fact, after the jury had heard all of the testimony and retired to consider McLaughlin's fate, Newman came forward to the judge with serious allegations that he had been threatened prior to testifying.

Newman described how he had arrived in Chicago on a Sunday, the day before the trial began, and hoped to slip into the city unnoticed. "I did not think anyone knew I was in town," he told the judge. Newman explained that he visited his attorney and then went to a barbershop on Dearborn Street for a haircut. While in the barber's chair, he was approached by Bob McLaughlin, brother of Red and president of the Checker Taxi Company. "Robert McLaughlin came in with his hands in his pockets, handed me his card and said: 'You know me,'" Newman described. "I said I did and asked him if it was a friendly meeting. He said yes, if I wanted to make it so." Newman went on to describe how Bob McLaughlin appeared to have a gun in his pocket and suggested that Newman might change his testimony to make it sound as if Red McLaughlin had not been robbing Newman after all, but was instead acting in self-defense.

Upon hearing these serious allegations of witness intimidation, the judge told the defense attorneys to produce Bob McLaughlin to answer the accusations. "Newman's statements indicate an attempt to obstruct justice and to commit the crime of subornation of perjury," the judge declared, and added that Newman would receive police protection. Instead, faced with the prospect of having to accuse Bob McLaughlin face-to-face in court, Newman fled the jurisdiction and went into hiding.

When the jury came back from their deliberations, they found Red McLaughlin guilty of the burglary, and the judge sentenced him to up to fourteen years in prison. Satisfied with this outcome, the prosecutors decided to drop the murder charge against McLaughlin in the Wokral case due to a lack of witnesses. The judge then immediately opened a hearing into Newman's accusations of witness tampering. "There is an atmosphere of lawlessness about this case," the judge declared. "And the court is prepared to meet the situation."

In fact, Newman was not the only person to come forward with such accusations. After Red McLaughlin's guilty verdict was announced, the jury foreman, Fred W. Eicke, told detectives a similar story. He claimed that, prior to the trial, he had been approached by two men who had attempted to influence his vote on the jury in favor of McLaughlin. Eicke said that a man he happened to know, secretary and treasurer of the International Brotherhood of Teamsters Gust Steinweg, brought a man to meet him and introduced the man as Bob McLaughlin. The two urged Eicke, if he was placed on the jury, to give Red McLaughlin "a good break." They suggested that if Eicke did so, he would be well taken care of. Hearing this, the judge was outraged. "The situation at present seems to this court to be unprecedented in the history of Cook County," he declared. "We have had testimony that witnesses have been intimidated in this case, and a prospective juror approached with bribery and threatened." The judge adjourned for the day, with the intention of hearing more testimony in the morning.

Then the stakes were raised further. Early the following morning, Eicke was at the East Side police station to positively identify Steinweg in a criminal complaint when police informed him that a bomb had just exploded at his home on the city's far southeast side. Eicke's wife, Martha, and their sons—thirteen-year-old Fred Jr., eleven-year-old Herman, and nine-year-old Kirk—were in the home at the time, as were Martha's sister and her husband, who were entertaining a breakfast party of six people in their second-floor apartment. The bomb exploded at the front of the home, tearing away part of the front porch, shattering the windows, and blasting a hole about a foot in diameter through a front bedroom wall. Fred Jr. was closest to the blast and suffered a concussion with temporary deafness. No one else was injured.

Following the bombing, police went immediately to the home of Bob McLaughlin to question him, and then brought him to court to answer the allegations against him. The judge had arrived to the courtroom an hour early that day, spending the time "in heated conference" with three assistant state's attorneys regarding the alleged witness- and jury-tampering. Resuming the hearing, the judge called first Steinweg and then Bob McLaughlin to the stand to answer questions under oath. Steinweg initially denied the accusations against him, as did McLaughlin, who arrived in the courtroom "dapper, smiling and entirely at ease." Eicke claimed that Steinweg and McLaughlin told him "it would be worth my while to see that Red got a fair trial." Under questioning, Steinweg admitted that he had approached Eicke but denied any attempted bribery. McLaughlin similarly denied any wrongdoing in his testimony, but the judge remained unmoved by these statements and declared the alleged incidents to be a "ruthless and fiendish assault on this court and the lives of our wives and children."

Fearing for his own family's well-being after Eicke's house was bombed, the judge made the unusual request to have a police detail assigned to his own home. "My request for police guard is the first of its kind that I have made in seventeen years on the bench," he said. "I believe I owe it to my family, however, to give them protection at this time. I feel that the situation is serious." The judge also set Red McLaughlin's bail at an unheard-of $100,000, a record-high bail at the time. When McLaughlin's attorneys objected, the judge explained that a customary bond amount was insufficient because of the wild accusations and attacks swirling around the case. "A most extraordinary situation . . . exists in this case," he explained.

After setting the bail, the judge then referred the allegations of witness- and jury-tampering to a grand jury, which was rapidly assembled the following day to hear the evidence. Eicke minced no words, testifying before the grand jury that his home had been bombed as a result of the verdict of the McLaughlin trial. After hearing this testimony, members of the grand jury chose to indict four men—Red McLaughlin, Bob McLaughlin, Gust Steinweg, and a fourth man known only by the alias Ed Donohue, who Steinweg had implicated in his statements.

The judge then doubled down, issuing contempt-of-court citations to Bob McLaughlin and Gust Steinweg for interfering in the trial, and gave them four days to show cause why they should not be punished with jail sentences. The men failed to convince him. On June 2, the judge sentenced Bob McLaughlin, still the president of the Checker Taxi Company, to thirty days in the county jail on a contempt-of-court charge. Steinweg got sixty days. During the hearing, Checker attorneys Cook and Albert accused the judge of bias against Checker Taxi and, once again, attempted to cast aspersions on Cook County state's attorney Robert E. Crowe by claiming he was "one of the largest stockholders of the Yellow Cab Company." The judge shut down these arguments immediately and instead accused McLaughlin and Steinweg of having "poisoned the wells of justice itself."

MARKIN PLOTS HIS REVENGE

As Bob McLaughlin was sentenced to jail time for his role in the jury tampering, Morris Markin may have sensed an opportunity. After his initially successful attempts to gain de facto control of Checker Taxi through the presidencies of Emanuel Goldstein and Joseph Wokral, Markin had seen the tables turned on him by the union- and gangland-affiliated McLaughlins. Since they had taken over the leadership of the company in January of 1926, Markin managed to keep a remarkably low profile, while resenting the brothers and the kickbacks they reportedly now demanded from the Checker Cab Mfg. Co. on every car they ordered from his company.

Despite the number of vehicles Markin's company was making each year, on paper the Checker Cab Mfg. Co. was failing to make a profit. From 1923 to September of 1927, Markin claimed, the company made no money at all. In fact, at the end of 1927, the company had lost more than $300,000. So on December 31, 1927, incidentally just days after Charlie Gray was killed in Jackson Park, the shareholders of Checker Cab Mfg. Co. had removed Markin as president, placing the company under the control of the Commercial Credit Company, a syndicate of auto executives. Markin was demoted to vice president.

Over the first six months of 1928, the Checker Cab Mfg. Co. underwent a series of restructuring tactics, which included taking out new loans and issuing new common stock. This seemed to have the intended effect: First-quarter earnings were up more than 100 percent over the previous year, and the company had sold 1,430 of its 1,512 manufactured cabs. In June, the Commercial Credit Company sold its controlling interest, and Markin was reinstated as president of Checker Cab Mfg. Co., just as Bob McLaughlin was weakened at Checker Taxi due to his role in his brother's trial. The stage was set. By the end of the year, Markin would go on the offensive, taking a swing at McLaughlin and the other Checker leaders.

THE MURDER OF EUGENE THIVIERGE

Convicted of the attempted burglary of Walter Newman and sentenced to prison, Red McLaughlin began his sentence at Joliet Penitentiary on

June 30. A deceptive calm settled over the court system and the Chicago taxi industry for the rest of the summer, interrupted only by the usual holdups of cab drivers for their fare money, and one unsolved murder of a Checker Taxi driver, who was found shot in his cab after what police assumed to be an attempted burglary.

However, starting around September 1, the tensions between Checker Taxi drivers and Yellow Cab drivers began anew. For the past several years, while Checker Taxi went through its contentious and bloody civil war and its takeover by the gang-affiliated McLaughlins, Yellow Cab had mostly managed to stay clear of the violence. But beginning that September, the two rival cab companies were about to clash once again over their claims to specific turf. That night, 150 Checker taxis arrived en masse and began circling a Yellow Cab stand near the Polk Street police station in a threatening manner. Police later described their "difficulty . . . keeping the cab men in line." The next night, two Yellow Cabs were overturned on Lower Wacker Drive.

A few weeks later, early in the morning of September 22, 1928 in front of the Granada Café, the Taxi Wars claimed another victim. The cafe was one of several entertainment venues in Woodlawn that attracted Chicagoans who wanted to experience a little Prohibition fun, both legal and illicit. In addition to hosting cabaret acts and musicians like Guy Lombardo and Louis Armstrong, the cafe had a reputation as a brothel and gambling den and was known to be frequented by some of the city's most well-known gangsters. As a result of this cachet, the taxi stand in front of the Granada Café was a busy one, and Yellow Cab drivers had recently been jockeying with Checker Taxi drivers over their positions in front of the club.

That night, a thirty-five-year-old Checker driver named Eugene Thivierge parked his cab on the curb across the street from the cafe and waited to pick up a fare. Two off-duty Yellow Cab drivers, Robert Mooney and Bernard Reicter, approached Thivierge in a roadster and told him he couldn't park his cab there. The Checker driver argued back, asking on what authority they could prevent him from parking where he had. The argument escalated to a physical fight, though the primary witness, a colleague of Thivierge's, declined to say who threw the first punch.

In the brawl, Reicter, one of the Yellow Cab drivers, suffered serious injuries. Checker Taxi's Thivierge was shot and killed.

Reicter and Mooney initially fled the scene, but police found Reicter two miles away and rushed him to the Auburn Park Hospital suffering from a fractured skull. Not long after Thivierge's death, the attorneys for Yellow Cab and Checker Taxi set up a meeting to try to "settle certain difficulties between the two companies," as the *Chicago Tribune* reported. A similar meeting the previous year had reportedly resulted in an arrangement that kept these turf battles at bay. But when it came time to renew those agreements in September of 1928, the attorneys' negotiations fell apart, and Checker Taxi representatives walked away without finalizing any agreements. It turned out Thivierge's death was just a hint of more violence to come.

The First Wave of Bombings

One week after Thivierge was shot to death, and shortly after the meeting that failed to produce a truce, the Taxi Wars escalated again. On the North Side, twenty Yellow Cab employees were working in a company garage not far from the opulent Edgewater Beach Hotel, the pink-hued, luxury high-rise hotel preferred by movie stars and gangsters alike. At 10:15 p.m. on Sunday, September 30, two men in a Stutz sedan drove into the alley and hurled a bomb at the back door of the garage. When the bomb detonated, a massive explosion erupted, destroying the door and wrecking several cabs inside. Every window in the building shattered, and the twenty employees fled through the front door. The force of the blast damaged surrounding buildings, and the deafening noise could be heard for blocks throughout the otherwise quiet neighborhood.

Fifteen minutes later, another Yellow Cab garage—this one in the Lakeview neighborhood, about four miles south of the first blast— became the target of a similar attack. A mechanic and two drivers were standing near the back door of that garage when a bomb exploded there, throwing them to the ground. The explosion destroyed the back door and blew out all of the windows. Slivers of broken door frame flew into the garage and knocked the fenders off some of the cabs parked inside.

Initial police investigations suggested that the bombs may have been intended to do even more damage. At the Edgewater garage, an employee discovered eight sticks of dynamite that had failed to detonate, and turned them over to police. In the immediate wake of the attacks, the acting police chief ordered increased police presence around all Yellow Cab and Checker Taxi garages. John Hertz announced a $5,000 reward for information leading to the arrest of the bombers.

The following night, acting on information gathered as part of the investigation into the bombings, police raided an apartment in an unassuming, two-story brick building located at a busy intersection just a few blocks away from the bombed garage in Lakeview. The apartment was a known headquarters of the North Side gang headed by Bugs Moran, and police knew the McLaughlins were regular visitors there. Police didn't find the McLaughlins there that night, but they found ten other men in the apartment and arrested all of them on suspicion of involvement in the bombings. The men were also charged with possession of several weapons—including a machine gun, pistols, and a rifle—and large amounts of ammunition, all of which police discovered during the search. The most prominent members of the group arrested that night were the brothers Frank and Peter Gusenberg, well-known contract killers who would lose their lives just a few months later in an infamous attack by the rival Capone gang, one that would come to be known as the St. Valentine's Day Massacre. Police had hoped that by arresting these ten men in one of Bugs Moran's headquarters, they could blunt this latest outbreak of the Taxi Wars. However, there was no concrete evidence connecting Moran's men to the bombings of the Yellow Cab garages. Within two days, all but the Gusenbergs were released.

THE FIRE AT LEONA FARMS

The same day that the police arrested the Gusenbergs and their accomplices, tragedy struck in an unlikely place: McHenry County, forty miles northwest of Chicago. At 8:00 p.m. on Monday, October 1, a ten-year-old girl named Authora Naylor was getting ready for bed in her family's home on the Hertzes' Leona Farm in Cary, Illinois, when she looked out the window and saw that one of the stables was on fire. She told her father, the farm's superintendent Arthur Naylor, who shouted for his employees' help and ran across the field toward the fire. The brick building that was now in flames sheltered a portion of the Hertzes' impressive stable of racing thoroughbreds, including the phenom Reigh Count, who had won the Kentucky Derby the previous spring. Following his win at the "Run for the Roses," John and Fannie Hertz spent a portion of the purse winnings to construct a top-of-the-line brick stable to house their racing steeds. The new stable had only been in use for a month when it went up in flames.

Hearing Naylor's shouts, an assistant trainer and former jockey named Jimmy Allen ran with him toward the fire. When they reached the building, Allen ran into the smoke-filled stable to Reigh Count's stall and began quickly blindfolding the horse with jockey silks and then leading him to safety in a pasture. Other stable hands arrived and followed Allen's lead, rescuing as many horses as they could. The building was filled with fire and smoke everywhere, the sound of horses bleating and whinnying in panic and men shouting as they desperately tried to coax the thoroughbreds out of the stable. In the chaos and terror, some of the horses that had been led outside panicked and ran back into the burning building. Eventually the men had to abandon their efforts, as the fire spread to the hayloft and completely engulfed the stable.

Flames from the fire rose so high into the night sky that farmers from neighboring Crystal Lake, five miles away, rushed to the scene to try to help. But by the time they arrived, it was too late. Firefighters from Cary, Algonquin, and Crystal Lake had arrived on the scene within minutes, but the fire was already so hot that they found themselves powerless to stop the flames. Ultimately, eleven horses perished in the fire, including a two-year-old presumed future Derby contender named Sandalfan, valued at $50,000 (more than $1 million in today's money). All of the stable's staff survived the fire, including Allen. But the total damages were ultimately valued at $225,000, and the loss of the horses' lives was devastating to everyone on the farm.

Once the blaze burned out, the McHenry County sheriff's department began investigating the fire, which had spread rapidly through the brick building in a way that caused the sheriff's investigators to suspect arson. They could find no logical, natural cause of the fire. On top of this, the gate at the main entrance to the farm had been broken down, and employees of the farm reported smelling oil in the stable prior to the fire. But when the sheriff questioned Hertz and Naylor about their theories on the fire's cause, the two men were tight-lipped. Publicly, they would proffer no accusations of arson, saying only that they harbored no suspicions and "did not suspect the cause of the fire was incendiary." Investigators did not share that opinion.

In Chicago, the police and the state's attorney's office opened separate investigations into the fire and any possible connections with the bombings of the Yellow Cab garages the night before. The *Tribune* reported that, on the day of the fire, investigators "were still working at midnight on the theory that the blaze was incendiary in its origin and premeditated." State's attorney Robert E. Crowe personally took charge of his office's investigation. Hearing this, Checker Taxi counsel Arthur F. Albert objected on the grounds that Crowe was biased against him politically. In addition, just a few months earlier, during Red McLaughlin's trial, Albert had accused Crowe of favoritism toward Yellow Cab and asserted that Crowe in fact held a significant amount of Yellow Cab stock. Crowe denied this allegation.

Hertz continued to deny that the cause of the fire was arson, claiming that he had no enemies and didn't know anyone who would do something so horrible. But despite Hertz's denials, attorneys for Yellow Cab minced no words. Yellow Cab Counsel George F. Barrett described the fire to a reporter as "vandalism" and claimed that the attack was a direct attempt to intimidate Hertz because of his connection with the cab company.

When Checker Taxi officials were confronted with questions about the fire and its possible connection to the Taxi Wars, they denied any involvement and blamed "turf enemies" of John Hertz. "The Checker company is in no-wise concerned in any so-called war, nor is it to be blamed for the violent activities of gangsters, race horse racketeers, bootleggers and the crooked political element of this city and county," they announced, conveniently overlooking the fact that the president of Checker Taxi had recently been ordered to serve jail time for witness- and jury-tampering in support of his gangster brother.

The Raid on Checker Taxi

A little more than twenty-four hours after the fire at Hertz's stable, Robert E. Crowe was ready to strike at Checker Taxi. He had been investigating the fire for the past day, during which time he had discovered what he described as "important new angles" in the case. Acting on his authority as state's attorney, on Tuesday night, Crowe ordered a raid on the Checker headquarters. Six police patrols descended on the building, confiscating and carrying out hundreds of boxes containing all of the company's records, and delivered them to the criminal courts building for review. During their search of the Checker offices, police also confiscated two shotguns and three revolvers.

Checker attorneys Albert and Cook were outraged and immediately appeared before a judge demanding the legal justification for the raid and subsequent records seizure, claiming Crowe lacked the authority to open a grand jury investigation on his own. On top of this, they again repeated their accusation that Crowe was financially invested in Yellow Cab and therefore biased in his decision-making. Albert and Cook then went a step further, writing an open letter to Crowe which they distributed to the press. "In your indignant outburst over the barn burning and the Yellow Cab garage bombings, you make no mention of any intention to indict and prosecute the cold-blooded killers of [Checker driver] Eugene Thivierge," the letter asserted. "While Mrs. Hertz weeps publicly for her beloved race horses, Mrs. Eugene Thivierge sorrows in silence and obscurity for her breadwinner and husband."

The letter went on to disparage Crowe's character while denying any existence of a Taxi War. The company also took out a large ad on page 20 of the *Chicago Tribune* refuting the accusations against them.

> Please let us register this big fact first, last and always. There is no "taxi war." What fools we would be, as stockholder-drivers of these cabs of ours, to engage in a "war" with the cabs operated by a mammoth corporation. . . . This talk of a "taxi war" is, in our opinion, propaganda engineered to hurt our business.

The ad insisted (incorrectly) that no Checker driver or officer of the company had ever been arrested or charged with any act of violence. Despite Checker Taxi's assertions in this ad and the open letter to Crowe, the chairman of the City Council's local transportation committee introduced a resolution to address the newest outbreak of the Taxi Wars. It read, in part: "If this situation is permitted to continue, it will undoubtedly lead to murder and other violent crimes which will menace life and property in Chicago and will especially endanger the public patronizing cabs."

It still remained unclear to police whether or not a fresh battle in the Taxi War had officially been declared. The following day, however, a judge sided with Albert and Cook, saying that Crowe's records seizures amounted to "practical theft." Two days after the records had been removed from the Checker offices, the judge demanded they be returned, on the basis that the seizure was "clearly illegal without a court order." Following the ruling, Checker leaders Bob McLaughlin, Max Raifman, and Harry Gordon posed for press photos holding stacks of documents that had been confiscated and then returned, each man wearing a different expression: McLaughlin looking smug, Raifman looking threatening, and Gordon looking extremely nervous.

However, the Checker Taxi officials were not content to merely accept their win in the courts. Instead, Albert and Cook then asked the judge to open an official grand jury investigation into the alleged Taxi Wars, in the hopes that such an investigation would clear the company's name. To ensure fairness, they requested that the judge remove Crowe from the process and appoint a special state's attorney. The judge granted part of their request, ordering the state's attorney's office to open a proper and official grand jury investigation, but he declined to remove Crowe.

GETTING TO THE TRUTH: A GRAND JURY INVESTIGATION

As Checker went on the counteroffensive, the threats to John Hertz and his family multiplied. By the time the judge ordered the grand jury investigation, Hertz was no longer asserting that the fire was accidental. He confessed that he had continued to receive threats to his life and property following the fire. The day after the grand jury investigation was ordered, a mailman discovered what appeared to be two sticks of dynamite near the offices of the Chicago Motor Coach Company, where Hertz served on the board of directors. Upon close examination, however, these were discovered to be dummies. At the same time, Hertz also went to the police to report that he had received threats to his life, as well as a warning that his five-year-old grandson would be kidnapped.

When the grand jury convened on Friday, October 19, the prosecutor—assistant state's attorney George Gorman—opened the proceedings by inviting Checker Taxi attorneys Albert and Cook to present their complaints. This was the moment they had been waiting for, and the reason they had advocated for this investigation in the first place. Albert and Cook opened by accusing the city of favoritism toward Yellow Cab, citing the Department of Vehicle Bureau's refusal to issue city cab stand permits to Checker taxis, despite having accepted payment for them. Checker president Bob McLaughlin entered into evidence a handwritten receipt from 1926 that he claimed proved he had paid for cab stand permits for all Checker taxis. He said that despite taking the money, the city didn't grant the permits.

A representative from the vehicle bureau admitted that he had not issued any cab stand permits to Checker Taxi, but explained that this was due to Checker's refusal to comply with the city regulations, specifically the regulation requiring that the name of the owner be prominently displayed on the side of the car. The vehicle bureau representative flatly denied ever accepting any money, offering any kind of receipt, or even interacting with Checker leaders in person.

As Cook and Albert argued their case, Checker's internal disputes suddenly roared to life once again. While the Cook County state's attorney was hearing testimony from Checker leaders in the city's court system, on Tuesday, October 24, three Checker driver-shareholders presented a separate petition to a federal judge. In it, they accused McLaughlin, along with Raifman, Gordon, and treasurer Barney Mitchell, of conspiring with automobile manufacturers and gasoline companies to receive illegal "kickback" payments in exchange for Checker Taxi's business. The federal judge considering the petition described the accusations as the "most savage ever made before him," and ordered a hearing into the matter.

The grounds upon which the three men brought their petition to the federal judge involved a pending lawsuit against Checker Taxi. About a year earlier, a business officially known as the "Checker Cab Company of New Jersey" sued the Checker Taxi Company of Chicago for $1.5 million for an alleged breach of contract. (Today the lawsuit would be the equivalent of around $26 million.) That case was still pending in the courts. Those not closely following the taxi industry might have thought it was unusual that a cab company in New Jersey would sue a cab company in Chicago. But in fact, the "Checker Cab Company of New Jersey" was a well-known player in the Chicago taxi industry: From February 28, 1923, this (somewhat misleading) moniker had been one of the official business names of the Checker Cab Mfg. Co. of Kalamazoo, Michigan, owned and operated by Morris Markin. And now, with this lawsuit, he was trying once again to take back effective control of Checker Taxi from the gangsters who had usurped it from him in 1926.

CHAPTER 12

Put It in the Rearview

The End of the Taxi Wars (1928–1932)

SINCE BOB MCLAUGHLIN HAD TAKEN OVER CHECKER TAXI IN 1926, ousting Markin's ally Joseph Wokral from the presidency, Markin had been cooling his heels and playing a long game. Markin realized that a cab manufacturing company was dependent on taxi companies to keep it profitable; no one else would buy a cab. Early on, he also understood that having effective leadership control of Checker Taxi ensured a steady demand for his cabs, under the most favorable terms for his business. The phrase "vertical integration" was not yet commonplace, but Markin understood the concept well. However, when McLaughlin staged his takeover at Checker Taxi, Markin lost this piece of vertical integration, and so he continued a quiet campaign to regain control. The $1.5 million breach-of-contract lawsuit he filed against Checker Taxi in October of 1927 represented a new move in Markin's chess game to control the taxi industry, and by extension, ensure steady business to the Checker Cab Mfg. Co. At the heart of the lawsuit was an accusation of graft.

Shortly after Markin's ally Goldstein had been elected president in 1923, he had signed a contract with the Checker Cab Mfg. Co., agreeing to purchase all of the new Checker cabs from Markin's company for a period of five years. In the lawsuit, however, Markin alleged that since 1926, Checker Taxi officials had been demanding that he pay them a $200 "commission" on each cab he delivered to a Checker driver. If he did not pay the commission, the company would not approve the cab for use in its fleet. When Markin refused to pay these kickbacks, Checker leaders failed to uphold their end of the purchasing contract, instead sending their drivers to buy cabs from auto dealers who would pay the commissions.

It took nearly a year after Markin first filed the lawsuit for this strategy to begin to bear fruit. Following the initial, week-long grand jury investigation into the Taxi Wars in October 1928, the jury members found the evidence of improper business dealings by Checker Taxi leadership compelling. Seeking more information, they asked the judge to order the confiscation of the company's records again, this time legally. In response, the chief justice of the Cook County courts ordered police to once again impound the company's records dating back to 1924, and named an impartial accounting firm to audit them. The grand jury also recommended a continuance of its investigation, to commence the following month, when Robert E. Crowe would be replaced as state's attorney by John A. Swanson, who had defeated Crowe in the recent election. In requesting the continuance of the grand jury investigation, the jury members explained that they had "heard only part of the evidence, but enough to convince us that unfair and bitter competition between the Yellow Cab Company and the Checker Taxi Company has resulted in such crimes as murder, arson and assault with intent to commit personal injury and property damage."

The independent firm completed the audit of Checker's records the day before Thanksgiving, and the judge indicated that he planned to turn over the results to Swanson on his first day in office on December 3. Before the judge had a chance to do that, however, the lawsuit between Markin's Checker Cab Mfg. Co. and McLaughlin's Checker Taxi Company came up before federal judge James H. Wilkerson in the federal courts building.

In the past month, several additional driver-shareholders had filed petitions with Wilkerson accusing McLaughlin and the other leaders of graft, and seeking to join Markin's lawsuit against the company. They alleged that McLaughlin and company officials had been manipulating the drivers and taking illegal kickbacks on the sale of not just taxis, but also gasoline and taximeters, pocketing the money for their own personal use. Judge Wilkerson took the allegations seriously, and convened a federal hearing to consider the complaints. To oversee the hearing, he appointed a master in chancery, Thomas J. Peden. With Peden set to open the hearing, it became clear that McLaughlin's steel grip on the Checker drivers was coming loose.

Graft, Influence, and an Accusation of Murder: The Opening of the Federal Hearing

The federal hearing opened the last week in November in the Chicago Federal Building in the Loop, a grand, Beaux-Arts structure topped with an eight-story gilt dome. The first day, Peden heard testimony from two of the petitioners—driver-shareholders Herman Friedman and Ross Ancelone—who described a company culture at Checker Taxi that forced drivers to purchase gasoline only from company-approved garages, despite a 1-cent markup over free-market gas stations. They also described how drivers were only allowed to purchase new vehicles from those auto dealers or manufacturers who had agreed to pay kickbacks to Checker leadership in exchange for their business. Additionally, Friedman and Ancelone alleged that when they spoke out against these practices, Checker leaders defrauded them of their stock in the company and forced them out.

By testifying in federal court that day, Friedman and Ancelone displayed courage. Friedman's wife, Rose, told the judge that she had received phone calls at their home from an anonymous caller who said that her husband would be shot if he testified. She also claimed that Checker Taxi vice president Harry Gordon had offered her $50 per week if she could convince her husband to withdraw his petition to join Markin's lawsuit. This claim was reinforced by the fact that two other men who had initially filed petitions had indeed withdrawn them, with little explanation.

However, Friedman could not be intimidated. So instead, the Checker leadership attempted to raise questions about his character and his motivation in filing the petition. Another driver-shareholder went to the judge and claimed that he had recently been approached by Markin. The driver claimed Markin had promised him a role in the new Checker leadership if he would file a petition against McLaughlin and the current leaders. He played along with the scheme, he said, to gather evidence of the plot. The driver claimed that Markin "wanted to be king of the Checker cab business," and that several men were complicit in the plot, including Friedman. Additional names he mentioned in connection with this plot included a member of the International Brotherhood of Teamsters, an attorney named Price, and former Checker president Emanuel Goldstein.

However, these accusations did not dissuade the judge from the seriousness of the graft charges against McLaughlin. He ordered Peden to continue hearing testimony on these charges. Next on the stand was a sales manager for a North Side auto dealership, who testified that he had been forced to pay a $100 "commission" to a Checker Taxi official to get a car approved by the company as an acceptable vehicle for one of the Checker drivers to purchase. His testimony seemed to corroborate the complaint in Markin's original lawsuit against the company.

Then, on November 28, the courtroom drama multiplied exponentially. On the schedule to testify that day was Max Raifman, the current secretary of Checker Taxi whose involvement with the seamier side of the business dated to at least 1923, when he was accused, with Jack Rose, of murdering Checker Taxi road supervisor and union slugger Frank Sexton. Back then, Raifman had given testimony that indicated he was working for Markin in the factional disputes at Checker. But since that time, he had switched sides and strongly allied himself with McLaughlin. Raifman had been acquitted on the 1923 murder charge, but he had not forgotten it. It was certainly on the top of his mind that day, as the hearing would reveal.

Over the course of the day's testimony, as Raifman answered questions regarding the current graft accusations, he became more and more agitated at the line of questioning directed at him by Markin's attorney, Paul L'Amoreaux. In an attempt to deflect the graft accusations, Checker Taxi attorneys Cook and Albert had already filed a complaint against L'Amoreaux's firm, accusing the attorney of exerting undue influence over Checker driver-stockholders and coercing them into joining Markin's lawsuit in the first place. Then, as Raifman became more and more angry at the questions posed to him by L'Amoreaux, he doubled down on attacking the attorney. First, he accused L'Amoreaux of corruption, claiming that the attorney had been making payments to former Checker Taxi president Emanuel Goldstein on behalf of Markin since 1923. "I have seen you give him money many times," Raifman said. "You paid him money and [then] he testified falsely, so it must have been paid for that purpose."

On the stand, Raifman continually denied the graft charges against the company, saying that no kickbacks were demanded or accepted on gasoline, automobiles, or taximeters. Becoming increasingly frustrated, Raifman then began shouting about what he perceived to be the injustice of the hearing. "There is an influence somewhere to discredit the Checker Taxi Company and to disrupt it!" he yelled. "I noticed every time charges are made in the newspaper, the Yellow Cab Company comes out with an advertisement that it is trustworthy. It ought to be stopped—these foolish questions!"

By the afternoon, Raifman's patience had completely run out, just as L'Amoreaux began asking questions designed to needle at Raifman's past arrest record. "I have paid money to you, haven't I?" L'Amoreaux asked him. "I paid for your bonds and attorney fees." At the mention of this, Raifman exploded in anger, and shouted words that stopped the hearing cold. "Yes, but I saved you from a murder rap!" he yelled at L'Amoreaux, appearing to reference Frank Sexton's 1923 murder. "I have kept quiet about this for a long time, but I will tell it now if you want me to." L'Amoreaux invited him to continue. "You would have been indicted for murder, Mr. L'Amoreaux, if it hadn't been for me. I saved your neck and Markin's! I took the rap myself."

Raifman's accusation of murder against the attorney questioning him was a shocking turn of events in the hearing, and it threw the courtroom into an uproar. Peden was forced to adjourn for the day. Exiting the courtroom past a line of reporters, L'Amoreaux simply shrugged off the accusations against him. "There is nothing to it," he told them. Raifman's testimony that day made it clear he no longer held any allegiance to Markin, but it failed to reveal the circumstances, which had led him to switch his support to Bob McLaughlin, where it clearly remained.

KICKBACKS AND ALIASES: THE FEDERAL HEARING, CONTINUED

Over the next week, following this bombshell accusation in the courtroom, the hearing shifted to more prosaic territory: money. At the heart of the graft charges was the accusation that Checker Taxi officials had been demanding illegal payments in exchange for their business, so L'Amoreaux began methodically tracing the whereabouts of the alleged kickback payments. He asked the judge to summon a man named Walter Fesselmeyer, director of personnel at Checker Taxi and the person in charge of cab approvals for the company. Under oath, Fesselmeyer testified that he had in fact asked the sales manager of a car dealership to make out a check for $100 to "Jack Friedman," saying that was the first name that popped into his head. The sales manager in question had previously testified that he understood the payment to be necessary to gain the company's approval of a car sold to a Checker driver. L'Amoreaux then showed the check to Fesselmeyer, showing him the endorsement signature reading "Jack Friedman" on the back. Under questioning, Fesselmeyer declared that he couldn't say whether or not the signature was in his own handwriting.

In fact, as L'Amoreaux had made clear earlier in the hearing that day, between April of 1927 and October of 1928, "Jack Friedman" had received at least $140,000 worth of payments, or nearly $2.5 million in today's money. The funds had been held in an account under the fictitious Friedman's name at the West Side Trust and Savings Bank. The account had been closed just a few weeks earlier, shortly before the federal hearing began. Under questioning, another car dealership employee connected the "Jack Friedman" account to Sidney "Shorty" Gordon, a salesman for the United States Taximeter Company and the brother of Checker Taxi vice president Harry Gordon. When L'Amoreaux questioned Fesselmeyer, the director of personnel, about Shorty Gordon's involvement, Fesselmeyer was cagey. "I may and I may not have given [the check] to him," he testified. "I cannot recall. My mind is hazy on this." Fesselmeyer's hedging angered Peden, who ordered the US district attorney to recommend a charge of perjury against him.

A few days later, Fesselmeyer took the stand again to "correct" his original testimony. This time, he positively identified Sidney "Shorty"

Gordon as "Jack Friedman," holder of the bank account. He explained that Gordon had instructed him to have the check made out in Friedman's name. The vast majority of those checks made out to "Jack Friedman" amounted to payments of $100 or less. In just under eighteen months, these payments had added up to $140,000, implying a wide-ranging scheme of graft.

With the evidence stacking up against the current leaders of the Checker Taxi Company, attorneys Albert and Cook complained to the judge that the court was being "overzealous" in investigating the charges. "You cannot collect a great fund like this without reporting to the United States government," the judge retorted. He pointed out that the mere fact that Checker failed to disclose the additional "Jack Friedman" income on its tax returns the previous year justified the investigation. "There appears to be a very serious conspiracy to defraud the United States," he went on. "The officers of this court cannot be overeager to emphasize that phase of the investigation."

By this point in the hearing, L'Amoreaux had successfully proven that Checker Taxi officials had been requiring kickback payments from car dealerships and taximeter companies, so the next phase of the trial turned to the third aspect of the scheme: extortion of gasoline companies. On Friday, December 7, L'Amoreaux called J. L. Stone to the stand. Stone was the former head of the United Petroleum Company, an oil company that was allegedly connected to Checker's grafting scheme. However, when Stone took the stand, he refused to answer any questions. Peden reported him to the judge, who rescheduled his testimony for a later date and ordered him placed in the custody of US marshals. Later that day, it became clear that L'Amoreaux may have simply called the wrong oil company official to testify—Stone's former partner, R. L. Eggert, proved to be more than willing to share his knowledge about the kickback scheme with reporters covering the day's hearing. According to Eggert, the United Petroleum Company had entered into a contract to serve as the sole provider of gasoline to Checker garages, marking up the gas price by a little more than 1 cent per gallon over the free-market rates. In exchange for this contract, United Petroleum then offered McLaughlin a "rebate" of 1¾ cents on every gallon of gas purchased by the company.

Eggert claimed that the rebate payments came in the form of checks made out to Checker vice president Harry Gordon.

As the hearing continued into the middle of December, L'Amoreaux's strategy to methodically undermine the power of McLaughlin, Raifman, Gordon, and treasurer Barney Mitchell was proving successful. On December 12, a Checker driver named James De Guida took the stand and testified that he and other Checker drivers had been intimidated into submission as far back as 1923, when McLaughlin had hired four sluggers to threaten and punish any drivers who sided with Markin during the run-up to that year's shareholder's election. When L'Amoreaux asked De Guida why he had declined an invitation from Markin at that time to attend a "business conference," De Guida replied that he "was afraid of the sluggers." On the stand, De Guida named two of those sluggers: gangster Danny Stanton and Mitters Foley. The men were two of the six who had been arrested shortly after that election for the murders of Israel Rappart and Leo Gistenson, which took place during the shift of power when Markin's ally Goldstein first assumed the presidency.

In an attempt to counter this potentially damning testimony against the current Checker Taxi president, the company attorney Albert presented a petition signed by twenty-three hundred current Checker drivers requesting that the present officers of the company be allowed to continue in office. Presumably, Albert meant this as a show of confidence from the driver-shareholders, intended to demonstrate their loyalty to McLaughlin, Gordon, Raifman, and Mitchell. However, the drivers' motivations in signing the petition were unclear. It's possible this petition, rather than countering De Guida's testimony, in fact inadvertently reinforced it.

The next day, two more Checker drivers took the stand against McLaughlin and company, testifying that when they went to an auto dealership to finance the purchase of their vehicles, they had been charged exorbitant interest rates—some in excess of 25 percent—by the Imperial Acceptance Finance Corporation. Further investigation revealed that the Imperial Acceptance Finance Corporation was overwhelmingly concerned with these predatory loans to Checker Taxi drivers, which made up more than 90 percent of Imperial's business. On top of that, Sidney "Shorty" Gordon was revealed to be a major stockholder in the Imperial Acceptance Finance Corporation. Both of the drivers further testified that they had been threatened by the current leadership for daring to speak up about this injustice. "I squawked about it," one of them said. "Max Raifman . . . called me in and told me not to talk so much, or something would happen," he went on, adding that he had also been threatened by McLaughlin himself just the previous day. Both men testified that they had arrived to work to find their cars chained in the company garage.

Nowhere Left to Hide

For the past four years, through murderous attacks on the Checker headquarters, targeted shootings of Checker employees like Lefty Wright and Harry Morley, the cold-blooded murder of Joseph Wokral, and the bombing of a jury foreman's house, McLaughlin and the other men now in charge of Checker Taxi had escaped any real accountability. But that was about to end. Finally, after many days of hearing testimony, it was time for the Checker Taxi leaders to take the stand. First, L'Amoreaux questioned vice president Harry Gordon, but he refused to answer questions on Fifth Amendment grounds. Then, the following day, McLaughlin took the stand. L'Amoreaux began by questioning him on his decision, made just three weeks earlier, to suddenly attempt to settle the lawsuit brought against Checker Taxi by Markin's Checker Cab Mfg. Co. L'Amoreaux seemed to be inferring that McLaughlin had become eager to resolve the lawsuit to avoid the very federal hearing in which they were now engaged and, perhaps, to avoid being called to the stand to testify. No sooner had L'Amoreaux begun asking questions than Checker attorney Cook began interrupting both L'Amoreaux and the master in chancery, Peden, raising objections and generally disrupting the hearing. Peden became outraged at Cook's behavior. "I'll certify you to Judge Wilkerson," he warned Cook. "I want you to shut up."

"I won't shut up!" Cook countered. "I want you to certify me."

"Furthermore," Peden continued, "I'll have you excluded from this hearing if you do not conduct yourself differently."

Peden adjourned the hearing for the weekend, as Cook continued to argue. Still angry on Monday, Peden did in fact escalate the matter to Judge Wilkerson, who determined that Cook's behavior was "grossly improper." However, his behavior may have been advantageous to his client as well, successfully distracting from McLaughlin's testimony, and removing McLaughlin's need to invoke his Fifth Amendment rights. Raifman and Barney Mitchell, who took the stand after McLaughlin, were not so lucky. Under questioning both men denied the general charges of graft, but on more detailed questioning, they repeated a similar phrase many times: "I refuse to answer on the ground that, in my opinion, it might tend to incriminate me or degrade me." No one reading about the Checker leaders' testimony in the newspaper that night could have doubted that the men were at least partially complicit in the graft they had been accused of. It was a modest victory for L'Amoreaux and Markin, but one which would have long-reaching effects.

The Removal of Bob McLaughlin

Although it would be several more years before McLaughlin and company finally tumbled from their post atop the power structure of Checker Taxi, in many ways, this hearing—and the breach of contract lawsuit that had inspired it—proved the beginning of the end of the group's iron grip on the company. For more than a month, news of the hearing had been an almost daily occurrence in the city's newspapers. Every day, McLaughlin, Gordon, Raifman, and Mitchell appeared less and less trustworthy to the public, while the company itself appeared more toxic and dysfunctional. The act of bringing the allegations of graft to light before a federal judge seemed only to empower and embolden those Checker Taxi drivers who had been cowed and intimidated by these men for so long. While Checker leaders continued to threaten the drivers even as the hearing progressed—on December 27, one driver complained to the judge that Raifman had told him "the healthiest thing you can do is keep your mouth shut"—Checker's once defeated driver-shareholders were proving increasingly willing to speak out against McLaughlin and company.

Then, on Saturday, December 29, while the hearing was still under way, the Checker Taxi board of directors announced that Bob McLaughlin had voluntarily stepped down as president of the company and would be replaced by a South Side banker and politician, Thomas J. Healy, whose duties would encompass those of the president of the board of directors as well as general manager of the taxi business. Healy's appointment was an admission of the toll the federal hearing was taking on public perception of Checker Taxi. In announcing Healy's new role, attorney Albert explained that "at this crisis in its affairs, [the Checker Taxi Company] needs a Landis to prove to the public the company is operated on the square." (This was a reference to Kenesaw Mountain Landis, the US federal judge who also served as the first commissioner of baseball beginning in 1920, and helped to bring respectability to the sport following the famous "Black Sox" scandal.) McLaughlin's willingness to step down as president at that critical moment may also have been a strategic decision on his part to temporarily maintain a lower profile and keep his name out of the newspapers while the hearing focused the spotlight on Checker Taxi's illegal business methods.

After more than six weeks of testimony, the federal hearing finally concluded the third week of January 1929. Master in Chancery Peden then spent another month compiling a report on the hearing to present to the judge. When Peden's report landed on Judge Wilkerson's desk in the middle of February 1929, it minced no words. The first of five major recommendations in the report read, in part:

> The master finds that there has been gross mismanagement of the affairs of the company and an extravagant and illegal expenditure of its funds by its officers and directors, and therefore recommends that appropriate action be taken to correct the evils, mismanagement, misuse and misapplication of funds by the officers and directors of the company.

Peden went on to recommend that the court should take steps to "institute and install . . . efficient business methods and systems" and concluded in no uncertain terms that the current officers of Checker

Taxi were indeed engaged in schemes of illegal graft. It was the end of McLaughlin and company escaping the consequences of their actions.

At the conclusion of the hearing, Judge Wilkerson had ultimately allowed Markin's breach-of-contract lawsuit to stand, as the court awaited Peden's final report and recommendation. The Checker Taxi board of directors knew that the company could not afford to pay the $1.5 million in damages sought, and this meant that if his lawsuit succeeded, Markin would soon be in a position to request that the company be put into receivership. In fact, this was the very strategy Markin had used nine years earlier to gain control of the Lomberg Auto Body Company, a move that had ultimately formed the Checker Cab Mfg. Co. It was an effective strategy, but one that worked at the often glacial pace of the US court system. So to hedge his bets, Markin had also begun quietly acquiring stock in Checker Taxi through a recently purchased subsidiary company. Although it would take a few years and the worst stock market crash in the history of the country, Markin would eventually hold a majority of the stock of the Checker Taxi Company, and in 1932, Bob McLaughlin and his associates were finally removed from power permanently, replaced by a familiar name from Checker Taxi's past: Michael Sokoll.

JOHN HERTZ RETIRES FROM THE TAXI BUSINESS

Following the devastating fire at his stable, John Hertz took stock of what remained of his beloved Leona Farms, his world-class thoroughbred breeding and training program. Although he tried to appear unflappable in the press, the violent events of the autumn of 1928 had shaken him. Hertz's concern went beyond the loss of personal property and the tragic death of eleven horses. In the aftermath of the fire and the subsequent grand jury investigation, Hertz had continued to receive threats against himself and his family.

Hertz's businesses had proved vulnerable to attack as well, as evidenced by the bombings of the Yellow Cab garages, as well as a new outbreak of violence in front of the famed jazz cafe The Green Mill that left at least one Yellow Cab with a bullet hole in its windshield. Adding strain to Hertz's position was the fact that he was forced to navigate these incidents without the companionship and advice of his longtime friend and second-in-command, Charlie Gray. Hertz had tried to step away from the day-to-day management of Yellow Cab, only to be drawn back in the previous Christmas by Gray's death, and his friend's absence surely weighed on Hertz's mind as he contemplated the future of his involvement at Yellow Cab. Hertz was about to turn fifty, and he had amassed a huge personal fortune by revolutionizing the taxi industry in its earliest years of development. He owned homes in Chicago; Cary, Illinois; and Miami Beach. He held a diversified portfolio of business interests. At that very moment, Hertz was also in talks to purchase Arlington Park Race Track with a group of similarly sports-minded businessmen from Chicago and the East Coast. It had become clear that Chicago's taxi industry was a business where you could lose everything, including your life. And these days, Hertz had a lot to lose.

And so, the man who had first partnered with Walden Shaw to come up with a simple yet brilliant new idea—automobile livery using vehicle trade-ins—reached out through mutual business connections to his former rival, Morris Markin, to inquire about selling his stock in Yellow Cab, the company he had conceived and helped found fourteen years earlier. On January 8, 1929, while the federal hearing into Checker Taxi was still under way, an item in the business section of the *Chicago Tribune* carried the headline, "Hertz, Builder of Taxi Service, Sells Holdings: Yellow Cab Co. Chief Will Retire." The news was picked up and carried in papers around the country. Hertz also stepped down from the Yellow Cab board of directors. It took several more months and a complicated transfer of stock designed to deter market panic, but by the end of the year, all of John Hertz's Yellow Cab stock was controlled by Morris Markin, who emerged from the deal the majority shareholder in Chicago's Yellow Cab Company. It was the end of a very contentious era, and the beginning of a business monopoly.

Markin's Triumph

As Markin solidified his control of Chicago's two largest cab companies, Checker Taxi and Yellow Cab, he also managed to acquire the city's third-largest cab company, so that by the end of 1932, Markin and his allies controlled 86 percent of the city's cab market. And just like that, Chicago's bloody Taxi Wars, which had gripped the city throughout the late 1910s and the 1920s, claiming so many lives and inspiring so much terror across the city, came to a screeching halt.

Markin's outstanding legal troubles, namely his conviction for violating the Blue Sky Laws in 1922, had disappeared as well. For five years, Markin had successfully postponed serving his thirty-day prison sentence from that conviction. Finally, in December of 1928, as Markin's attorney Paul L'Amoreaux faced off with Checker Taxi officials in the city's federal courts building, Illinois governor Len Small announced that he would pardon Markin for the 1922 offense. Small, who had been indicted during his term for embezzlement and money-laundering, and was later accused of patronage and jury tampering in securing his own acquittal, issued the pardon as one of his last acts in office. Markin was once again a free man with no federal record.

Eventually, Markin's business success reached well beyond Chicago and Kalamazoo; through his many mergers and acquisitions, he eventually ended up in control of major taxi fleets in New York City, Pittsburgh, Minneapolis, and Cleveland as well. By the early 1950s, at the height of his business empire, Markin was the most powerful taxi owner in the country, operating more taxis than any other person or organization. Almost all of them were built by his Checker Cab Mfg. Co., ensuring a steady stream of business to the company he had founded in 1922 after foreclosing on a loan. In fact, Markin's business expansion sometimes seemed nearly limitless—well into the second half of the twentieth century, he continued to make and operate taxis, adding to his vast empire the operation of airport limousine, bus, baggage handling, fuel, and insurance companies as well. When he died in 1970, Markin's understated obituary said simply that he "ran Checker Motors and subsidiaries," and gave no hint that he had once had a front-row seat to Chicago's dramatic and deadly Taxi Wars. By then, they were nearly forgotten.

Afterword

Today, the modern taxi landscape has changed significantly since the era of the Taxi Wars. We no longer worry that our cab driver might be shot by a rival while taking us to the airport, or dinner, or the theater. In cities throughout the country, there are longstanding regulations that govern the industry, and many of those regulations trace their origins back to this contentious (and sometimes dangerous) early period of transportation history. Anyone who has ever stepped into a taxi with the company's name clearly identified on the outside of the vehicle, or stared at a placard in the backseat identifying the cab number, the driver, and the last city inspection date and status, and then gone on to pay a standardized, metered rate no matter the time of day, amount of traffic, or level of rider demand, has benefited from rules and regulations passed in Chicago in response to the Taxi Wars, and then adopted around the country. It is easy to forget that to achieve our modern expectations of taxi safety, fairness, and convenience, the blood of many had to be spilled on the streets.

When ride-hailing services first debuted in the United States in the past decade as a new breed of transportation company, they famously flouted many of these government rules regulating taxis, arguing that the world had changed and the rules were outdated. The ride-hailing companies simply refused to abide by them. (This professed "disruption" of the industry also had the added benefit of promising to put more money directly into the pockets of ride-hailing company investors.) Many riders, lured by the ease of modern technology and the initially low prices that these services offered, chose to overlook this rule-breaking. No matter that the cars were no longer inspected for safety by the city. No matter that the only background checks performed on the drivers were done by the companies themselves, if at all. No matter that the lack of a meter or regulated rates meant that at times of high demand, you could end up paying fifteen times the regulated taxi rate.

There's a popular adage that says you have to learn the rules before you can break them. As the Taxi Wars prove, we did learn the rules—the hard way. In some cases, the hardest way. Over the many decades that separate the appearance of the first automobile taxis on the streets of Chicago and the world we find ourselves in today, we have indeed learned the rules, but we have also forgotten what we learned. The stories of men like Walden Shaw, John Hertz, Charlie Gray, Ernest J. Stevens, Max Raifman, Joseph Wokral, Morris Markin, and Bob and Red McLaughlin form a riveting and often heartbreaking human drama. They also serve as a reminder of these hard-won lessons, and a warning of what happens when we fail to learn from past mistakes. As the playwright Eugene O'Neill (a contemporary of the Taxi Wars era) once wrote, "There is no present or future, only the past happening over and over again, now."

BODY COUNT

Although **Bob McLaughlin** stepped back from the presidency of Checker Taxi in December of 1928, his influence continued to loom over the company. By the end of 1929, when so many businesses had entered financial freefall or failed entirely following the stock market crash in October, McLaughlin was reinstated as Checker Taxi's president. However, earlier in the year, Markin had begun a quiet and concerted effort to acquire the majority of stock in the company. This effort was aided by the Great Depression, as more and more Checker drivers fell delinquent on their car payments to his Checker Cab Mfg. Co. and Markin acquired their owner shares. At the end of 1932, Markin finally succeeded in ousting McLaughlin for good.

McLaughlin went on to purchase a bar northwest of the Loop, where he reputedly ran a gambling operation as well. Ten years later, on Christmas Day 1942, a milkman discovered Bob McLaughlin's body, clubbed over the head and then shot to death, three bullet holes piercing his head and neck. His only surviving brother told police that McLaughlin had lived in fear of a gangland killing for over ten years; they suspected that he was murdered by remnants of Al Capone's gang, men who were running a rival gambling operation in the area. No one was ever convicted for his murder. He was forty-two years old.

McLaughlin's brother **Red** had met an even more untimely end. Appealing his prison sentence for the jewel heist, Red was released on a $15,000 bond in April of 1929 pending a new trial. However, before he could appear in court again, Red's checkered past caught up with him. On June 7, 1930, a tugboat lumbered through the Chicago Ship and Sanitary Canal in Summit, Illinois, just west of the city, and in its wake a fisherman spotted something bobbing to the surface. Arriving on the scene, police recovered the body of Red McLaughlin from the river. His hands had been tied behind his back with telephone wire, his body weighed down by 75 pounds of angle iron, and he had been shot twice in the head from behind, execution-style. No one was ever convicted for his murder. He was twenty-six years old.

Just a few months earlier, police had sought Red in connection with another murder related to the Checker Taxi Company, one that had hit very close to home. Late on the night of Wednesday, January 29, 1930, the four Checker Taxi officials who together ruled by intimidation—Bob McLaughlin, Howard Gordon, Max Raifman, and **Bernard J. "Barney" Mitchell**—spent the evening at McLaughlin's home to celebrate their host's birthday and wedding anniversary. Shortly before 3:00 a.m., the group ordered a cab to take Mitchell home to his wife, while the other three stayed behind. Mitchell never made it home. Less than a mile away from the party, the police found the cab that had picked up the Checker treasurer. Both Mitchell and the cab driver lay dead, shot by attackers inside the vehicle. In the immediate investigation that followed, the three remaining Checker officials proved uncooperative, and police failed to turn up any solid leads. Red McLaughlin, out on bail, was called in for questioning but released for lack of evidence. No one was ever punished for Mitchell's murder. He was thirty-three years old.

After Markin took back control of Checker Taxi in 1932, **Max Raifman** effectively disappeared. Leaving Chicago behind, he moved to Los Angeles with his wife, Lillian, and their daughter, Anita. After

Lillian died in 1947, Raifman married a second time. Despite once serving as a key player in the Taxi Wars, he went on to live a quiet life, keeping his name out of the newspapers for three decades until he died in L.A. in 1965. He was seventy years old.

Though he was never a major character in the Taxi Wars, onetime Yellow Cab garage supervisor **Al Weinshank** went on to great notoriety after leaving the company. During Prohibition, he became affiliated with the North Side gang headed by Dean O'Banion and then by Hymie Weiss. When Bugs Moran took over leadership of the gang, he financed Weinshank in opening a club and speakeasy called the Alcazar in Uptown. Weinshank eventually joined Moran's inner circle, entrusted with the presidency of one of Moran's profitable rackets. On February 14, 1929, Weinshank walked into a garage at 2122 N. Clark Street to meet with a bootlegger. Mistaking Weinshank for Moran, members of the rival gang headed by Al Capone followed him into the garage. Two of Capone's men were dressed as policemen, and they ordered Weinshank and the six other men present—including the Gusenberg brothers, who had been arrested in the wake of the 1928 Yellow Cab garage bombings and the fire at Leona Farms—to line up against a brick wall, before opening fire on the group with Thompson submachine guns. Everyone was killed. These cold-blooded murders would come to be known as the St. Valentine's Day Massacre. No one was ever convicted for the crime. Weinshank was thirty-five years old.

After deciding to shut down the taxi department of the Hotel La Salle in 1922, **Ernest J. Stevens** and his father went on to build one of the biggest and most luxurious hotels in the country, on Michigan Avenue across from Grant Park. Designed by their favorite architects, Holabird & Roche, the Stevens Hotel opened in 1927 and boasted three thousand guest rooms, making it the largest hotel in the country at that time. The massive building contained four dining rooms, a banquet room that could hold up to four thousand people, a gallery of exclusive shops, a five-lane bowling alley, a hospital, a twenty-seven-chair barbershop, a pharmacy, a twelve-hundred-seat movie theater, a miniature golf course, and an ice cream and candy factory, among other amenities. Ernest

J. Stevens was the primary planner of the new hotel, undoubtedly drawing on his years of experience managing the Hotel La Salle.

However, the arrival of the Great Depression caused the Hotel Stevens to falter financially. Just a few years after opening, the hotel was in danger of defaulting on its loans, so the Stevenses dipped into their personal finances, as well as the finances of the family's Illinois Life Insurance Company, to provide loans to keep the hotel afloat. It didn't work. In 1932, the Stevenses declared bankruptcy and found themselves facing a lawsuit from Illinois Life Insurance policyholders when they couldn't repay the loans they had made from their insurance company to their hotel venture. Facing a trial, Ernest's father, James W. Stevens, suffered a debilitating stroke. Shortly thereafter, overcome by financial and emotional distress, Ernest's brother Raymond committed suicide. So Ernest J. Stevens stood trial alone and was initially convicted of defrauding the policyholders. The following year, however, the Illinois state supreme court overturned the conviction. The dramatic legal experience had a lasting effect on one of Ernest J. Stevens's sons, John Paul Stevens, who would eventually go on to serve as a justice of the US Supreme Court for thirty-five years. Today, the Stevens Hotel is the Hilton Chicago, one of the largest and grandest flagships of the internationally famous Hilton hotel brand. Ernest J. Stevens died in 1972. He was eighty-seven years old.

Walden W. Shaw retired from the taxi industry by the end of 1920, before the most violent period of the Taxi Wars began. By 1930, Shaw and his wife, Jean, had relocated to their home in Pasadena, California, leaving the Lake Geneva estate to their daughter and her new husband. Shaw spent the remainder of his life focusing on his family, which grew to include six grandchildren and nine great-grandchildren, and died in 1962. He was eighty-three years old.

After selling all of his Yellow Cab stock and stepping down from the presidency and the board of directors, **John D. Hertz** went on to even greater business success than he had seen with Yellow Cab and Yellow Cab Manufacturing. Although Hertz had initially sold his "Hertz Drive-Ur-Self" concept to General Motors in 1926, the business continued to expand rental car access across the country, and eventually around the world. In 1932, the company opened the first airport rental car counter, at Chicago's Midway Airport.

In 1933, Hertz became a partner at Lehman Brothers investment bank. Throughout the 1930s and 1940s, his Leona Farms continued to experience great success in breeding thoroughbred racehorses. During World War II, Hertz's racehorse Count Fleet—whose sire, Kentucky Derby winner Reigh Count, had been rescued from the devastating Leona Farms stable fire in 1928—went on to win the Triple Crown. In 1953, Hertz bought back the rental car business bearing his name for $10.8 million, and by the time he retired two years later, Hertz Rent-A-Car had continued to flourish as an international industry leader, a position the company retains to this day. John Hertz died in 1961. He was eighty-two years old.

As he acquired more and more subsidiary companies, **Morris Markin** eventually changed the name of his Checker Cab Mfg. Co. to Checker Motors. By 1953, Checker was the only manufacturer still making five-passenger, purpose-built cabs. Having dominated the market of both cab manufacturing and taxi service, Markin then led Checker to an era of building and marketing non-taxi passenger vehicles. However, beginning as early as 1937, Markin's wild success invited a series of lawsuits against Checker Motors, and by the 1960s, rulings in various cities would crush Checker's taxi monopoly. Checker Motors ceased making cabs in 1982, but vintage Checkers still have a devoted following among collectors and automobile historians today. Markin died in 1970. He was seventy-seven years old.

Author's Note

I never met my grandfather, John Hertz Wellington Gray. He and my grandmother divorced in 1968, well before I entered the world, and in the aftermath of their marriage, he became estranged from the family. I grew up knowing only a handful of stories about him—how he was seriously wounded storming the beach on the tiny Pacific island of Tinian during World War II; how he learned to play the ukulele while recovering in a Honolulu hospital; how he nearly died on a golf course after returning stateside, when he was struck in the face by a golf ball. But there was one story about him that I found most affecting: On Christmas Day when my grandfather was just seven years old, his father left the house to go horseback riding in Chicago's Jackson Park, and never came home. My great-grandfather, Charles W. "Charlie" Gray, died in a freak riding incident that day, and what is supposed to be one of the happiest days of the year for a seven-year-old boy turned into one of the most tragic days of my grandfather's life.

I knew that Charlie Gray's death was officially ruled an accident. I knew that there had always been rumors in the family that this ruling was inaccurate. I also knew that he died at the height of a period known as the "Taxi Wars." Over the years, I wanted to know more about this chapter of Chicago history. The more I researched, the more complex the Taxi Wars revealed themselves to be. It's a story firmly rooted in its time and place—Chicago in the 1910s and 1920s. So it is not surprising that, as I dug further and further into the archives, I discovered a wide range of adjacent crimes: labor racketeering, corrupt politicians, voter intimidation, jury tampering, corporate graft, and plenty of Chicago gangsters with their Thompson submachine guns. Although she was just a young girl at the time, one of my grandfather's sisters even remembered people shooting at their house in an incident she understood to be related to the battle for cab company dominance.

And yet despite the drama of the Taxi Wars, this conflict is an aspect of Chicago history that has been almost entirely forgotten today. When I first started this project, I would tell people I was working on a book about the Taxi Wars in Chicago in the 1920s, and very few people I spoke with had ever heard of them. Despite the fact that the topic had become newly relevant in the twenty-first century with the introduction of ride-hailing services like Uber and Lyft, the struggles of the taxi industry in its infancy—struggles which had led to the very regulations these services were now attempting to overthrow—had mostly been lost to our collective cultural memory.

Because of this, I was delighted to find myself at the release party for my previous book chatting with my hostess's adult son. When he asked what my next project might be, I mentioned the Taxi Wars, expecting the usual blank look. Instead, his face lit up. "Oh, fascinating!" he said. "My great-grandfather founded the Yellow Cab Company in Chicago." I hadn't made the connection until that moment, but my hostess that evening was the granddaughter of Walden W. Shaw, and hearing about my interest in the topic, she offered me access to boxes of research she had collected on "Puppa Shaw's" business ventures from that time period. Later in my research, I discovered that Shaw and my own great-grandfather, Charlie Gray, had in fact been closely acquainted. I marveled at the series of events that had to happen to put their descendants in that room together nearly one hundred years later.

Over the thirteen or so years that the street battles raged in Chicago, the story of the Taxi Wars filled thousands of column inches in the city's daily newspapers. In this case, journalism truly was the first rough draft of history. Until now, it has been the only draft. In writing this book, I have tried to tell the full story: the shootings, the bombings, the mysterious accidents, the arrests and the trials, yes . . . but also the human stories. I tried to never forget that, for every man who was gunned down in the street, or surprised in his driveway by attackers, or ambushed in his office, there was a brother or a mother or a wife or, perhaps, a seven-year-old son waiting for him to come home on Christmas Day.

Acknowledgments

I could not have written this book without the support of many people. Thanks, first and foremost, to my parents, Thomas and Laurie Morrissy. They passed down a love of history and a talent for writing, and have provided unwavering support to me throughout my life and especially throughout this project. (The idea to write a book about the Taxi Wars can rightfully be credited to my mom.)

I am indebted to the following people, who provided advice, support, or invaluable connections, volunteering their time, talents, and tools to help me along the journey of writing this book: Sean Cannon, Keith Ulrich, Katie Weinert, Lauren Harrigan, and Steven Case.

My conscientious intern, Abby Foster, provided invaluable research assistance, without which I could not have finished the book in a timely manner.

I am also grateful for the thoughtful feedback provided to me by beta readers: Laurie Morrissy, Scott Kenemore, Zac Cassel, Nima Shirazi, Erin Eckert, Megan Buhr, Avani Narang, Catherine Clark, Amy Black, and Marion Baumgarten.

I am further indebted to the following people for additional research inspiration and assistance: Joy Phaphouvaninh, Wendy Singer, Nita Trapp, Lucy Reuter, and Michael Angelich.

Thanks to all the librarians and archivists who have helped me conduct research along the way, including Colleen and the research librarians at the Chicago History Museum, as well as the librarians at the Chicago Public Library (especially the Harold Washington branch, fifth-floor microfilm department), the Cook County Law Library, and the special collections department at the University of Illinois at Chicago.

Special thanks to Eugene Brissie at Lyons Press for seeing the potential in this story.

Very special thanks to the late Joy Rasin, her son Steve Rasin, and the entire Rasin family.

It would have been impossible to write this book without the digitization of countless newspapers. I am forever indebted to the thousands of librarians and archivists who have labored away in obscurity over the past two decades scanning and uploading old copies of newspapers. You are the true heroes of history.

Notes

A note on sources: Researching this nearly forgotten piece of Chicago history came with predictable challenges. After nearly one hundred years, some of the primary resources I would have loved to consult were simply no longer available: police and court records, business documents, anyone with a living memory of the era. Despite this, nothing in this book has been invented. Every fact, quote, and incident was reconstructed from newspaper articles, newsletters, contemporary interviews, published memoirs, summaries of court decisions, or modern academic research about the era. Everything that appears between quotation marks is quoted directly from one of these sources and cited appropriately in the following section. References regarding sensitive information, facts, or details that might be questioned or disputed are cited in this section as well.

In addition, census and vital records, city directories, and gravesite details were useful in providing background information about the main players in the Taxi Wars, and in verifying the most common spelling of the names of the supporting players. Dollar amount equivalencies were calculated using the Inflation Calculator on the U.S. Bureau of Labor Statistics website. I would also be remiss not to mention a series of particularly thorough articles about Yellow Cab, Checker Taxi, and Checker Cab Mfg. Co., written by Mark Theobald and published on *CoachBuilt. com* in 2004, which proved to be an invaluable resource for creating an outline of the Taxi Wars and finding additional research material.

INTRODUCTION

"hog butcher for the world": Carl Sandburg, "Chicago." Poetry (Poetry Foundation: 1914).

"stood at the peak of its economic power and influence": Neil Harris and T.J. Edelstein, *The Chicagoan: A Lost Magazine of the Jazz Age* (University of Chicago Press: 2008).

"extrovert of cities"; "never embarrassed, never apologizes, never blushes." Quoted in Neil Harris and T.J. Edelstein, *The Chicagoan: A Lost Magazine of the Jazz Age* (University of Chicago Press: 2008).

CHAPTER 1

"defying gusts of wind and low-hanging clouds…": "Buyers Throng City for Opening of Market Week," *Chicago Daily Tribune*, August 3, 1915.

"the Yellow Cab will be picked up on the street…"; "clean as a whistle…"; "The whole thing is an experiment…"; "every inducement to become courteous…": Yellow Cab ad, page 8, *Chicago Daily Tribune*, August 2, 1915.

"were in a condition which rendered travel vexatious…" and "millions of pounds of manure…": quoted in Greg Borzo, *Chicago Cable Cars*, (Arcadia Publishing, 2012).

"such a vulgar thing as a horse…": "Chicago As It Will Be One Hundred Years from Today, a City of Wonders Unbelievable," *Chicago Daily Tribune*, Dec. 12, 1897.

"practicable, self-propelling road carriage": Keith R. Gill, electronic *Encyclopedia of Chicago* entry for "Chicago Times-Herald Race of 1895" (Chicago History Museum: 2005).

"a better test of the utility…": "Duryea Wagon Is Winner," *Chicago Chronicle*, Nov. 28, 1895, 7.

"not to worry about money…": interview conducted by the author with Joy Peterkin Rasin, Nov. 15, 2019.

"on the theory that if there are going to be any road mishaps…": quoted in Mark Theobald, "Yellow Cab Manufacturing Company, 1919-1925; Yellow Cab Co. 1919-present; Chicago, Illinois" (*CoachBuilt. com*: 2004).

"Chicago has the most imposing automobile row…": "No Motor Row like Chicago's," *Chicago Daily Tribune*, Feb. 6, 1910, 66.

"to encourage all sports…"; **"unique mix of sports and clout"**: quoted in Lisa Holton, *For Members Only: A History and Guide to Chicago's Oldest Private Clubs*. (Lake Claremont Press: 2008), 190.

"single, highly urbanized venue…": Edward W. Wolner, *Henry Ives Cobb's Chicago*. (University of Chicago Press: 2011), 155.

"My first sight of America…"; **"My problem was that I had to eat…"**; **"stood in a long line…"**, **"Working nights, picking up a meal…"**; **"The doctor warned me…"**; **"I wouldn't have dared…"**; **"always considered the real turning point…"**; **"It was by chance…"**: Evan Shipman, *The Racing Memoirs of John D. Hertz as told to Evan Shipman*. (privately printed, 1954).

"waif's home"; **"good, plain food to eat"**: "The Newsboys' Home, to the Editor of the Chicago Tribune," *Chicago Tribune*, June 12, 1881, 16.

"so poor, and the soles of his shoes…": George Ade, *John Hertz, an appreciation*. (Miami, Fla.: privately printed by the Central Press, 1930).

"doubtless richly deserved"; **"I was as wild and untamed…"**; **"I was making fairly good money…"**; **"I was determined…"**; **"The main reason I succeeded…"**; **"As my customers weren't buyers of second-hand cars…"**; **"commissioned a local university…"**: B.C. Forbes and O.D. Foster, *Automotive Giants of America*, (New York: B.C. Forbes Publishing, 1926).

"the 'Contract Company'…": "The Taximeter in Chicago," *The Horseless Age*, Aug. 18, 1909.

"Company Will Operate 'Yellow Cab'…"; **"So we are making…"**: "Cut Rate Taxi at $2 an Hour, New Shaw Plan," *Chicago Tribune*, March 31, 1915, 3.

"When the Yellow Cab Company began operations…": "'Yellow' Backed By Our Service," *The Taxigram*, Vol. 4, Number 1, Sept. 2, 1920, 1.

"exclusive right to paint…": "Taxicab Companies Merge," *The Horseless Age*, Vol 29. May 29, 1912, 950.

"In London and in Paris…"; **"The taxicab companies in this city…"**: Department of Public Service Bureau of Valuation Statistics,

"Report on Taxicab Rates and Vehicle Traffic," (City of Chicago reports, Oct. 5, 1914).

"A Chicago taxi doesn't look like one...": "Our Own Travelogues," *New York Tribune*, Aug. 4, 1915, 7.

"World's Most Famous Restaurant": Neal Samors and Eric Bronsky, *Chicago's Classic Restaurants: Past, Present and Future*, (Chicago's Books Press, 2011), 37.

"Stink Bomb Hurled...": "Stink Bomb Hurled in Taxi War Hits Hotel," *Chicago Tribune*, Oct. 20, 1914, 13.

"The burden of expense..."; "afford every convenience...": Yellow Cab ad, *Chicago Examiner*, April 1, 1915, 7.

CHAPTER 2

"tower among men": "Life Story of Charles W. Gray," *The Taxigram*, Vol. 9, January 1928, 4.

"I didn't have a dime...", "I cannot afford it";: "Poor Man's Friend, Says Woodruff," *The Taxigram*, Vol. 9, January 1928, 15.

"It was by far the biggest...": "Big Night for Taxis," *Chicago Tribune*, Jan. 2, 1916, 9.

"no matter where they were...": "500 Taxicab Drivers Are Out On Strike," *The Inter Ocean*, April 5, 1910, 1.

"right of the city to pay..."; "their property was in danger...": "Pledges Support to Taxi Strikers," *Chicago Tribune*, June 20, 1910, 4.

"prohibiting the strikers...": "Labor Official is Denied Cell," *Chicago Tribune*, July 2, 1910, 4.

"a dearth of nonunion drivers": "Taxi Club Gives In to Striking Chauffeurs," *The Inter Ocean*, Sept. 2, 1910, 12.

"being disloyal to the company...": "Yellow Cab Blackboard," *Chicago Day Book*, June 28, 1916, 23.

"withdraw the finest taxicab service...": "Ten Cent Cut in Taxi Rate, Alderman's Plan," *Chicago Tribune*, March 14, 1915, 13.

"wearing a cap": "Bomb Exploded in Loop Near Hotel, Taxi War Blamed," *Chicago Examiner*, July 29, 1916, 3.

"We have evidence...": "Shaw Company Fights Against Bomb Throwers," *Chicago Tribune*, August 8, 1916, 18.

first automatic windshield wipers…: Gilbert Gorman and Robert E. Samuels, *The Taxicab: An Urban Transportation Survivor*, (University of North Carolina Press, 1982), 44.

"As rapidly as possible…": "Shaw Company Incorporates; Stock $900,000," *Chicago Tribune*, Dec. 28, 1916, 9.

"Our men are salesmen…": "Shaw Company Sells Interest to its Employees." *Chicago Tribune*, November 22, 1916, 11.

"strictly confidential"; "prompt pay…"; "We count among our assets": Ernest J. Stevens papers, Chicago History Museum, boxes 8 & 28.

"in the florid style…": "Ex-Wife Clings to Old Home of the Stevens Family in Faded South Side Residential Area," *Chicago Tribune*, March 26, 1933, 2.

"a single meal meant bankruptcy": David Lowe, *Lost Chicago*, (New York: American Legacy Press,) 1985, 120.

…rejecting the $12,000 per year…: "Asks Injunction of US Court in Taxicab War," *Chicago Tribune*, Sept. 28, 1919, 9.

CHAPTER 3

"purple cabs"; "A stranger would have imagined…": "Yellow Cabs and Purple Stage a War," *Chicago Tribune*, Jan. 9, 1917, 17.

"comfortable, easy-riding…": Ernest J. Stevens papers, Chicago History Museum, boxes 8 & 28.

"like sparrows": "Taxi Drivers Make War on Hotel's Private Line," *Chicago Herald*, January 9, 1917.

"no desire to monopolize…": Yellow Cab ad, *Chicago Tribune*, Jan. 10, 1917, 10.

"Such a thing might be all right…": "O'Shaw Taxi's," *Chicago Eagle*, March 10, 1917, 1.

"if it is not passed…"; "a few alderman…": "20 Cent Taxis Imperiled by Law Blockade," *Chicago Tribune*, March 15, 1917, 11.

"passage of this ordinance…": "Taxed to Death," *Chicago Eagle*, March 24, 1917, 1.

"We want to let you in on a secret..."; "Ninety Days Ago..."; "not that kind of businessman": Yellow Cab ad, *Chicago Tribune*, March 21, 1917, 4.

"riotous mob": "One Cop Quells Street Battle of Taxi Drivers," *Chicago Tribune*, Nov. 11, 1917, 12.

"The Yellow Cab has created...": Yellow cab ad, *Chicago Tribune*, Nov. 6, 1917, 7.

"No alderman rides free..."; "You can't talk..."; "Mr. Stevens, your remark..."; "The chauffeurs' union...": "Hotels Protest, But Cab Stands are Approved," *Chicago Tribune*, Nov. 22, 1917, 9.

"It seems to be the old trouble...": "Stink Bomb at Brevoort Hotel Taxi War Move," *Chicago Tribune*, Jan. 5, 1918, 1.

"They are 100 per cent more efficient...": "Negro Women Car Washers Take Men's Places in Chicago Plant," *Chicago Tribune*, Oct. 27, 1917, 3.

"Black Bohemia of crowded streets...": Quoted in Margaret Moos Pick, "Swinging on the South Side: The Heartbeat of Chicago Jazz," (riverwalkjazz.standford.edu: 2010), P2.

"Sporting Set": William Howland Kenney, *Chicago Jazz, A Cultural History, 1904-1930,* (Oxford University Press: 1993), 15.

"free-for-all": "Two Fights, Two Shots; Casualties, Ear and Finger," *Chicago Tribune*, March 20, 1918, 1.

"intense rivalry among the taxi drivers...": "Hotel LaSalle Guests in Panic Over Rumors of 'Mickey Finns,'" *Collyer's Eye*, July 6, 1918, 1.

"soliciting business away from a machine...": "Taxi Drivers Arrested in Front of Hotel La Salle," *Chicago Tribune*, July 1, 1918, 17.

"originated and developed...": "Can't Imitate Yellow Taxis, Court Ruling," *Chicago Tribune*, June 5, 1918, 8.

"All private [taxi] owners ...": "Manager of Yellow Cab Company States His Case," *Chicago Tribune*, June 10, 1918, 17.

"We are a success...": Yellow Cab ad, *Chicago Tribune*, Dec. 31, 1918, 8.

CHAPTER 4

"I would say you lie...": "Maclay Hoyne, Crime Fighter, Is Dead at 66," *Chicago Tribune*, October 2, 1939, 14.

"For Chicago, Thompson has meant filth...": "Thompson," *Chicago Tribune*, April 9, 1931, 14

"intoxicated by absurd ambitions...": Harry Elmer Barnes, *Hizzoner Big Bill Thompson: An Idyll of Chicago*, (Chicago: J. Cape and H. Smith, 1930), xiii.

"I protested to Sheriff Peters..."; "in police court..."; "that afternoon..."; "Stevens is romancing"; "The Yellows are out to get...": "Grand Jury to Look Into Taxi Warfare Today," *Chicago Tribune*, May 28, 1919, 19.

"through the maintenance of a coterie of sluggers..."; "I didn't think it was wise..."; "It looks to me...": "Hoyne Says He's 'In Middle' of Taxicab War," *Chicago Tribune*, June 5, 1919, 13.

"systematic war of intimidation...": "La Salle Driver Sues Yellows for $100,000," *Chicago Tribune*, June 10, 1919, 7.

"true in substance"; "slugging crew"; "no right to violate..."; "if they are guilty...": "Star No Shield to Taxi Feudist, Ettelson Rules," *Chicago Tribune*, July 25, 1919, 11.

"If you have never driven a cab...": Yellow Cab ad, *Chicago Tribune*, Feb. 3, 1920, 12.

"by early 1920s, the motorist...": Paul Barrett, *The Automobile and Urban Transit: The Formation of Public Policy in Chicago, 1900-1930*, (Philadelphia: Temple University Press) 1983, 132.

"didn't like Yellow Taxi...": "Dislikes Taxi Drivers, So He Shoots Up Cab," *Chicago Tribune,* March 4, 1919, 1.

"The Yellow Cab Company wants to be your father...": B.C. Forbes and O.D. Foster, *Automotive Giants of America*, (New York: B.C. Forbes Publishing, 1926), 152-153.

"When any of [the drivers] succumbs..."; "Before new drivers..."; "Every boss in the operating department...": "No Bosses from Swivel Chairs," *The Taxigram*, Vol. IV, Number 1, June 21, 1920, 1.

"Attention of drivers...": "The Blackboard," *The Taxigram*, Vol. III, Number 11, June 20, 1919, 4.

"just came back with bullet holes…": "Race Riot Zone, Seen from Taxi, Quiet, Ominous," *Chicago Tribune*, July 29, 1919, 3.

"taxi companies thrived": "Loop Is Cleared by 6:30; Crowds Lorry Home," *Chicago Tribune*, July 31, 1919, 7.

"gloom pervaded the Loop…"; "I don't think many of the places": "Loop's 'Flowing Bowl' Gives Way to Coffee Pot," *Chicago Tribune*, Oct. 30, 1919, 17.

"changing unions so frequently…"; "There's the big [expletive]…"; "Well, if you want to fight…"; "unprovoked"; "I recognized him…": "Geary Kills Again; Gets His Man and Escapes," *Chicago Tribune*, May 28, 1920, 1.

"rank miscarriage of justice"; "Yellow Cab was after me…": "Jurors Acquit Geary; Verdict Arouses Hoyne," *Chicago Tribune*, March 7, 1920, 1.

CHAPTER 5

"pimply-faced"; "throw up [their] hands"; "taking only the most valuable…": "'Amateur' Gang Gets $100,000 in Loop Store," *Chicago Tribune*, Dec. 9, 1919, 1.

"in great detail"; "alleged participation…"; "certain high-up officials": "Seek Motive of Cohns' charge against Abrams," *Chicago Tribune*, March 3, 1920, 2.

"wanted it robbed…"; "The confessions should be…"; "the whole affair is a frame-up…": "Halt Trial as Loop Robbers Accuse Sleuth," *Chicago Tribune*, March 2, 1920, 1.

"In justice to the Yellow Cab Company…": "Hoyne and Aid State Stand on Klein Bank Case," *Chicago Tribune*, March 4, 1920, 6.

"as a bludgeon…": "I.W.W. Lynching Resented Here By Union Labor," *Chicago Tribune*, Aug. 6, 1917, 3.

"three or four cabs a month"; "certain city officials"; "By organizing into these associations…"; "immediately took the offensive…"; "suppress[ing] the trouble": "Taxi War Quiz On," *Chicago Tribune*, March 11, 1921, 17.

"license and inspect public vehicles…"; "no public vehicle shall be licensed…"; "The Commission shall refuse…": Journal of the

Proceedings of the City Council of the City of Chicago for the Council Years 1919-1920.

"We are forced to comply…"; **"It's an honest man's law…"**: Yellow Cab ad, *Chicago Tribune*, Feb. 10, 1920, 12.

"lamps or wheels are similar…"; **"imitative appearances of taxis"**: "Freelance Taxi Men Say License Board is Unfair," *Chicago Tribune*, March 9, 1920, 19.

"jockeyed for position…": "Taxi War Breaks Out in Chicago Again; Man Shot," *Rock Island Argus*, August 5, 1920, 1.

"acting as a scout"; **"For hours, the battling drivers…"**; **"empty their pistols…"**: "Chicago Taxicabs Used As Tanks in Big Street Battle," *San Antonio Evening News*, July 27, 1920, 1.

"war of rival taxicab companies": "Shot May Cost Life of Checker Cab Chauffeur," *Chicago Tribune*, August 6, 1920, 3.

"fighting was resumed…": "Two Taxi Drivers Shot in War Between Two Rival Chicago Companies," *Belvidere Daily Republican* (Belvidere, Illinois), August 7, 1920, 4.

"a rival taxicab organization": "Bomb at Yellow Cab Garage Just Misses Tank," *Chicago Tribune*, August 15, 1920, 7.

"In leafy seclusions…": "Sunday Jazz in Dance Building Rouses Council," *Lake Geneva Regional News*, June 24, 1920, 1.

…questionably legal tactics: "Names Checker Cab Officials in Fraud Charge," *Chicago Tribune*, Feb. 18, 1923, 16.

CHAPTER 6

"The attacks made on our cabs…"; **"Yellow Cab is doing no fighting…"**; **"almost powerless to defend…"**; **"gangsters and products of the pool room…"**; **"a subterfuge to avoid liability"**; **"recent decrease in rates…"**; **"We can't indulge…"**: Yellow Cab ad, *Chicago Tribune*, March 6, 1921, 24.

"war for supremacy…"; **"put in the middle"**: "Hoyne Says He's 'In Middle' of Taxicab War," *Chicago Tribune*, June 5, 1919, 13.

"Contemporaries described him…": Dean Jobb, *Empire of Deception: The Incredible Story of a Master Swindler Who Seduced a City and Captivated the Nation*, (New York: Algonquin, 2016), 64-65.

"I am going to stop...": "Taxi War Quiz On," *Chicago Tribune*, March 11, 1921, 17.

"The hidden flaw..."; **"be aware of any other incidents..."**; **"who was not easily..."**; **"hardened combatants"**; **"aggressive, industrious..."**; **"What this for?"**; **"beaten, kicked, vilified..."**; **"Come clean..."**; **"Do you know anything..."**; **"given the third degree"**; **"Look at my lips..."**: Myron H. Fox, *Through the Eyes of Their Children*, (Chicago Jewish Historical Society: 2001).

"of the opinion that they are not entitled...": "City Favors Monopoly," *Chicago Eagle*, March 12, 1921, 1.

"If this was a hint..."; **"riddled with bullets"**: "Confesses Taxicab Killing," *Chicago Tribune*, June 10, 1921, 1.

"several Yellow and Checker chauffeurs...": "Taxi Men Fight in Loop; Several Hurt, Arrested," *Chicago Tribune*, June 8, 1921, 1.

"malicious mischief..."; **Any taxi drivers..."**; **"the taking of the law..."**; **"revolver or other deadly weapon"**: "Chief to Revoke Permits if Taxi Warfare Goes On," *Chicago Tribune*, June 10, 1921, 9.

"slugged"; **"We have gone just as far..."**: "Driver Slain in Taxi War; $5000 reward," *Chicago Tribune*, June 9, 1921, 1.

"All of the Checker drivers...": Yellow Cab ad, *Chicago Tribune*, June 12, 1921, 25.

"The Yellow Cab Company..."; **"Time and time again..."**; **"Police officers look on..."**; **"Mangan is not assigned..."**; **"He told me that if he caught me..."**: "Heated Charges Hurled at Quiz Into Taxi War," *Chicago Tribune*, June 14, 1921, 14.

"This thing has... been but a campaign...": "Checker Cab Co. Sues to Secure Cab Stand Licenses," *Chicago Tribune*, October 13, 1921, 15.

CHAPTER 7

"usual jam and hurly-burly": "How New Signal Towers Aid Rush Traffic," *Chicago Tribune*, Sept. 27, 1923, 3.

"erstwhile pompous man..."; **"I am gratified..."**: "Signal Towers First Day Finds Motordom Dizzy," *Chicago Tribune*, Sept. 26, 1923, 3.

"There is practically no limit…"; "Watch the crowds…": "Sees Big Cut in Taxi Rate With Traffic Relief," *Chicago Tribune,* March 29, 1922, 4.

"like clockwork": "Signal Towers Offered to City To Speed Traffic," *Chicago Tribune,* April 23, 1922, 5.

"its complete reorganization…"; "With this reorganization…": Checker Taxi ad, *Chicago Tribune,* Feb. 27, 1922, 6.

"twelve persons, commonly described…"; "clique of control"; "intends to impair…"; "sufficient good faith": "Taxi Co. Hires Gunmen, Says an Ex-Director," Chicago Tribune, May 25, 1922, 17.

"growing concern"; "bona fide corporation…": "Checker Cab Co. Given Legal OK," *Chicago Tribune,* June 4, 1922, 6.

"Having closely watched…": "Announcing the Checker Cab (Formerly the Mogul)," July 15, 1922, retrieved from the Internet Checker Taxi Archives.

"freeze out": "Accounting in Checker Cab Co. Affairs Sought," *Chicago Tribune,* March 3, 1923, 12.

"Mr. Markin has no interest…"; "Of course, he also is anxious…": "Taxicabs Fight Duel; 'Terror Reign' Is Seen," *Chicago Daily News,* June 8, 1923, 1, 3.

"trouble with some": "Seven Men in Autos Fire on Former Taxi Driver," *Chicago Tribune,* June 4, 1923, 16.

"slugging and pistol battle"; "attempted to make him pay": "1 Shot, 2 Held as Taxi and Union Agents Battle," *Chicago Tribune,* June 6, 1923, 16.

"proxy gatherers"; "several businessmen and lawyers"; "reign of terror"; "One man has been murdered…": "Crowe Works for Taxi Confessions," *Chicago Tribune,* June 9, 1923, 3.

"There is no safety…": "Drive Thugs Off the Taxicabs," *Chicago Tribune,* June 9, 1923, 8.

"majority shareholders": Checker Taxi ad, *Chicago Tribune,* June 20, 1923, 24.

"ruling minority;" "hauled before a trial board…"; "flying squadron"; "routed by sluggers": "Stop Gun Rule in Checker War," *Chicago Tribune,* June 12, 1923, 13.

"firearms and knives...": "Courts Order Bars Sluggers at Taxi Election," *Chicago Tribune*, June 14, 1923, 5.

"nearly unconscious": "Two 'Cops' Lure, Beat Up Checker Taxi Co. Head," *Chicago Tribune*, October 9, 1923, 11.

"clearly tended to obstruct...": *People v. McDonald*, 233 Ill. App. 389 (1924)

"a union official"; "I'm going to take a crack"; "a forceful lecture": "Nab Guntoters as Checker War Kills Another," Chicago Tribune, February 10, 1924, 3.

"Other thugs and sluggers...": "One More Dead in Taxicab War; Police Take Two," *Chicago Tribune*, February 11, 1924, 5.

"get the truth without fear or favor": "Order Six Held for Murder of 2 Taxi Drivers," *Chicago Tribune*, February 12, 1924, 19.

"About the first thing...": "Checker Taxi Drivers Ousted from Union," *Chicago Tribune*, Feb. 16, 1924, 5.

"forced peace": "Crowe Wars on Gangsters and Taxi Feudists," *Chicago Tribune*, Feb. 21, 1924, 11.

CHAPTER 8

"started to rush at me"; "Now I'm satisfied": "Father Shoots 'Son's Slayer' at Court's Door," *Chicago Tribune*, April 22, 1924, 3.

"The Taxicab of Distinction"; "each of these men...": Premier cab ad, *Chicago Tribune*, Sept. 15, 1924, 20.

"organized labor"; "the leader of one of the city's...": "Investors May Lose Million in Taxicab Failure," *Chicago Tribune*, July 8, 1926, 3.

"partially wreck[ing]": "Bombs Blast Home, Flats of Landlords," *Chicago Tribune*, May 5, 1924, 1.

"Sure, I know who shot me...": "Another Shot; Checker Men's Private War," *Chicago Tribune*, July 10, 1924, 1.

"hijacker, gunman and extortionist": "Seize Hijacker, Finch Slaying Solved, Belief," Chicago Tribune, Dec. 20, 1924, 3.

"the toughest guy in Chicago": "Interviewing Bob 'Doc' Graham: part 1," Studs Terkel Radio Archive, Chicago History Museum, 14:07.

Wickersham Commission...: *Enforcement of the Prohibition Laws: Official Records of the National Commission on Law Observance and*

Enforcement Pertaining to Its Investigation of the Facts as to the Enforcement, the Benefits and the Abuses Under the Prohibition Laws, Both Before and Since the Adoption of the Eighteenth Amendment Of the Constitution, Volume 4, United States, Wickersham Commission, 1931.

"If he hadn't tried to get me...": "Held for Trying to Shoot Man in Hospital," *Chicago Tribune,* July 21, 1924, 1.

"an official of the company": "Robber is Shot; Ex-Taxi Official Found Wounded," *Chicago Tribune,* Sept. 14, 1924, 1.

"demolishing the machine..."; "union troubles": "Two Checker Cabs are Bombed Here," *Suburbanite Economist* (Chicago, Ill), Sept. 25, 1924, 18.

"sell building lots in the blue sky": Paul G. Mahoney, "The Origins of the Blue Sky Laws: A Test of Competing Hypotheses," *The Journal of Law and Economics,* Vol. 46, Number 1, April 2003, 34.

"We have rescued the people...": Yellow Cab ad, *Chicago Tribune,* July 29, 1924, 12.

"Think back 9 years!": Yellow Cab ad, *Chicago Tribune,* Nov. 8, 1924, 18.

"Each day, Joe took a sheet of paper...": Ted Schwartz, *Joseph P. Kennedy: The Mogul, the Mob, the Statesman, and the Making of an American Myth,* (New York: Wiley, 2003), 102.

"I knew something...": B.C. Forbes and O.D. Foster, *Automotive Giants of America*, (New York: B.C. Forbes Publishing, 1926), 154.

"probably in revenge..."; "rival gangster": "Gunman Found Dead," *Chicago Tribune,* Nov. 23, 1924, 1.

Chapter 9

"terrific force"; "a dirty touring car with its curtains drawn"; "threw 1,000 Saturday night shoppers into a panic"; "It's a wonder...": "Bombs Wreck Two Taxicabs; One Man Hurt," *Chicago Tribune,* Jan. 18, 1925, 1.

"very anxious": Ernest J. Stevens papers, Chicago History Museum, boxes 8 & 28.

"taxi war without casualties"; "crashed head-on...": "Wire Shorts," *Waukegan News-Sun* (Waukegan, Ill.), Feb. 24, 1925, 3.

"wild west display of revolvers"; "The present taxi drivers' war…": "Dever Warns Taxi Drivers War Must End," *Chicago Tribune,* July 19, 1925, 7.

"administered a beating": "Seize Gangster, He Confesses Fatal Shooting," *Chicago Tribune,* Sept. 13, 1925, 11.

"would feel safer in a cell…": "Gangster, Freed of Gun Carrying, Kills Gangster," *Chicago Tribune,* Sept. 14, 1925, 9.

"carried mortgages…": "Investors May Lose Million in Taxicab Failure," *Chicago Tribune,* July 8 ,1926, 3.

"to insure responsibility…": "Yellow Puts 'Screws' On," *Collyer's Eye,* Dec. 19, 1925, 1.

"protect the claims of the public…": "Busch Order Taxicab Bonding Law Enforced," *Chicago Tribune,* August 15, 1926, 26.

"During the past 10 years…"; "The reports that our corporation…": "Taximen Flay Yellow Menace," Collyer's Eye, Sept. 4, 1926, 1.

"thugs" and "gangsters"; "Anything you have to say…"; "'I didn't know…"; "Mr. Wokral, if you…"; "If those fellows…"; "lengthy hearing": John H. Lyle, *The Dry and Lawless Years,* (Hoboken, NJ: Prentice-Hall, 1960), 143.

"nemesis of gangsters": "Ex-Judge John Lyle 'Gangster's Nemesis'," *The New York Times,* Nov. 25, 1964, 37.

"I think one bullet…"; "The McLaughlins knew…": "Ex-Official of Checkers Shot in Taxicab War," *Chicago Tribune*, Dec. 10, 1926, 3.

"unidentified persons": "Murder of Joseph Wokral Still Mystery, Says Jury," *Chicago Tribune,* Dec. 29, 1926. 12.

Chapter 10

"instituted a reign…": "10 Deputies to Watch Election of Checker Cab Co.," *Chicago Tribune,* Jan. 9, 1927, 27.

"Vote early, vote often": John Kobler, *Capone: The Life and World of Al Capone,* (New York: Da Capo Press, 2003), 293.

world's largest martini: "10 Things You Might Not Know About Chicago Elections," *Chicago Tribune.com,* Feb. 20, 2011.

"true story that rivals fiction"; "ace of chauffeurs"; "many hundreds of them…"; "work hard and be one hundred percent…": "Former

Taxicab Driver Now Big Business Chief," *Belvidere Daily Republican* (Illinois), Jan. 20, 1926, 1.

"While complete figures…": "Business Moves Forward with Cautious Step," *Chicago Tribune,* Feb. 2, 1927, 37.

"one of the most beautiful…": "Yellow Cab Co. Magnate Takes $115,000 Home," *The Miami News,* March 7, 1927, 4.

horse had stumbled…; "This is a terrible shock…"; "He took a personal interest…": "Yellow Taxicab President Is Killed," *Chicago Tribune,* Dec. 26, 1927, 1.

found on the ground…: "Yellow Cab Co. Chief Killed," *The Decatur Herald (Illinois),* Dec. 26, 1927, 1.

Yet another reported…: "Charles W. Gray Meets Death," *The Herald (Crystal Lake, Illinois),* Dec. 26, 1927, 2.

"the boys from Valentine's…": "Friends Remember With Flowers," *The Taxigram,* Vol. 9, January 1928, 4.

CHAPTER 11

"I did not think anyone…"; "Robert McLaughlin came in…"; "Newman's statements indicate…": "Jury Convicts Red McLaughlin of Gem Holdup," *Chicago Tribune,* May 16, 1928, 3.

"There is an atmosphere…"; "The situation at present…"; "My request for police…"; "A most extraordinary situation…": "Police Guard Judge from Terrorists," *Chicago Tribune,* May 18, 1928, 1.

"a good break": "True Bills Voted in McLaughlin Case Jury-Fixing," *Chicago Examiner,* May 18, 1928, 1.

"in heated conference"; "dapper, smiling, and entirely at ease"; "ruthless and fiendish assault…": "Demands Inquiry in Juror Bombing," *Chicago Examiner,* May 18, 1928, 1.

"one of the largest stockholders…"; "poisoned the wells…": "Robert McLaughlin Gets 30 Days for Court Contempt," *Chicago Tribune,* June 3, 1928, 18.

From 1923 to September of 1927…: "Checker Cab Mfg. Co.," *San Francisco Examiner,* June 16, 1928, 19.

In June, the Commercial Credit Company…: "Topics of Finance, Trade and Industry," *Chicago Tribune,* June 20, 1928, 26.

"difficulty...keeping the cab men...": "Bombs Shatter Two Garages in Taxicab Wars," *Chicago Tribune*, Oct. 1, 1928, 1.

"settle certain difficulties..."; **"did not suspect the cause..."**: "Burn Hertz Racing Horses," *Chicago Tribune*, Oct. 2, 1928, 1.

"were still working at midnight..."; **"vandalism"**; **"turf enemies"**; **"The Checker company..."**; **"important new angles"**: "Firebug Clews Found in Hertz $200,000 Blaze," *Chicago Tribune*, Oct. 3, 1928, 1.

"In your indignant outburst..."; **"If this situation is permitted..."**: "McHenry Sheriff Hunts Hertz Fire Clew in Chicago," *Chicago Tribune*, Oct. 4, 1928, 2.

"Please let us register...": Checker Taxi ad, *Chicago Tribune*, Oct. 9, 1928, 20.

"practical theft": "Court Battles Tie Up Inquiry into Hertz Fire," *Chicago Tribune*, Oct. 5, 1928, 2.

"clearly illegal without...": "Return Taxicab Records, Court Order to Crowe," *Chicago Tribune*, Oct. 6., 1928, 2.

"most savage ever made before him...": "Checker Taxi Chiefs Hit by Graft Charges," *Chicago Tribune*, Oct. 24, 1928, 9.

CHAPTER 12

"heard only part...": "Jury Asks New Prosecutor to Continue Taxicab Quiz," *Chicago Tribune*. Nov. 1, 1928, 23.

"wanted to be king...": "Tells of Plot to Bankrupt Checker Cab Co.," *Chicago Tribune*, Nov. 28, 1928, 4.

"commission": "Drivers Accuse Checker Taxicab Chiefs of Graft," *Chicago Tribune*, Nov. 27, 1928, 11.

"I have seen you give him money..."; **"There is an influence..."**; **"I have paid money to you..."**; **"You would have been indicted..."**; **"There is nothing..."**: "Slaying Charge Upsets Hearing on Checker Taxi," *Chicago Tribune*, Nov. 29, 1928, 20.

"I may and I may not have...": "Checker Taxi Official Faces Perjury Charge," *Chicago Tribune*, Dec. 1, 1928, 6.

"correct": "Checker Officer Revises Story; Tells of Graft," *Chicago Tribune*, Dec. 5, 1928, 27.

"overzealous"; "There appears to be…": "Judge Upholds U.S. Tax Quiz on Checker Taxi Co.," *Chicago Tribune*, Dec. 7, 1928, 8.

"rebate": "Ex-Oil Official Held by Court in Taxi Hearing," *Chicago Tribune*, Dec. 8, 1928, 8.

"business conference"; "was afraid of the sluggers": "Sluggers Guard Checker Affairs, Charges Driver," *Chicago Tribune*, Dec. 13, 1928, 15.

"I squawked about it…": "Checker Drivers Testify Against Taxi Officials," *Chicago Tribune*, Dec. 14, 1928, 14.

"I'll certify you…"; "I won't shut up!"; "Furthermore…": "Lawyer Clashes with Master at Checker Hearing," *Chicago Tribune*, Dec. 15, 1928, 18.

"grossly improper": "U.S. Judge Gives Checker Lawyer a 'Calling Down'," *Chicago Tribune*, Dec. 18, 1928, 17.

"I refuse to answer…": "Checker Chiefs Dodge Quiz on Graft Charges," *Chicago Tribune*, Dec. 19, 1928, 38.

"the healthiest thing…"; "at this crisis…": "Banker Will Be Named Czar of Checker Taxi Co.," *Chicago Tribune*, Dec. 29, 1928, 7.

"The master finds…"; "institute and install…": "Report Attacks Management of Checker Affairs," *Chicago Tribune*, Feb. 15, 1929, 10.

It took several more months…: *United States vs. Yellow Cab*, 332 U.S. 218, 1947.

In fact, Markin's business expansion…: Michael Angelich, *The New York City Taxicab: The First Hundred Years*, (Self-published: 2015), 112.

"ran Checker Motors and subsidiaries": "Services Set Tomorrow for Morris Markin," *Chicago Tribune*, July 9, 1970, 122.

AFTERWORD

"There is no present or future…": Eugene O'Neill, *Before Breakfast*, (Stage Door: 2014), cover.

His only surviving brother…: "Tavern Owner Shot to Death on Ride," *Chicago Tribune*, Dec. 25, 1942, 1.

INDEX